THE PEOPLE MOTIVATORS

THE PEOPLE MOTIVATORS

Consumer and Sales Incentives in Modern Marketing

HOWARD M. TURNER, JR.

McGRAW-HILL BOOK COMPANY

New York   St. Louis   San Francisco   Düsseldorf   Johannesburg
Kuala Lumpur   London   Mexico   Montreal   New Delhi
Panama   Rio de Janeiro   Singapore   Sydney   Toronto

Library of Congress Cataloging in Publication Data
Turner, Howard M
  The people motivators.
  1. Sales promotion. 2. Marketing. 3. Motivation
(Psychology) I. Title.
HF5438.T79   658.8'2   73-1890
ISBN 0-07-065530-8

1234567890 KPKP 76543

*The editors for this book were W. Hodson Mogan and Carolyn
Nagy, the designer was Naomi Auerbach, and its production was
supervised by George E. Oechsner. It was set in Alphatype
Astro by University Graphics, Inc.
It was printed and bound by The Kingsport Press.*

TO J. R. T.

CONTENTS

PREFACE

This book was written to give the reader an understanding of consumer and sales incentives—not only what they are as used in marketing, but also how they work to produce results. Incentives cover a very wide variety of applications, ranging from a toy worth only a few cents inside a cereal box, to a luxury trip to Europe won by a dealer for selling hundreds of thousands of dollars' worth of merchandise.

In all their diversity, incentives are constantly used in one form or another in marketing products by almost every business. The reader will become familiar with the marketing strategy used in developing incentive programs, the advertising and promotion of incentives, and analyses of how they work to produce results.

The author is indebted to Bill Communications, Inc., publishers of "Incentive Marketing" for much of the source material used in this book; to the Premium Advertising Association of America for case material; and to the A. C. Nielsen Company for statistical data related to price-off coupons and coin refund offers. I would also like to acknowledge the cooperation of many other businesses whose incentive promotions are used to illustrate this book.

Howard M. Turner, Jr.

THE PEOPLE MOTIVATORS

INTRODUCTION

CONSUMER AND SALES INCENTIVES—THE PEOPLE MOTIVATORS

Incentives are the people motivators used in marketing to offer rewards to consumers or salesmen over and above what they normally expect to receive in the routine course of business. These rewards can take the form of a wide variety of inducements designed to motivate an individual to action. They can include a chance to win, a special price offer, a free sample offer, a chance to buy a premium product at a special price (or get one free), sweepstakes offers, trading stamps, price-off coupons, free samples, distributor prize trips, sales contests, sales incentives. These are all typical examples of incentive offers or programs.

The marketing of products in a competitive economy involves spending money on distribution in order to make a profit. These distribution costs include direct sales expense—salesmen's com-

pensation and travel; warehouse and freight costs; adminis-
trative expenses; and advertising and sales promotion.

Incentives form an important part of the sales promotion
area in the marketing of products and are vital to their success.
When product differences are minimal and when distribution
factors such as selling expense and warehouse and manufacturing capacity are relatively evenly matched between competing
products, incentives are often used to gain a competitive advantage and to contribute to increased profits through additional
sales volume. In other cases, when a product with real competitive advantage is endeavoring to gain a foothold in the marketplace against large established competitors, incentives can provide
vital assistance in obtaining distribution or consumer trial usage.

There are two major types of incentives: consumer incentives
and sales incentives. Consumer incentives are used to motivate
the customer of products and services; sales incentives are used
to motivate manufacturers' salesmen, distributors and their
salesmen, and retailers and their salesmen. A complete incentive
program may involve incentives directed at every level of distribution. At the same time, a complete incentive program may include more than one form of incentive at a given level, for example,
a prize sweepstakes and a price-off coupon directed at the consumer in a single promotion.

The Size and Importance of Incentives in Today's Marketing

The importance of consumer and sales incentives is illustrated
by a few simple statistics:

Item 1: total wholesale value of all forms of incentives currently
run in excess of $4 billion annually.[1] This figure includes all forms
of premiums, trading stamps merchandise, sales incentives, and
sweepstakes and contest prizes.

Item 2: over 10 billion price-off coupons are estimated to be
distributed annually, and one billion are redeemed with an approximate value of $100 million.[2]

---

[1] *Incentive Marketing Facts,* Bill Brothers Publishing Corporation,
New York, N.Y., 1969.
[2] A. C. Nielsen Clearing House.

Item 3: over $500 million is spent by advertisers annually in promoting incentives (this figure includes point-of-purchase display and direct mail).[3]

Item 4: over 350 sweepstakes and contests are run every year, involving tens of millions of entrants. Adding regional events would easily double these figures.[4]

Incentives not only help U. S. business promote its products but also enable consumers to get more at lower cost, either through price reductions or through purchase of premiums which are sold at less than prevailing retail prices.

A source of deep concern to most marketing men is that excessive government regulations in important areas of incentive programs may deprive the consumer of legitimate sources of satisfaction and cost saving in the name of consumer protection. No one can deny that incentive offers should be subject to full disclosure or that clear communications with the consumer are necessary. However, an overrepressive atmosphere appears to be developing; in such an atmosphere, legitimate ways to promote products may be hampered to an extent that would stifle legitimate promotional efforts by business.

Consumer Incentive

There are four basic types of consumer incentives.

1. A premium

The customer receives an article other than the product itself, free or at a low price. In this category are included trading stamps (and other programs where gift coupons are collected to get merchandise rewards).

Typical examples of premiums include: a free toothbrush packed with a tube of toothpaste; pantyhose for $1 with a label from a skin cream; free glassware with every purchase of $3 worth of gas; free camera with purchase of portable typewriter; free miniature car with visit to automobile dealer's showroom.

---

[3] *Incentive Marketing Facts,* Bill Brothers Publishing Corporation, New York, N.Y., 1969.
[4] Premium Advertising Association of America booklet.

2. A bargain

For a limited time the customer gets a price reduction or a cash refund when she purchases the product.

Typical examples: 10-cent price-off coupon on a box of cake mix; 50-cent refund for sending in three labels of cat food; buy two cakes of soap, get the third one free; buy a major appliance and receive a forty-five-piece set of melamine dinnerware.

3. A sample

The prospective customer gets a sample of the product free, or for a token price. Typical examples; a free sample of powdered soft drink is sent through the mail; a sample of bath oil is offered for 25 cents in a magazine ad; a sample of cheese is offered to shoppers in a supermarket.

4. A chance to win

The entrant gets a chance to win prizes, cash, or trips in a sweepstakes or contest.

Typical examples: go to the store and match symbol against package on shelf to see if you are a winner; write twenty-five words "I like this face cream because. . . ." Send in entry with label from product.

Consumer incentives are means of getting direct consumer action, i.e., product trial or product purchase. The choice of which approach or combination of approaches to use provides a constant and fascinating challenge to marketing men. In most cases, the most effective and most costly consumer incentive promotions fall within the "bargain" category, because they offer immediate savings on the product itself. In many cases, however, the offer of direct savings on the product is too expensive; and a more indirect approach, such as sweepstakes or premiums, offers a more affordable approach.

In many cases, consumer incentives are offered to some extent (or primarily) for trade reasons, i.e., for greater distribution or to help the product displayed in retail stores. Quite often, a combination of trade and consumer objectives is involved.

Sales Incentives

There are five basic types of sales incentives.

1. Sales incentive plans

Sales incentive plans offer rewards to all participants on an equal basis, that is, a specific performance is rewarded with a specific prize. These plans may be used with manufacturers' salesmen; distributors' salesmen; or, as in the case of bank programs, with all employees.

Typical objectives of these plans are to increase sales on selected products or services over a period of time; to get broader distribution at the distributor or retail level; or to get product displays or promotions.

2. Sales contests

Sales contests are set up where individuals or groups compete with one another to win prizes offered to those who perform best against a specific set of objectives. They can be applied to manufacturers' salesmen, distributors' salesmen, or (less frequently because of difficulty of administration) to retail salesmen. Sales contests are usually most effective when a "team" approach can be applied, i.e., one region or branch competes against another. In many cases, the features of the sales incentive plan can be combined with sales contests so that both individual and group performance are recognized through the contest.

3. Sales awards and other recognition plans

Sales recognition plans differ from sales incentive plans and sales contests in that they are based mainly upon the pride of a salesman doing a superior job within his own organization and receiving management recognition for his efforts. Sometimes the physical recognition is in the form of an award, sometimes in cash or merchandise, and sometimes both. However, the key thing is that the pride of the salesman is of overriding importance in this form of program. Naturally, the sales recognition plan can be part of either a sales incentive plan or a sales contest.

4. Trade incentive programs

Trade incentive programs are directed at either distributors or retailers. They involve free merchandise or trips in return for purchases; trade allowances for specific periods of time on merchandise; premiums given to wholesalers or retailers with merchandise orders, or with agreement to display certain merchandise.

5. Retail salesmen's incentive and contest programs

Retail salesmen's incentive programs usually consist of cash rewards for selling a manufacturers' merchandise. These rewards are known as "spiffs" or "PMs." They are characteristically common in certain areas of the home-furnishings industry where a large, "big ticket" unit of sales is involved.

Other forms of retail salesmen's programs involve contests in which prize merchandise is offered in return for filled-out entry forms which relate to product facts. Thus, these contests provide a form of sales training in these applications.

Incentives: the People Motivators

Incentives, both consumer and sales, work because they offer people not only something extra but also a little fun and excitement. To most housewives, sending away for a premium she wants is certainly not on an equal level of importance as the purchase of a new car, or her husband's livelihood; but it does give her a chance to get something that will add to her pleasure in a small way. By the same token, the fact that a good salesman, by exerting himself for a couple of months, can win a set of golf clubs he has been wanting not only gives him something he wants, but also gives him a sense of personal satisfaction which results in a better performance on the job. Then, too, incentives often bring a sense of participation to people who are joining in a sweepstakes or become part of a sales incentive program.

1

PREMIUMS—THE EXTRAS THAT MAKE THE SALE

Enter the world of self-liquidators, on-packs, traffic builders, bounce-backs, and continuities.[1] These fascinating terms apply to incentives—the people motivators. They are the physical things that often can make people do what they would not do otherwise.

Consumer premiums are items of merchandise which are offered to help make a sale or otherwise motivate people to come into a store or to observe a product demonstration. Some premiums

---

[1] *Self-liquidator:* a premium offer for which a price is charged which generally covers the cost of the item. *On-pack:* a premium which is physically attached to the product. *Traffic builder:* a premium which is offered free to attract people to a store or special event. *Bounce-back:* a price-off coupon which is packed with a product to attract a second purchase. *Continuities:* premium offers which are sets of merchandise collected through a series of purchases, e.g., chinaware, glassware.

are offered free; others are offered at a very advantageous price. Premiums become an extra reason for people to take action, and as such they represent one of the most basic of consumer incentives.

Premiums account for the movement of more than one and a half billion dollars' worth of merchandise annually.[2] They range all the way from a comic booklet worth only a few tenths of a cent inserted in a package of bubble gum, to a mink coat worth a thousand dollars offered at a bargain price with labels from a food product. From the consumer's point of view, these premiums can offer real bargains because the purchaser of premiums can place very large orders with the premium supplier. At the same time, premiums often provide the marketing man an opportunity to promote effectively at a considerably lower cost than that provided by other promotional techniques.

The challenge of selecting an effective premium lies in choosing an item which will appeal strongly to the majority of customers for the product being promoted—an item which will influence purchase or promote other positive action, e.g., a store visit or a product demonstration.

In addition to simply offering an unusual value, a successful premium usually exerts its appeal to the potential consumer in other ways:

- A premium can be appealing because of a built-in relationship to the product itself: a coffee carafe forms an instant coffee package; highball glasses are offered by a liquor brand; Campbell Soup mugs are offered to soup lovers.
- A premium can be chosen because of its relationship to the consumer audience: a child's toy or game in a cereal package; a decorating booklet for promoting a carpet.
- A premium idea can stimulate consumer interest through its relationship to a special promotion: a record which features the star of a TV show; a booklet containing game schedules, tying in with sponsorship of football.
- A premium may be suggested by a seasonal or holiday pro-

---

[2] *Incentive Marketing Facts*, Bill Brothers Publishing Corporation, New York, N.Y., 1970.

motion: a barbecue grill for summer; a school-oriented premium in September.

One major reason for the challenge in successful premium selection is the problem of finding an item which is different and unusual yet has a broad consumer appeal among the product's users and, at the same time, is available in sufficient quantity to satisfy anticipated consumer demand.

TYPES OF PREMIUM OFFERS

Consumer premium promotions represent an extremely flexible activity which can be applied to the broadest range of products and services. It is helpful, therefore, to categorize these offers into classifications which can simplify an understanding of them and how they work.

Self-Liquidators

Self-liquidators are premiums which are offered at extremely reasonable prices made possible by volume purchasing. The price charged for a self-liquidator generally covers all or most of the cost to the promoter, hence the term self-liquidator.

Free Premiums

Free premiums are offered in a variety of ways:

- At the time of purchase, with the product
- Through the mail, by sending in proof of purchase
- As an incentive to send for a product on a trial basis
- As an incentive to visit a retailer's place of business or to attend special event (traffic builders)
- As a means of getting a product demonstration
- As a good-will builder, given to the prospective customer by a door-to-door salesman (door openers)

Trading Stamp Plans

Trading stamps are given out at the time of purchase by individual retailers, especially by supermarkets and gasoline stations. Their value is usually set at a rate of ten stamps per dollar purchased. When accumulated, as with coupon plans, they are traded in exchange for merchandise. As a rule of thumb, a book of 1,200 stamps is worth about $3. This book represents $120 in purchases by the consumer.

Coupon Plans

Coupon plans are premium offers in which special coupons are made available with purchase of the product. When accumulated, these coupons are convertible to premium gifts. In some cases, they are offered with individual products (e.g., Raleigh/Belair Cigarettes); in other plans, they are offered through a wide range of participating products (e.g., Gift Star Coupons).

Total Amount Spent on Consumer Premiums

Incentive Marketing's annual survey estimates the relative importance in dollar volume of the various types of consumer premiums. In looking at these figures, one should realize that the amount spent on self-liquidating premiums comes, for the most part, out of the consumer's pocket; whereas free premiums, trading stamps, or coupon plans are part of the promotional cost borne by manufacturers or retailers.

Type of premium[3]	Millions of dollars
Self-liquidators	$ 337.4
Free Premiums	347.7
Coupon Plans	140.6
Trading Stamps	773.0
	$1,598.7

SELF-LIQUIDATING PREMIUMS

Self-liquidators are premiums which are sold to the consumer at very advantageous prices made possible by purchasing in volume.

The reason for the popularity of self-liquidators is that the promoter pays only for the promotion of the premium, while the consumer pays for the premium itself. Obviously, this is a very inexpensive form of promotion. However, while it appears that

[3] *Incentive Marketing Facts*, Bill Brothers Publishing Corporation, New York, N.Y., 1971.

the marketing man is getting a "free ride" with a self-liquidator, these promotions can be very tricky in the actual execution.

Unless the premium actually fulfills the marketing objectives set for it, it can end up being a very expensive failure. If the premium does not attract customers or stimulate the retail trade, the money spent in promoting it, the sales time spent in selling it, and the management time spent in planning it will be wasted. Unfortunately, a significant percentage of self-liquidators do fail because this type of promotion is fairly easy to "sell" to management as opposed to more costly ones. However, this is not to say that good self-liquidating promotions are not extremely effective. They can be, and they are. But it requires extremely careful evaluation and solid planning to produce a successful self-liquidator.

What then, are the ingredients of a successful self-liquidating promotion? The best self-liquidators have a very strong appeal to the prospective buyers, and they offer an extremely good value immediately apparent to the consumer. Many self-liquidators offer a distinctive change from run-of-the-mill merchandise through design or special features so that the customer instinctively knows that she cannot purchase the item elsewhere. Then, too, the attributes of the premium and its value must register very strongly on the consumer through the advertising or point of purchase material so that she will be motivated to act on the offer.

Examples of Self-Liquidators

The various types of appeals that make a self-liquidator successful are illustrated through a number of examples covering a variety of different products.

Offer directly related to product use

Gold Medal Flour offered a set of four aluminum mini-loaf bread pans for $1 plus proof of purchase. The miniature loaf promotes bread-baking at home by featuring the unusual mini-loaf. (Gold Medal has a healthy share of the market; so if they promote the use of flour at home, they will get their share of any increase in business.)

In every great cook's bag of tricks, you find the fresh lemon. How come?

Leaf through any good cookbook. From Betty Crocker to Julia Child, the fresh lemon pops up all over the place.

Why?

Because it can make the difference between good and great. It's a sign you care. And know.

The fresh, sharp taste and aroma of lemon can enhance a sauce, a dessert, a main dish. Take it from ordinary to extraordinary.

And, good cooks like the great look of lemon. Fresh, wet wedges on a platter of fish, or the rim of a glass, or nestled among vegetables are just plain stunning to look at.

So remember the Sunkist lemon. Like the experts always do.

It shows you care.

Special offer:

Would you like a copy of the new Good Housekeeping Cookbook plus the Sunkist Cookbook at a special reduced price?

You can get both for $5.00. A $10.75 value. Be sure to look for the details on the special Sunkist display at your grocers. Price slightly higher in Canada.

Sunkist.

Remember the fresh lemon. It shows you care.

Fig. 1.1 *"Sunkist uses strong combination of an appealing headline, combined with a 'double-header' self-liquidator offer — two cookbooks for $5. This is an excellent example of a well-executed premium offer. Advertisement appeared in* Woman's Day, *May 1971." (Sunkist Growers, Inc.)*

Offer related to the product's name or symbol

Green Giant   The friendly *Green Giant* (Ho, Ho, Ho,) has been established as the symbol of their products. Accordingly, they have offered a succession of self-liquidating premiums which serve as reminders of the Jolly Green Giant name, as well as being intriguing premiums. For example, a scatter rug in the shape of a huge green footprint for $2.50 plus two labels.

Offer using the manufacturer's own product

Westinghouse Light Bulbs   Westinghouse appliances are some-times used to promote their bulbs. Some examples: Westinghouse transistor radio, $4.95; Westinghouse electric knife, $9.95; At other times, they promote general items, e.g., sportsman's hammock, $3.55; choice of four art prints, $3.98.

The Pricing Structure of Self-Liquidators

A study conducted by the Premium Advertising Association of America shows the pricing structure of a representative group of self-liquidators.

Of the 664 offers studied, 62.5 percent were under $3, and another 29.3 percent were under $10. Thus 91.8 percent were under $10. Table 1.1 shows the detailed breakdown.

While the majority of self-liquidators fall into the price range under $4, there has been a definite increase in the value of self-liquidators over the last few years.

In this study, the average price of self-liquidators was 46.6

TABLE 1.1

Price range	Number of offers	Percent	
$ 0.10–$0.99	105	16.6	51.6%
1.00– 1.99	221	35.0	under $2.00
2.00– 2.99	89	14.0	79.2%
3.00– 3.99	92	14.6	under $4.00
4.00– 4.99	31	5.0	
5.00– 5.99	34	5.4	
6.00– 6.99	12	1.9	
7.00– 7.99	10	1.6	
8.00– 8.99	7	1.1	
9.00– 9.99	8	1.2	
10.00 & over	23	3.6	

SOURCE: Self-Liquidator Promotions. Premium Advertising Association of America, 1969.

percent of the average retail price claimed for the premium. This indicates that these premiums represented an excellent value to the consumer. It also reinforces the point that the premium buyer, if he is to be successful, must shop for real bargains in order to attract his purchaser. (See Table 1.2.)

In general, the lower the price of the self-liquidator, the greater is the consumer advantage in terms of retail price savings. Thus, the items at $1 and below offer greater values (in terms of percentage of saving) than those in the higher price brackets.

FREE PREMIUMS

Near-packs, reusable containers, door-openers, traffic-builders, in-packs, on-packs, and continuities are some of the colorful names applied to free premiums offered in a wide variety of ways to motivate a consumer to buy a product, visit a store, send for a subscription, try a product, buy one brand of gas regularly, or take some other action leading to a sale.

On-Packs, In-Packs, Near-Packs, and Reusable Containers

The food and drug business, distributing their products principally through supermarkets, drug chains, and large discount stores

TABLE 1.2

Average price item	Average offered price	Average retail price	Percent offered price of retail price
Under $0.50	$ 0.21	$ 1.05	20
$ 0.50–$ 0.99	0.68	2.12	32
1.00	1.00	2.92	34
1.01–1.95	1.47	3.80	39
2.00	2.00	4.72	45
2.01–2.99	2.60	5.87	44
3.00	3.00	6.48	48
3.01–3.99	3.70	7.40	50
4.00–4.95	4.61	8.65	53
5.00–5.99	5.60	11.50	49
6.00–6.99	6.63	12.77	52
7.00–7.99	7.32	15.31	48
8.00–8.99	8.88	16.80	53
9.00–9.99	9.77	22.23	44
10.00–19.99	12.33	22.03	54
Over $20.00	45.99	68.75	66

SOURCE: Self-Liquidator Promotions, Premium Advertising Association of America, 1969.

TABLE 1.3 Free Premiums by Type and Use

Type	Description	Principal users	Principal retail outlets
On-pack	Premium attached to package	Packaged goods	Supermarkets, drug stores
In-pack	Premium inside package	Packaged goods	Supermarkets, drug stores
Near-pack	Premium near package at point of sale	Packaged goods	Supermarkets, drug stores
Containers	Premium is package container itself and is reusable	Packaged goods	Supermarkets
Free with purchase: send-away	Premium is sent through the mail	Packaged goods Major purchase products	Supermarkets, drug stores
Free with purchase: at point of sale	Premium is given with purchase	Major appliances, automotive, gasoline companies, banks, book publishers, etc.	Appliance stores, automobile dealers, gas stations, banks, mail order
Free with purchase: continuity	Premium given with purchase: multiple items form a set; encourage repeat purchases	Gasoline companies, major retailers, banks	Gas stations, banks, supermarkets
Traffic builder	Premium given for store visit	Wide range higher-priced items: major appliances, home furnishings, automotive, banks, all types of store openings	Appliance dealers, furniture stores, department stores, automobile dealers, banks, specialty stores
Door opener	Premium given at customer's home as good-will builder	Door-to-door salesmen	Door-to-door selling

(mass merchandisers), represent the principal channels of distribution for on-pack, in-pack, near-pack, and reusable container premiums.

On-Pack Premium

The on-pack premium is attached to the outside of a product by banding, by a plastic blister or bubble pack, or by using some other single packaging device. As the products involved are volume sellers, the retail price is relatively low (average around $1); and the on-pack usually costs only a few cents. To obtain a real value, the premium buyer must make a large volume premium purchase. Furthermore, the logistics of special packaging also usually require a large volume operation.

The on-pack premium has certain advantages. It is immediately perceived as a free offer, and the customer can see exactly what she is getting. However, the on-pack also has some immediate drawbacks. The retailers handling this type of volume-selling product are often reluctant to handle packages which vary from the norm. On-pack premiums often do not stack properly or have a bulkiness which causes them to take up extra shelf space. At the same time, unless the product offered is going to provide a large increase in volume in a profitable category, the retailer may balk at handling this product with an on-pack premium affixed to it.

Some Typical Examples of On-Pack Premiums

Examples of various types of on-pack premiums illustrate how this form of premium is used.

On-pack related to product use

Vicks Cough Syrup attached a no-spill spoon to the bottle. The idea of making it easier to dispense the syrup to a coughing child has immediate practical appeal.

On-pack which appeals to the typical customer for the product

Clark Gum included a plastic hand puppet on a polybag with six packs of gum. Here multiple purchase was encouraged through a premium which intrigues the kids.

Fig. 1.2 *Adorn Hair Spray provides an on-pack with a special comb for teenagers who are using the product to style their hair. The kicky comb smooths, curls, swirls, poufs, and waves . . . a good example of a product-oriented premium. (The Gillette Company.)*

In-Pack Premiums

In-pack premiums, like on-packs, must be included within the regular cost of the product to the consumer. As in-packs and on-packs are generally used in products which cost between 75 cents and $2, in the food and drug category, the cost of these premiums may not exceed a few cents. However, mass purchasing can make possible some extremely interesting and intriguing values. While on-packs require packaging solutions which are often difficult to work out, on-packs can be seen and therefore "speak" for themselves. In-packs, on the other hand, are inside the carton or package; and therefore they do not present the problem of bulkiness on the shelf. They do, however, pose another problem because the in-pack must instantly convey the premium offer through the message on the package. Therefore, the in-pack premium must lend itself to a clear word and/or picture description which makes the premium immediately desirable to the consumer. This desirability can be a function of utility, value, or uniqueness—or combine all three. In-pack premiums are used with products which are normally packaged in boxes as opposed to jars, tubes, or bottles. While the package must be adapted to the premium offer, the logistics involved with special printing on cartons are easier to deal with than providing new packaging solutions for on-packs. Incidentally, one bottled product, a liquid shampoo, did successfully use an in-pack—a simulated pearl inside the bottle which demonstrated how thick the shampoo was when the bottle was turned over.

Typical Example of In-Pack Offer

Examples of in-pack premiums give an indication of the variety of ways in which this form of premium can be used.

In-pack premium related to product use

Brillo Soap Pads offered a household sponge, related to practical cleaning problems in bathroom and kitchen. This premium is certainly not a unique item, but it is very practical. (Premium buyers should never forsake practicality because it produces results!)

In-pack premium related to customer needs

Breeze Detergent Powder offered Cannon Spring Bouquet towels in red, gold, green, and blue. Towels are an excellent in-pack premium. They are universally needed in the household and provide no problems in packing or shipping.

General Mills Trix offered whirligig toys. Instructions on the back panel of the box taught kids how to assemble them. They were produced in the three Trix colors, lemon yellow, raspberry red, and orange.

Near-Pack Premiums

Near-packs, as their name implies, are not attached to or inside the package but are placed on a display, or otherwise near the product on the shelf. Because they are not physically connected to the product they are not used very often since they present a lack of distribution control. The promoter must expect a certain percentage of those who inadvertently, or purposely, take advantage of the offer without making a purchase. In addition, it is difficult to gain special displays which will give proper exposure to the near-pack premium offer. In general, it can be stated that those products which tend to be important to the store in terms of volume and profit are the only ones with which this type of premium should be attempted. These products may have the necessary leverage in the store to make sure that check-out people are informed of the offer and that proper displays are set up showing the premium and the product together.

Typical Example of a Near-Pack Premium

Eversharp Pen Company promoted its $2.50 Reporter ballpoint pen using two 6-inch bayberry candles which were placed in a counter display unit. Here the major outlets were drug stores and stationery stores where a retail clerk was instructed to give out the premium to those who purchased the pen.

Reusable Container Premiums

Every time a housewife uses a jelly jar as a water glass or a coffee can as a receptacle for bacon grease, she is using the principle of the reusable container. When these containers are pur-

Fig. 1.3 *Kellogg's Sugar Smacks offers a series of Famous Indian Chiefs on the back of the packages. There are a total of eleven in the series to attract repeat purchasers. (The Kellogg Company.)*

posely designed for a special reuse, and then promoted as such, they can become a very effective form of premium.

The reusable container either involves use of the package as a container for something other than the product or use of the package to make something else. For example, using a jelly jar as a water glass provides a second use for the container; printing cut-out illustrations on the back of a cereal box provides a different use of the package after the product has been used up. In general, most reusable container premiums are useful either in the serving of food or drinks or in the children's toy and game category. In either case, the shape and color of the reusable package are extremely important in making the premium immediately communicate its purpose to the consumer.

Examples of Reusable Container Premiums

Good Seasons Salad Dressing Mixes, in foil packages, were packed in a plastic mixing bowl enclosed in a cardboard sleeve. The mixing bowl provided a convenience element, immediately perceived.

Free with Purchase—Send-away Premiums

In-packs, on-packs, and reusable containers are physically part of the package or in immediate proximity at time of purchase. In many cases, however, where use of premium is indicated, it is more desirable to offer a separate premium through the mail, as opposed to one which is immediately available with purchase. Send-away premiums work in the same way as self-liquidating offers. The send-away premium which is offered through the mail does not require a change in the packaging of the product. It can be offered through advertising and thus can be put into effect in a relatively short time. The preparation and placing of a full-color magazine advertisement can usually be accomplished in a couple of months, while a premium which involves packaging changes usually requires several months' lead time for planning and execution. Therefore, the send-away premium enables the marketer to move more quickly than does the premium available at point of sale.

On the other hand, send-away premiums involve additional costs in handling and mailing which are not involved with premiums offered with the package at the point of sale. In order to amortize these costs, these send-away premiums often require multiple purchases. While this approach sells more products, it also cuts down on the number of customers responding to the offer.

If you buy 12 cans of Campbell's Tomato Soup, 13 wonderful things can happen.

1 TOMATO CHEESE SAUCE. In pan, combine 1 can (10¾ oz.) Campbell's Tomato Soup, ¼ cup cheese spread with smoke flavor, 2 tbsp. water. Heat slowly until cheese melts; stir. Serve over hamburgers on toasted buns. Makes 1½ cups sauce.

5 HOT TOMATO-ORANGE TODDY. In pan, combine 1 can (10¾ oz.) Campbell's Tomato Soup, 1 cup water, ½ cup orange juice, dash ground cloves. Heat; stir. Garnish with orange slices. Also may be served cold. 2 to 3 servings.

7 TOMATO SALAD DRESSING. Combine 1 can (10¾ oz.) Campbell's Tomato Soup, ¾ cup prepared Italian-flavored salad dressing in covered container; shake well. Chill. Makes 2 cups salad dressing.

10 CHICKEN PAPRIKASH. In skillet, brown 2 lb. chicken parts in 2 tbsp. shortening; pour off fat. Stir in 1 can (10¾ oz.) Campbell's Tomato Soup, ½ cup sour cream, 1 cup sliced onion, 2 tsp. paprika. Cover; simmer 45 min. or until tender; stir. Serve over noodles. 4 servings.

2 YANKEE POT ROAST. In large heavy pan, brown 3 to 4-pound boneless beef pot roast in shortening. Pour off fat. Stir in 1 can (10¾ oz.) Campbell's Tomato Soup, 1 cup chopped onion, 1 large clove garlic, minced. Cover; simmer 3 hours or until tender. Stir. Skim off fat. Thicken gravy, if desired. 6 to 8 servings.

6 SPAGHETTI SAUCE WITH BEEF. In pan, brown ½ lb. ground beef; stir to separate. Pour off fat. Stir in 1 can (10¾ oz.) Campbell's Tomato Soup, 1 can (10¾ oz.) Franco-American Spaghetti Sauce with Mushrooms, ¼ cup water. Simmer 10 min. Stir. Serve over spaghetti. Makes 3 cups sauce.

8 TOMATO TARTAR SAUCE. Combine 1 can (10¾ oz.) Campbell's Tomato Soup, ½ cup mayonnaise, 2 tbsp. pickle relish, 2 tsp. grated onion. Chill. Serve with cooked seafood. Also may be served hot. Makes 1½ cups sauce.

11 TOMATO BARBECUE SAUCE. In pan, combine 1 can (10¾ oz.) Campbell's Tomato Soup, ⅓ cup chili sauce, 2 tbsp. salad oil, 1 tbsp. horseradish mustard, 2 tsp. grated onion, generous dash hotpepper sauce. Simmer 5 min. Stir. Makes 2 cups sauce. Use as barbecue sauce for frankfurters, hamburgers.

3 HEARTY TOMATO SOUP. In pan, brown 2 thinly sliced frankfurters in 1 tbsp. butter or margarine. Stir in 1 can (10¾ oz.) Campbell's Tomato Soup, 1 soup can water, ½ cup cooked mixed vegetables, dash marjoram, dash pepper. Heat; stir. 2 to 3 servings.

9 TOMATO TWINS. In pan, combine 1 can (10¾ oz.) Campbell's Tomato Soup, 1 can Campbell's Bisque of Tomato Soup, 2 soup cans water. Heat; stir. 4 to 6 servings.

12 TOMATO SOUP GARNISH. Garnish Campbell's Tomato Soup with any one of the following: sour cream and chives, packaged cereal, shredded cheese, sliced green onion, watercress, croutons, toasted slivered almonds.

13 GET A THERMAL MUG FREE. Send us 12 Campbell's Tomato Soup labels, and we'll send you the exclusive Campbell's Tomato Soup Thermal Mug absolutely free! (Or you can get your mug for 2 Campbell's Tomato Soup labels and 50¢.) See? Something wonderful happens every time you open a can of Campbell's Tomato Soup.

4 SKILLET PORK CHOPS. In skillet, brown 6 pork chops (about 1½ lb.); pour off fat. Stir in 1 can (10¾ oz.) Campbell's Tomato Soup, ¼ cup water, ¼ cup chopped chutney. Cover; simmer 45 min. or until tender. Stir. 4 servings.

Send to: TOMATO SOUP MUG, BOX 425
Maple Plain, Minnesota 55359
Please send me_____Tomato Soup Mug(s).
For each mug, enclosed are either 12 Campbell's Tomato Soup labels or 2 Campbell's Tomato Soup labels and 50¢

Name_____
(please print)
Address_____
City_____State_____Zip_____

Offer expires December 31, 1970, but is subject to existing supply. Please allow 3 weeks for delivery. Offer good only in U.S.A. and Puerto Rico. Subject to state and local regulations. Void if taxed, restricted or forbidden by law.

Fig. 1.4 *Campbell's Tomato Soup customers get a free soup mug for twelve labels or for 50 cents with two labels. In any event, the mug stays around the house as a reminder to buy Cambell's soup. Advertisement appeared in* Family Circle, *September 1970. (Campbell Soup Company.)*

Example of a Send-away Premium Offer on Packaged Goods

Hi C Orange Drink offered personalized stationery, fifty sheets and twenty-five envelopes for twelve labels from 46-ounce cans. This offer is aimed at the large family consumer, those who purchase the 46-ounce size and use canned orange juice regularly. The purpose of this promotion is to gain mass purchase of the product among heavy users of canned orange juice.

Send-away Premiums — Major Purchase Products

Send-away premiums are not only used in packaged goods. They also have important uses in a variety of other product categories.

One of these important categories is in mail-order selling, where the premium is used as an incentive to urge the prospective purchaser to place an order for a product to be sent to him by mail. Frequently, a premium is offered which the purchaser is allowed to keep, regardless of whether he returns the merchandise to the seller or not. Usually, in these cases, the merchandise is offered for ten days free trial or examination. A variation of this type of promotion occurs when a book club or record club membership which is contingent upon purchase of a certain number of items yearly offers a book or record as a premium when a member signs up. In either of these cases, the premium offer makes the mail-order solicitation more attractive to a prospect who may be strongly considering filling in the order but is postponing action.

A second variation of the send-away premium offer used with major purchase products applies to premium offers as a means of locating or influencing prospects for these products.

Typical products or services for which this type of premium is used include insurance and home furnishings. In the insurance field, the premium offer is used to locate prospects who are attracted to a certain type of insurance presented in an advertisement or in direct mail. The premium offer is not featured but is contained within the text of the advertisement, so that only those who have actually read most of the proposal will respond. Once the prospect has responded, a salesman will be assigned to telephone him to try to set up an appointment to follow up on the contact.

Typical Examples of Insurance Send-away Premiums

Liberty Mutual Life offered a soft cover book, *The Flying Fisherman*, written by R. V. Gadabout Gaddis, star of their TV show.

Another product category which relies upon the send-away premium extensively is the home furnishings industry. Those who are active in the market for home furnishings may either be furnishing a new home or redecorating. However, those who are engaged in a major home furnishings project are in the market for furniture, carpets, and draperies within a relatively short period of time. During this time, the manufacturers are interested in making these prospects aware of their products—their special features, where they can be bought, and how to use them in their decorating plans. Through their advertising, the manufacturers often offer decorating information in booklets which advise the homemakers, as well as giving them product information.

As in the case of insurance premium offers, those used in the home furnishings field are frequently referred to within the text of an advertisement, as opposed to being featured. In these cases, only those who are interested in reading the ad carefully will see the offer and respond. To provide an additional deterrent to those who have only a cursory interest in the advertisement, a 25-cent charge is often included as a means of "screening out" disinterested individuals. Those who do respond are most likely to really be in the market for home furnishing products.

These booklets usually give general decorating information to the homeowner or apartment dweller as well as information on the products being promoted and where to buy them.

Typical Example of a Home Furnishings Send-away Premium

Armstrong Cork Company, manufacturer of hard surface and carpet products, offered the booklets *Before You Buy a Floor* and *What Every Homemaker Should Know about Floor Care.*

Free Premiums with Purchase—Major Purchase at Point of Sale

The seller of toothpaste or dry cereal uses an on-pack or send-away premium to give an immediate purchase incentive to the buyer. The sellers of a large number of more expensive items, both

This toaster does more than just toast. We're giving you two baking dishes to prove it. Free.

Life without a GE Toast-R-Oven* is like life without cherry tarts, hot bagels, English muffins. It can toast. It can top brown cheese sandwiches. It can warm muffins. It can bake loaves of bread, meat loaf for two.

When you buy a GE Toast-R-Oven, we'll give you (now through March 31, 1971) two free baking dishes. Ovenware of white porcelain decorated with sprays of garden herbs. Send in the upper right-hand corner from your GE Toast-R-Oven Use & Care book, along with this coupon.

A delicious offer like this is hard to resist, isn't it?

*TM General Electric Company

General Electric Company, Housewares Division, Bridgeport, Conn. 06602

GENERAL ⊕ ELECTRIC

Free.

GE Baking Dish Offer
P. O. Box 7500
Bridgeport, Conn. 06609

Gentlemen: As proof of purchase, I am enclosing the TOAST-R-OVEN* Model Number T-93 (located in the upper righthand corner) clipped from the front cover of my Use & Care Book. I made my purchase prior to March 31, 1971. Please send my 2 baking dishes to the address shown below:

Name_____
Please print clearly
Address_____
City_____State____Zip____
Please allow up to 4 weeks for delivery. Limit: One return per family. Deadline: all requests must be received with a postmark dated no later than midnight March 31, 1971. Note: Offer void where prohibited, taxed or otherwise restricted by law.

Fig. 1.5   *General Electric Toast-R-Oven* offers two free baking dishes with the purchase of the product. Offer is a send-away free premium using a coupon plus proof of purchase. Advertisement appeared in* Reader's Digest, *May 1971. (General Electric Company.)*
**TM General Electric Company*

goods and services, often use the same approach when they offer free premiums in return for purchase. Sometimes the premiums are immediately available with purchase; and in other cases, they are sent to the purchaser.

The free premium offered with the purchase of a major appliance usually represents a value of $20 or more, and a free premium offered with the purchase of an automobile usually has a value of well over $100. However, among "big ticket" items (e.g., major appliances, furniture, carpets, or tires), there is usually extremely active price competition. Thus, the ability to offer a premium within the manufacturer's price structure is usually limited to some degree. In general, the same situation applies to small appliances, and other items in the $10 to $30 range. Discount stores have a large percentage of the consumer market, and their operation is based on offering an extremely advantageous price to the consumer. This price does not allow the manufacturer to offer a premium and still make a profit. Indeed, the only time a consumer can buy most small appliances at a more advantageous price than that offered by discounters is when these items are offered as self-liquidating premiums.

Banks represent another important category in the use of free premiums. They use them to promote savings accounts, checking accounts, automobile loans, safe deposit boxes, and many other services.

Typical Examples of Free Premiums Offered with Purchase of Major Items

Motorola TV offered a 4-quart West Bend electric corn popper, four bowls, and a bag of popping corn—a $7.65 value—with a portable TV set. This offer appeals to teenagers, promoting the sale of a second or third TV to the family.

Indiana National Bank offered a free college dictionary for every new account or add-on of $100 or more or buying savings bonds. This offer was combined with an essay contest for teachers and a personal visit by Bennett Cerf to present prizes to the contest winners.

CONTINUITY PREMIUMS

Continuity premiums are offers in which items collected to make sets are made available one at a time, in order to encourage

Fig. 1.6 *The Seamen's Bank for Savings in New York promotes the opening of new branches to attract depositors, and to stimulate traffic to the new branches. Certain premiums are offered for $5,000 accounts. Others are offered for $500 accounts. Advertisement appeared in* The New York Times, *October 9, 1971. (The Seamen's Bank for Savings.)*

repeated transactions. Depending upon the situation, continuity premiums are offered either free, as self-liquidators, or as a combination of both types of offers.

The continuity premiums that are most familiar are chinaware, glassware, or flatware offers; but they can be adapted to any form in which a series of related premiums are collected. Typical examples are sets of books, matching towels, sets of commemorative stamps or coins, bracelet charms, or baseball trading cards.

The continuity premium is used in situations where a customer makes relatively frequent purchases and when there is very little variation in the products or services offered from one retail outlet to another. Gas stations, supermarkets, and banks are frequent users of continuity premiums because they have a major stake in getting repeat business from their day-to-day customers. If a housewife begins collecting a set of glasses, or an educational series on American history, there is a good chance that her interest will be sustained throughout the period of the promotion and that she will become a repeat customer. For example, if she wants to complete her set of eight glasses, she must refill her gas tank eight times, or make eight visits to the supermarket. If each visit averages $5, a total of $40 worth of business is represented by glassware which might cost $2 in premiums to the retailer or the manufacturer.

Banks or retail stores often use a combination of the free premium and the self-liquidating premium in promoting continuities. In this case, the initial item is usually offered free with a certain purchase or deposit. Then, for additional premiums to fill out the set, a charge is made which pays for the offer but is still well below retail price on the item.

Typical Examples of Continuity Premium Offers

First National Stores, Pittsfield, Mass., offered Funk and Wagnalls twenty-five volume encyclopedia: first volume for 49 cents, additional volumes for $1.49 with $3 purchase.

In another promotion, this time on a charm bracelet, they offered the first charm for 50 cents with charm bracelet free and additional charms 50 cents each with $3 purchase.

Enco Gas Stations offered five steak knives with wood-grained holder for 77 cents with each 8-gallon fill-up. Special additional offers: carving knife, fork, ham slicer, and sandwich spreader for $1.99 after collecting a full set of eight steak knives.

Traffic Builders

Attracting people to visit a retail store, a dealership, or a bank sometimes is the prime objective for a premium offer. The traffic builder premium fills this need. It is usually a rather low-cost item, but it has some particular utility or humorous appeal which makes it desirable. Quite often, the traffic builder is identified with the name of the product or retail location involved so that it serves as a reminder to the recipient.

Traffic builders are applicable in certain typical situations. The first of these is in connection with "big ticket" products such as automobiles, major appliances, and home furnishings. In these cases, a promotion which brings additional people into the dealer's showroom or retail store will create a certain amount of business, regardless of the fact that the majority do not buy. In these situations, relatively few sales can result in a large volume of new business. Traffic builders, however, will not generally represent the main promotional effort. In most cases, they are an additional element in a sale event or other special promotion. Another variation of the traffic builder is as a low cost self-liquidator, usually priced below $5, which represents an excellent value. Typically, tire and automobile accessory stores have found this type of traffic builder successful.

Traffic builders also play an important part in store openings, bank branch openings, or other similar situations. Here again, the traffic building premiums will not be the major promotional element, but will be an additional effort to help draw people to the new location. Traffic builders in these store openings promote goodwill and can serve as physical reminders to the public of a new and different location by being imprinted with the store's location.

Typical Examples of Traffic Builders

Firestone Tire and Rubber Co. have distributed free Burpee zinnia seeds through Firestone retail stores for three years to build spring traffic.

Firestone has also offered, as a traffic builder, a specially designed plastic litter box for automobiles — a $1 value for forty-nine cents.

Chevrolet Dealers distributed 2 million schedule books of college football programs in connection with their TV sponsorship of thirty-two NCAA college football games. This is a good example of an effective traffic builder which offers a very desirable low-cost premium, coinciding with new model introductions.

Door Openers and Good-Will Builders

Door openers and good-will builders, like traffic builders, are low-cost premiums which do not directly involve a sale. While traffic builders are used primarily to attract people to a retailer, these premiums are used to help set up a sales call, to establish a rapport between the prospective customer and the product or salesman, or to serve as a reminder of the sales call or service offered.

In door-to-door selling (e.g., cosmetics, housewares, or vacuum cleaners), the salesman often uses an inexpensive sample of one of his own products, whether he has received an order or not. In this way, he not only establishes good-will but also lets his prospect try out one of his products, thus paving the way for a second call.

In situations where a salesman is seeking an appointment in the home (e.g., carpet, home furnishings, encyclopedias), a more expensive premium may be offered as a door opener, which the prospect may keep regardless of whether or not she buys anything. In the case of carpet, for instance, a small decorative scatter rug is often used in this manner. In the life insurance business, another version of a door opener is used. A rather substantial premium, worth a dollar or more, is often advertised in order to select prospects out of general readership. The premium is used as a door opener. The salesman will follow up by telephone to set up a definite appointment on the very theory that anyone who sends for the premium would have been sufficiently attentive to the advertising to be a prospective customer.

Good-will builders are often just forms of reminder advertising used as part of a special promotion, in connection with a store opening, or to reinforce a continuing campaign for a product or service. These premiums include inexpensive imprinted pens, book matches, key chains, and similar articles which generally contain the name of a product or location of a retailer as a reminder to the customer.

Typical Examples of Door Openers and Good-Will Builders

Fuller Brush regularly provides their salesmen with small special-duty brushes, such as bottle washers. These are used as a "thank you" for a customer order, or simply as a good-will item, on the salesman's first or second call at the home.

Connecticut Mutual Life Insurance, Hartford, Conn., offers a free Rand McNally road atlas and travel guide for requesting information. This is a door opener which is followed up by a salesman's call asking for an appointment.

TRADING STAMPS

Trading stamps as a promotional technique account for over one half of all premium expenditures. At the same time, a downward trend has been apparent in the last few years, which clearly indicates that stamps have begun to lose ground as the dominant supermarket promotional vehicle.

In order to put this into perspective, we can go back to 1960 when trading stamp volume was estimated at $504 million. From 1960 to 1965 the trading stamp volume jumped to $748 million, during a period of relatively stable prices. However in 1970, despite the inflationary price increases which occurred during the late sixties, trading stamp volume was estimated at only $733 million (having reached $821 million in 1969).

In order to arrive at some understanding of stamps, it is necessary to examine the way in which they work, and how they are looked on by the consumer.

Trading Stamps as a Promotional Vehicle

Trading stamps, according to surveys made over a period of years by a leading stamp company (and corroborated by other independent surveys), are saved by over 80 percent of all U.S. families, either regularly or intermittently. So, regardless of present trends they still represent the strongest premium device in this country today.

Trading stamps are distributed by retailers, principally supermarkets, on the basis of ten stamps for each $1 of retail purchases. The customer collects these stamps in books, each of which hold 1,200 stamps. One filled book, therefore, represents $120 in sales.

If the average weekly supermarket check is $10 for an average customer, she will accumulate one book in twelve weeks. If she visits the store on the average of twice a week, a filled book will represent twenty-four store visits.

The filled stamp book (retail value approximately $3) is turned in for merchandise chosen from the stamp company's catalog.

The typical catalog contains over 3,000 items ranging from those worth less than $1, up to some worth over $1,000. However, in actual practice almost 70 percent of all books are turned in for items representing less than five books.

If the average book will be redeemed for merchandise worth about $3 at retail, what does the housewife pay for this book? The proponents of trading stamps state that the cost to the consumer averages about 1.8 percent over nonstamp supermarket prices. In return, she gets $3 worth of stamp merchandise for every $120 of purchases or 2.5 percent. These proponents say that the return on her dollar advantage to the consumer of 0.7 percent is accounted for by the fact that stamp companies buy their merchandise from the manufacturers of traded merchandise in huge volume at prices well below cost to retailers. Therefore the stamp companies claim they provide values below those offered even in discount stores.

The strength of trading stamps does not lie primarily in their offer to the consumer of a lower-priced way to buy merchandise. Instead, the strength of trading stamps is in their powerful continuity factor (the frequency with which a housewife can add to her stamp book), and the wide variety of merchandise which is offered (over 3,000 items) in the average stamp catalog book. Furthermore, through trading stamps, the average housewife can save for things she wants out of her own household money without asking her husband for extra money.

Compared to the typical continuity promotion which lasts a period of eight to sixteen weeks, and confines itself to a particular type of merchandise, the appeal of trading stamps is immediately apparent. Trading stamp promotions are offered by retailers on a year-to-year basis giving the customer a long term opportunity to save stamps in exchange for premiums. There is really something for every type of saver within the structure of trading stamp plans. For those who wish to cash in their books every few weeks, there are many low-denomination items to choose from; while those who prefer to wait six months or more are able to redeem their books for very substantial rewards. Figures for redemptions by size of book and total retail value are shown below:

TABLE 1.4   Redemptions by Book Values

Redemptions by number of books*	Estimated retail value (Author's estimate)	Percent of redemptions* by book values	Estimated average period of saving, in months (Author's estimate)
1/4–1 3/4	$ 0.75–5.25	20.7	1/3–2 1/2
2–4 3/4	6.00–14.25	47.8	3–7
5–9 3/4	15.00–29.25	19.4	7 1/2–14 1/2
10–19 3/4	30.00–59.25	7.9	15–29
20–29 3/4	60.00–89.25	3.3	30–45
30 or more	90.00 or more	0.9	Over 45

Incentive Marketing, Bill Brothers Publishing Corporation, New York, N.Y., March 1971.

Table 1.4 shows that while about one-fifth of all transactions are relatively small, the largest number of redemption transactions (almost 50 percent of them) are in the $6 to $14.25 range—representing substantial items. Another 30 percent are for even higher values.

A housewife spending $80[4] per month in a particular supermarket collects one book worth of stamps every six weeks, or two books in three months (which represents $6 retail value). We can see, therefore, the powerful continuity factor in the trading stamp psychology. Fifty percent of all transactions represent a saving period which approximates between 3 months and 7½ months; and another 30 percent represent an even longer period of saving.

The number of visits to the supermarket in order to collect the stamp books is particularly significant. The average housewife visits a supermarket about two times weekly. This represents about eight times per month. On this basis, the $6 to $14.25 category of stamp redemptions (47.8 percent of redemptions) represents between twelve and thirty visits to the supermarket which offers the trading stamps which she is collecting. While this does not prevent her from visiting competitive supermarkets, it does give her a continuing incentive over a long period of time to concentrate

[4] We are assuming that an average housewife will not concentrate all her expenditures in one supermarket but will spend about two-thirds of her household funds where she saves trading stamps.

more of her purchases in the store in which she is collecting her stamps. No other form of incentive promotion has ever been able to achieve this degree of long term appeal to exert a continuing influence on the housewife's purchase patterns.

The Variety of Merchandise Offered in Trading Stamp Plans

A typical trading stamp catalog is actually a small department store in print, offering over 3,000 items of merchandise. The merchandise is beautifully illustrated and represents the major brand names in every category.

Backing up the trading stamp programs of merchandise selection, and catalog display of these items, is a tremendous amount of specialized skill, paralleling the job of a merchandise manager in a comparable mass retail venture. Each category represents a different "department," in the department store sense, and the number of pages in the catalog must conform to tangible limits even as a store has physical limits on its display space.

The trading stamp merchandisers have had many years of experience, and they know which items are required for the one-book trade, which items are needed to satisfy the most popular two to five book categories. In addition, the higher redemption value items, such as furniture, higher-priced TV consoles, or expensive crystal ware, add elegance to the catalog; and they add to the assortment from which the trading stamp saver can choose. Of course, this variety and profusion is made possible by the long term relationship which exists between the supermarket and the trading stamp company. The supermarket commits to offer the trading stamp merchandise over a relatively long period of time to its customers; and, on the basis of this, the trading stamp company prints its catalogs, sets up its redemption centers (where the stamp merchandise offered is displayed and given out), and establishes its relationships with its many hundreds of suppliers.

The stamp saver's enjoyment in working with the catalog encourages her to consult it more often.

Recent figures show the categories of merchandise for which stamps are redeemed, as estimated by the leading industry source.

The range of merchandise represented by these categories shows that the stamp-collecting customer can get almost anything she wants if she is willing to patronize the trading stamp stores and wait for her books to accumulate.

Trading Stamp Promotions Outside the Supermarkets

The trading stamp business depends, as we have pointed out, on the supermarket. There are, however, many other retailers who can gain similar benefits from trading stamps. These other retailers are generally those who, like supermarkets, have customers who visit their stores quite regularly and who have essentially the same service to offer as their competitors. Filling stations are users of trading stamps, as are cleaning establishments and other local service retailers.

As soon as a supermarket is offering a particular brand of trading stamps, the local retailer has an opportunity to gain a potential advantage through offering the same brand of stamps to his customer.

TABLE 1.5   Stamp Redemptions by Category*

Merchandise classification	Total cost value estimated, %
1. Soft goods	15.1
2. Housewares	9.7
3. Small appliances	9.6
4. Furniture	8.9
5. Juvenile	5.6
6. Toys	5.1
7. Sporting goods	4.7
8. Gifts	4.6
9. Jewelry	4.5
10. Outdoor accessories	3.7
11. Luggage	3.5
12. Bathroom accessories	3.0
13. Clocks	3.0
14. Tools	2.7
15. Radios	2.6
16. Glassware and chinaware	2.3
17. Lawn supplies	2.3
18. Silver and flatware	1.6
19. Cameras	1.2
20. Books	0.9
21. Miscellaneous	5.6

Incentive Marketing, Bill Brothers Publishing Corporation, New York, N.Y., March 1971.

Trading Stamps: the Problem Areas

The success of trading stamps—the fact that more than three-quarters of all U.S. families save them, that they account for almost $800 million of goods moving into the hands of the U.S. consumer, that they comprise nearly one half of the value of all consumer incentives—has stirred up some strong detractors of trading stamp plans and their sponsors. At the same time, many supermarket chains have reconsidered their attitudes toward trading stamps and have decided to try promoting without them.

The first factor causing trading stamps to come under fire is occasioned by the consumerism movement. A very vocal segment of this movement at the state as well as at the national level puts forward the argument that a trading stamp plan "coerces" the buyer to accept a certain promotional program and that legislation should be enacted to protect the consumer. To this end, a number of states have passed legislation which requires a cash refund in lieu of trading stamps at the option of the customer. Other legislation on trading stamps has been enacted to protect the consumer against the trading stamp company or the retailer discontinuing the program and leaving them with books for which they have "paid" but which they cannot redeem.

Partly as a result of the consumerism movement and partly as a result of a move to offer lower prices in an inflationary situation, many food chains have eliminated their stamp programs. The basic merchandising theory of trading stamps is that stamps will yield a higher net profit because of the extra traffic to the supermarket. However, if two competitors both have stamp plans of equal merit, these stamp plans tend to offset one another so that each must turn to other promotional devices—specials, promotional games, or premiums—to attract additional customers.

In this situation, a large number of retailers have decided that they prefer to establish their image as "discounters," using advertised specials to support this approach. The Super Market Institute reported in 1963 that over 70 percent of their stores offered trading stamps. As of 1970, only 37 percent of their stores reported that they were offering stamps. As of 1963, the trading stamp volume was reported at $700 million; and in 1970, it was reported at $770 million representing an increase of only 10 percent during a period in which food prices increased by at least 60 percent. In other words, if trading stamp activity had remained at the 1963 level, trading stamp volume in 1970 would have reached $1.2 billion.

Trading stamp promotions are still an extremely potent promotional force, especially with food marketing. However, unless a new direction is taken, it would appear 'that their influence is far less powerful than it used to be. In the last analysis, one must conclude that the trading stamp concept still has great appeal for a large number of housewives; but, in a time of high food prices, the bargain appeal is essentially stronger. However, it would seem logical that, in a given area, certain stores will continue to offer trading stamp plans, because they will become the exclusive trading stamp promoters in their own markets.

COUPON PLANS

Akin to trading stamp plans, coupon plans provide a means of collecting coupons or labels on a relatively long term basis. They too may be exchanged for a variety of premiums offered in a catalog. While trading stamps are made available through retailers for the most part, coupon plans are offered through the purchase of individual products. Sometimes the product contains special coupons in the package and sometimes the labels themselves are collected for redemption against the merchandise.

While trading stamps as a category are on a downward trend, coupon plans have been increasing in importance. In 1968, coupon plans accounted for $197 million as opposed to $770 million for trading stamps.

There are many different versions of coupon plans. However, the two major categories are as follows:

1. Coupon plans in which an individual product or line of products makes the plan available, e.g., Chesterfield Cigarettes, Betty Crocker products (General Mills).

2. Coupon plans which, under one overall name, offer a variety of different products, e.g., Gift Stars, Bonus Gifts.

Coupon plans do not represent a new promotional technique. They are, in fact, among the oldest promotional methods dating back to the 1850s, when Mr. B. T. Babbitt offered his customers colored lithographs in exchange for twenty-five soap wrappers. However, recent developments in the marketplace have given them new importance in the field of incentive merchandising. One reason for the resurgence of coupon plans has been the development of cooperative plans in which many different products participate. Another has been the TV ban on cigarette advertising which has caused several major brands of cigarettes to go into coupon plans as new ways to gain an edge over their competition.

While new coupon plans are started every year, the solid success of well-established plans shows how well they work in getting and holding customers for a particular brand or a line of products. Brown and Williamson Tobacco Corporation has had a program on Raleigh and Belair Cigarettes for almost forty years. The merchandise distributed annually is estimated at $12 million; and their eighty-four-page catalog is distributed to 6 million people.[5]

The Betty Crocker coupon plan has been in effect since 1930. It offers coupons on over 100 General Mills' products. The plan offers a twenty-page catalog; and in one fifteen-year period, over 110 million pieces of Oneida silverplate were redeemed.[6]

Most coupon plans not only offer straight redemption against merchandise prizes, but also offer other options involving cash or trading stamps. Since coupon plans have not developed to the size and volume of trading stamp operations, their coupon plan catalogs are, by necessity, smaller and contain fewer items. However, they often offer convertibility into trading stamps, so that the housewife can also redeem her coupons against trading stamp catalogs.

The Chesterfield Cigarette LMC coupon program is an example of the flexibility which is being built into successful coupon plans.

The plan offers the participant four different ways to redeem coupons:

1. Use LMC coupons to order merchandise by mail from the LMC Catalog.

[5] *Giveaway Promotions*, Premium Advertising Association of America, 1969.
[6] Ibid.

Fig. 1.7 *Raleigh/Belair promote their gift catalog (with over 1,000 gifts to choose from) through a magazine advertisement with a special pop-up card coupon. $12,000,000 worth of premiums are handled each year through this program. Advertisement appeared in Life, September 13, 1971. (Brown & Williamson Tobacco Corp. Reprinted by permission.)*

2. Use LMC coupons and cash to order merchandise by mail. Many items in the LMC catalog can be redeemed for a minimum number of coupons plus cash. Under their speed plan, this enables the person who wants an item to get it faster than he normally would.

3. Exchange LMC coupons for cash. The coupon collector mails in exactly 375 coupons and receives a cash certificate worth $2.80 which is redeemable at a local cooperating retail store.

4. Exchange LMC coupons for trading stamps. LMC coupons may be redeemed in lots of 75 (equal to 300 trading stamps) at cooperating trading stamp gift centers.

Mr. Samuel White, corporate vice president, Liggett & Myers, Inc., explains, "We thought we would measure the single best and most exciting way to redeem our coupons. Instead, what we found was that customers like a variety of redemption methods with the comfort and freedom to choose."[7]

Under the Chesterfield LMC plan, each package contains one coupon and each carton contains four additional bonus coupons. Thus, a carton contains fourteen coupons. When a smoker orders the LMC catalog, he gets a certificate worth 300 coupons—so that when he buys 5 1/2 cartons of Chesterfields he has 375 coupons, which is sufficient to order the minimum gift in the catalog.

Another angle to the carton bonus coupons is that the retail trade collects the four coupons with each carton they break open for retail sale. Therefore, a retailer has an added incentive to promote Chesterfields, as he can save for gifts too.

The LMC catalog has sixty pages in full color and offers over 1,000 items to choose from. The LMC catalogs are distributed by mail on request only. Several million are currently in circulation. The LMC program is extensively promoted at point of sale and through natural advertising.

GUIDELINES FOR PURCHASING PREMIUMS

Locating and purchasing a consumer premium is an extremely demanding task. The premium buyer must find a reliable source of

[7] *Incentive Marketing*, Bill Brothers Publishing Corporation, New York, N.Y., March 1971.

supply, and, at the same time, seek new or unusual items which will have special appeal to his audience.

He often must commit ahead of time to a substantial quantity, or make sure that there is available stock for prompt fulfillment of his customers' orders.

This delivery factor becomes of utmost importance when dealing with premiums which are sent through the mails, by express or by other methods. If the premium is not delivered with reasonable promptness, which requires efficient order-processing procedures and sufficient stock of merchandise, the resulting consumer dissatisfaction reflects upon the promoted product rather than upon the premium supplier. In these cases, obviously, the promotion will create a negative reaction.

In the average self-liquidator offer, those ordering the premium are advised to allow three to six weeks for delivery.

A study conducted by the staff of *Incentive Marketing* illustrates the problem involved in delivery. This group sent away for thirty-two self-liquidators offered by advertisers.[8] The median time required for delivery was just under six weeks with only ten of the thirty-two items being delivered in less than four weeks. The longest delivery time required was fourteen weeks—over three months waiting time. When a premium purchaser has been kept waiting for more than two weeks over the time limit promised, it is no wonder that irritability sets in.

It is for this reason that the premium buyer must not only make sure that the premium he selects is of a quality standard which reflects well upon the product he is promoting, but also make sure that his premium supplier has a proven track record in being able to handle orders and ship merchandise efficiently. Once the premium project has been launched and the supplier fails to maintain inventory or to fulfil orders to the consumer promptly, there is very little the premium buyer can do for recourse. Checking the supplier for reputation, credit, and ability to deliver is therefore essential.

Just as premiums vary in price and type, they also vary, according to the needs of the promoter, in the way in which they are purchased. In this area there is room for some innovation and imagination so that the premium buyer avoids the run-of-the-mill

[8] *Incentive Marketing*, Bill Brothers Publishing Corporation, New York, N.Y., July 1970.

items and ends up with a premium which is different or exciting or which represents an excellent value. Some of the purchasing methods used may involve one or more of the following methods:

1. Locate merchandise which is overstock in a manufacturer's inventory and therefore available at an extremely attractive price.

2. Using a manufacturer's available stock merchandise, find a way to add a special feature at very low cost. Naturally, an aggressive manufacturer will be of great help in coming up with new ideas and setting up such a program.

This special feature can be a pattern or color in the case of textile, ceramics, or glassware: or the product's trademark or brand name can be included in the design. In other cases, the special premium can involve special product features.

3. In situations where an extremely large volume is involved, special merchandise can be commissioned. In these cases, a production commitment will be required; and the buyer must be certain that if the promotion is very successful he can obtain reorders within a reasonable period of time.

Proof-of-Purchase Requirements

In almost all send-away promotions, the consumer is required to submit proof of purchase, regardless of whether or not cash is required (as in the case of a self-liquidator).

When a product is packaged in a carton, such as a tube of toothpaste, the proof-of-purchase requirement is fairly easy. The end flap of the carton is removed and placed in the envelope with the premium order form and the check or money order (if the premium is a self-liquidator).

When a can, a jar, a bottle, or an aerosol container is involved, the proof-of-purchase requirement becomes a more difficult problem. In these cases, various solutions have been worked out. In some cases, the gummed label can be soaked off and sent in with the order. (However, this leaves the product without any label identification in the kitchen.) In other cases, a portion of the label can be detached and sent in with the order leaving the major identification intact.

In still other cases, an inner seal or liner from a screw-top lid can be used as proof of purchase. The drawback in this method is that a certain amount of product protection is sacrificed.

If a can or aerosol container is being promoted, a serial number is usually shown on the can and may be used as proof of purchase. It is possible that a customer could simply jot down the number of the can while shopping in a supermarket and thereby avoid the purchase requirement. However, it is the usual experience that only a small minority of housewives will take advantage of this possibility.

CONSUMER ADVERTISING OF PREMIUMS

Advertising of premiums differs from regular product advertising in that the premium offer must be clearly and forcefully communicated, while at the same time the product must be identified and presented to the reader, listener, or viewer.

In general, the print forms of media (magazine, newspaper, or direct mail) are preferred for premium advertising because of these complexities. In many cases, it is desirable to place a coupon containing basic information about the offer (i.e., where to send for it, cost, color and size, and delivery time) in the hands of the reader. Handling a premium offer on TV or on radio becomes difficult unless the offer is an extremely simple one to convey. An example of an offer which could be effectively handled on radio or TV would be a glassware offer for a major oil company. The offer would be simply stated, and the gas stations offering them would be well known to the consumer. However, in the case of the usual self-liquidator or free send-away premium offer, quite a bit of information must be imparted to the reader.

Among premium offer advertisements studied by *Incentive Marketing Facts*,[9] the amount of space devoted to the premium varied greatly but came out to an average of 40.8 percent of total advertising space. If it is possible to carry the product identification into the premium as Campbell Soup, Green Giant, Coca Cola, and many others have done, it makes it possible to picture the premium and the product identification as well. This makes the advertisement simpler and more effective. This approach, of

[9] *Incentive Marketing Facts*, Bill Brothers Publishing Corporation, New York, N.Y., 1969.

course, requires substantial resources on the part of the sponsor to order a sufficient quantity to customize his own premiums.

Advertising the premium serves to notify the consumer of the offer. However, in many cases, the consumer will not use the coupon in the advertisement but will use a coupon enclosed in a package or available at the point of sale. Many times, the consumer will be initially motivated by the advertisement with the point of purchase activity serving as a reminder or reinforcement to actually purchase the product.

For this reason, direct coupon response from a magazine or newspaper ad is not necessarily the true measure of that advertisement's effectiveness in promoting the offer.

A group of premium users reported on the origin of responses to self-liquidatory offers as follows: [10]

28.5%	Coupons from ads
22.0%	Package advertising
34.3%	Point of purchase order forms
15.2%	Letters and miscellaneous

In considering the most effective media for premium offers, the promoter must weigh the immediacy of newspapers with the fact that magazines, especially monthlies, stay around longer and have great multiple readership. Again, in comparing one magazine against another, the promoter will attempt to match the audience; not only against the audience for his product, but also against the premium he is offering. Thus, if a kitchen-oriented premium is offered, a women's magazine would have a greater pulling power than a general magazine.

In a recent survey of magazines, covering a six-month period, the following premium offers per issue were recorded: [11]

1. *Ladies Home Journal*, 14.2 offers per issue
2. *Redbook*, 12.2 offers per issue
3. *Cosmopolitan*, 11.3 offers per issue
4. *Good Housekeeping*, 10.2 offers per issue
5. *McCall's* and *Woman's Day*, 8.3 offers per issue

[10] *Incentive Marketing Facts*, Bill Brothers Publishing Corporation, New York, N.Y., 1969.

[11] *Incentive Marketing*, Bill Brothers Publishing Corporation, New York, N.Y., July 1971.

In national magazines, the survey shows an average of 2.250 pages devoted to premium offers annually.

In considering the advertising of premium offers, direct mail is a very high response medium. In cases where the premium offer might not warrant the expense of a direct mail effort, the offer is sometimes used as an extra incentive in a direct mail price-off coupon program to try to increase consumer participation and thereby create a lower cost per thousand responses from the direct mail list.

PREMIUM TESTING

It is a fact of life that most marketers talk about testing their premiums, but most of them don't do anything about it. Fifty-eight percent of premium users polled by *Incentive Marketing Facts* reported that they rarely or never market-test premium items.

There are various reasons for this situation:

1. Many premiums have a track record of performance which makes testing a futile exercise.

2. Premium testing becomes expensive under professional research guidance; yet its results are questionable if done without proper research expertise.

3. Most premium testing is a rather time consuming process. If there is urgency to get a promotion into the field, there may not be time for testing.

There are many methods of premium testing. They range from extremely simple personal interviews on a do-it-yourself basis to full scale in-store tests in which the premium is tested as part of an overall marketing program.

Premium testing is usually used when several premiums have been screened and are being considered for a particular promotion. The purpose of testing is to determine which will be the most effective.

Personal Interviews

In the most simple form of personal interviewing, the respondent is exposed to the actual premiums (or to pictures of them) and asked to rate the premiums in order of desirability. If the premiums are self-liquidators, the respondent is also given the price. This form of testing can be done with minimum expense and supervision, and the results obtained from it will be rather rudimentary. However, if several hundred interviews yield a big negative factor in connection with one of the premiums or show one to be an odds-on-favorite, the effort may well be worthwhile. In conducting this type of testing, it is important that those people interviewed fairly closely match the demographic characteristics of purchasers of the product. Where at all feasible, market research people should help determine those who are interviewed.

Mail Questionnaire

Another form of premium polling is conducted via direct mail. The respondent is asked to select from pictures which premium she would prefer or how she would rate them. Using selected lists for direct mail, the questionnaire can be directed to a representation of the target audience for the product. The direct mail questionnaire can reach many more people economically than personal interviews.

Direct Mail Offer

In the direct mail offer, the premium is actually offered for sale; and therefore, the results are judged on the basis of which premium actually pulled in cash.

There are two ways to conduct the direct mail offer test. In the first method, all premiums considered are offered in a single mailing with the respondent having to choose between them. In the second method, favored by larger premium users, a separate direct mail piece would be developed for *each* premium tested. Then these pieces would be sent to matched groups of respondents to determine which one sells the best. In this case, several thousand would have to be sent to each group in order to reach a reasonably accurate prediction.

If the premium user is experienced in direct mailing, he may well have a previously successful premium which can be used as a control item in a test. Thus, he may send out 3,000 direct mail offers on his control premium and 3,000 on each of four others. He can then judge how well his new premiums are doing against a known control factor.

Split-Run Newspaper Offer

When the premium is to be offered in newspaper advertising, a split run is sometimes used in the same way that the direct mail offer is run. A split run is two or more versions of the same advertisement run in alternating copies of the same edition of the newspaper. The premium tester then has a "head-to-head" comparison of which premium will pull more inquiries.

The outcome of a series of tests by one advertiser resulted in an interesting track record of premium testing. Here the results were reported in the percentage of return the winning offer had over its rival in a series of eighty five split-run comparisons.

Return of winning ad over losing ad, %*	Number of tests
0–4	27
5–9	5
10–19	9
20–49	36
100–135	8

* *Incentive Marketing Facts*, Bill Brothers Publishing Corporation, New York, N.Y., 1969.

In this series, forty-four advertisements revealed differences of 20 percent or more between one offer over the other. Thus, a significant difference was revealed in over 50 percent of cases tested. At the same time, this premium user also had a series of quantitative results. In some cases, the percentage of return would show *both* premiums to be well above average; in others both could be eliminated as "losers."

Store Panels

Various research organizations or media groups have available, through cooperation with food and drug store chains, a means through which a premium user can test his premium offers at the point of sale. In this type of situation, a control group of stores will show the product without any special incentive; another group of stores will have one premium offer; and a third group of stores will show an alternate offer. As many premium offers are largely supported by the point of sale activity (even when they are advertised), this type of testing can yield valuable information on the effectiveness of a premium to communicate itself to the consumer in the confusing supermarket or drug store situation.

Hypothetical Case No. 1—Product Q Dry Cereal

In the heavily competitive dry cereal market, the use of premiums is a way of life—a means of selling products both new and old to a consuming population, 70 percent of which is under seventeen years of age. A continual stream of in-pack, on-pack, and self-liquidating offers is directed at this audience.

In the case of product Q, let us assume a market share of 1 percent ($7 million) of a total market representing $700 million retail. This represents a total of 24 million packages of cereal per year at an average price of 29 cents. Product Q was successfully launched four years ago and has achieved as high as 1.2 percent share of the market.

The brand manager's task is to come up with a premium promotion which will help gain new users for product Q, a presweetened brand which appeals mainly to children under fourteen according to research studies.

The goal of the product manager is to try to increase his sales by 10 percent in the next six months. In order to do this, he is considering two premium proposals. The first promotion involves printing a series of ten famous American battle scenes (Valley Forge, Fort Sumter, The Alamo, etc.) on the packages. The second promotion is a self-liquidator in which a variety of five toy cars are offered at a price of 50 cents in the mail. In either case, the number of packages printed for the promotion will be one-half of the estimated annual sales (plus a 10 percent increase), or 13,200,000 packages.

In choosing between the two promotions, the product manager weighs the merits of these two promotions he has selected from a large number of potential premiums which have been suggested by his own sales promotion department, his advertising agency, and a great many outside suppliers.

Here are the considerations which lead him toward a final decision between the two premiums.

Premium No. 1: American battle scenes on the carton

Appeal   The appeal of the American battle scenes is considered to be excellent for the age group from eight to fourteen years with diminishing interest when the children are less than eight. However, the educational and patriotic aspects will probably be attractive to mothers, who are obviously an important purchasing influence. Finally, the product manager feels that the battle scene promotion is really different from most cereal premiums offered.

Continuity factor As the famous American battle scenes represent a series, there will be a good continuity factor built into the promotion. Many kids who get one package of product Q will want to collect all or many of the series, and therefore repeat purchase will be stimulated during the promotional period. This factor will also tend to develop regular users of the product.

Cost factors As there are ten different battle scenes, there is going to be some cost involved in printing a different scene for each 1,320,000 packages (13,200,000 divided by 10). The product manager has figured that with a printing run of over one million he has to allow for additional costs of one-tenth of one cent per package. In addition, he must allow $10,000 to pay for the rights to the art work he is going to use. This factor will cost him approximately one tenth of one cent for each package.

Premium No. 2: Choice of five cars—50-cent self-liquidator

Appeal The toy cars will have appeal to the three to eight year old age bracket, with diminishing interest as the child goes over eight years. The price of the premium is considered a good one, and it is not expected to provide any major deterrent as far as mothers are concerned. However, the nuisance of having to send away for a self-liquidator must be considered negative when compared with premium No. 1 which is right on the package. Finally, while the toy car premium is a proven item, it is not considered greatly different from the typical cereal premium offered.

Continuity factor A continuity factor is built in, as each toy must be redeemed for 50 cents plus one box top. While it is likely that some children will want to collect a full set of cars, the desire will probably not be as strong as the wish to have a full set of battle scene pictures.

Cost factor The premium is fully self-liquidating, and the large toy manufacturer involved has handled many premium offers before. The price is excellent, as the manufacturer considers that 13,200,000 advertising impressions of his brand name will be conveyed by product Q packages; and he has taken this fact into his price consideration.

Discussion leading to decision for product Q premium promotion

The product manager's market research shows that product Q has greater strength in the eight to fourteen year old age group, with 70 percent of sales coming from families where this age group predominates; while the less numerous five to nine year old age group accounts for only 33⅓ percent of product Q's sales.

In addition, the product manager feels that there will be a greater degree of appeal in a color picture right on the package as opposed to a send-away offer.

If the sales target is met using premium No. 1, the cost factors will work out as follows:

Retail sales.	$3,850,000
($7,000,000 + 10% ÷ 2) (1/2 year)	
Increase over previous year	350,000
Increase in gross margin over	
previous year (20% × 350,000)	75,000
Cost of Promotion:	
2/10¢ per package.	26,400
Net increase in gross margin . . . . $	48,600

If premium No. 2 were used and sales goals were met, the brand would enjoy an increase in gross margin of $75,000. However, the product manager decided in favor of premium No. 1 feeling that his primary objective is to regain share and that the battle scene picture premium had the best chance of helping him gain the extra business.

Hypothetical Case No. 2—Product A Desk Top Copier

A large business equipment firm has a problem with the sales of its desk top copier. The machine is not only competitive in price with other machines on the market, but also it has excellent speed and performance characteristics, making it a better value than its competition. When a demonstration of the machine has been made to a qualified prospect, such as an office manager or purchasing agent, the field sales managers report an excellent rate of conversions to sales—at a ratio of about one sale to four demonstrations. The sales promotion manager of the firm has been given the assignment of increasing the number of demonstrations made by the 200-man sales force so that the current rate of three sales per salesman per week can be greatly increased.

A premium given to a prospect for watching a demonstration seems to be appealing. The sales promotion manager reasons that if the prospects know that they can obtain a desirable premium for simply seeing a demonstration, a great many of them will respond. Of course, there will be some who request the demonstration simply because they want the premium; but if they are qualified respondents, they will be in the market sometime in the future anyway. From past experience, he knows he can set up a screening system to be sure that those who get demonstrations are qualified prospects.

A premium which would be given on the basis of a sale has been rejected because, in the first place, the objective is to get prospects to watch a demonstration. It is also felt that it would be better psychology to have the prospect sure he would get the premium regardless of whether he purchased a copier or not. Finally, a prospect, such as an office manager or a purchasing agent, might well feel it was unethical if he got a premium as a result of placing an order, but he would not feel that way in the case of the demonstration.

The selection of the premium is the next order of business. The sales promotion manager finds a very attractive hard cover atlas which would be a decorative item for any office and is obtainable for $3. He figures that if one demonstration in four results in a sale, then each copier sold will cost $12 against a $200 sale price. Actually the current cost of a sales call per machine has been running close to $30. He figures he could, by increasing the efficiency of his sales force, cut the cost per sales call to $12 per machine, thus allowing a budget to pay for most of the cost of the premiums and the advertising.

The next consideration is the means by which to promote the atlas offer. The sales promotion manager consults the advertising manager, and they select one broad-based business magazine to promote the offer. Direct mail has been considered but is discarded because of its expense, and also because the target group is an extremely broad business audience.

The advertisement features a return coupon at the top to focus attention on it. It provides about equal weight to a description of the atlas premium and to product A's benefits. Coupons are directed to the sales promotion manager whose office will screen them and then send them out to the field for personal follow-up by the sales force.

Cost analysis of the product A desk top copier promotion

The cost of the advertisement—one page, black and white—is $8,250; and the circulation of the magazine is 450,000. A return of 1½ percent on circulation is achieved.

Promotional cost is 8 percent. The percentage is considered allowable for this promotion which has the effect of placing a large number of machines in new locations where the superior quality of the machine will result in stimulating additional orders.

```
450,000 circulation. . . . . . . . . . . . . . . . . . . . . . . . . . .   6,750 returns
Cost of 1 page black and white. . . . . . . . . . . . . . . .   $8,250
Cost per return . . . . . . . . . . . . . . . . . . . . . . . . . . . .      1.22
Number of demonstrations actually reported . . . . . . . .   5,000
   (Balance of 1,750 did not work out)
Number of sales (1 out of 4). . . . . . . . . . . . . . . . . . .   1,250
Cost of promotion:
   Premiums                      5,000 × $3.00 =  $15,000
   Advertising                                      8,250
   Total                                          $23,250
   Total sales                                   $250,000
```

Hypothetical Case No. 3—Product F Facial Tissues

Product F, an established brand name with a 20 percent share of the market, has been under heavy pressure from competitive brands, particularly lower-priced products without established brand names. Meeting price competition head on is not possible, because product F has better quality and must command a higher price than its competition.

Among the least expensive promotions considered has been a self-liquidating premium which not only represents a minimal promotional cost, but also can bring prestige to product F if the right premium can be found.

A prominent producer of hair-care products has made available a new hair-care kit at a price of $6.95 delivered to the consumer. Excellent demand from users of facial tissues is anticipated on this offer, as a result of a series of personal interviews conducted by the market research department.

The objective of the promotion is to regain several percentage points of market share lost to competition in recent months.

In order to take advantage of the premium, clear sales objectives must be established. The brand manager says the promotion must produce a 5 percent increase in sales. He feels that this promotion can be carried out over a three month period and that if he enjoys a 5 percent increase, the brand's increased share will sustain itself for several additional months.

There are several ways this "hair care" promotion can be used to bring about increased sales:

1. Gain increased sales of product by featuring the offer prominently on the package.

2. Advertise the offer to the consumer to get direct response and awareness.

3. Advertise and promote the offer to the retail trade, attempting to get special retail displays. In this connection, offer a special display stand featuring a sample of the premium and containing the product. Also make it known to the store manager that the sample of the premium in the display is his to keep after the promotion period is over.

In order to quantify the estimated sales increase and to establish costs, let us assume that product F's present rate of travel is 40 million packages per month at an average retail of 25 cents or $10 million per month. The desired sales increase would produce 2 million additional packages per month or a total of 6 million packages worth $1,500,000 at retail.

Cost analysis—"hair care" premium three-month promotion

Let us assume that the promotion meets target increase of 5 percent sales. The promotional cost for increased sales has been approximately 12 percent since $1,500,000 represents $800,000 sales at the manufacturer's level. If the post-promotion sales increase is sustained for three months the brand manager will feel that this promotion has been justified, in view of the fact that brand erosion has been halted.

Magazine advertising to consumers, 8,000,000 circ..	$50,000
Trade advertising	10,000
Special feature displays, 5,000 at $4.00	20,000
Premiums for store managers, 5,000 at $4.00	20,000
	$100,000

Note that $100,000 spent in a straight price reduction against total product in a three-month period would not have represented a sufficient amount to achieve a meaningful price reduction to the consumer. ($100,000 applied to 6 million packages amounts to only 1.7 cents per package—insufficient for a consumer price-off.)

It is important to realize that many promoters would be tempted to cut back on the consumer advertising expenditure in order to reduce promotional costs. The magazine exposure works not only for direct response but also to reinforce consumer awareness at the point of sales. When the prospect sees the promotion, either on the package, on the shelf, or, less frequently, in a special display, she is aware of the offer and is inclined to act on it.

In addition, most retailers refuse to consider special displays on this type of promotion unless they are backed by consumer advertising.

2

THE BARGAIN APPEAL — COUPONS, DEALS, AND PRICE-OFFS

PRICE REDUCTION AS A MARKETING TOOL

It is believed by many who are not thoroughly experienced in marketing that any form of price reduction is a sign of weakness or ineptness on the part of marketing managers—that if they had done their jobs properly in the first place it would never have been necessary to take the price cut. In actual practice, this belief is not well-founded. While it is true that many price reductions are a sign of hasty or even panicky reaction to competitive situations, for the most part these actions are legitimate and necessary from time to time for effective marketing of almost every product.

To place strategic price reductions in the proper perspective, consider for a moment that in retail merchandising pricing is the most vital function in the process of retailing. The merchandising manager in the great retail operations—Sears, Penneys, and all department stores—is the key figure in management; and his job is not only to price the merchandise initially, but also to move the merchandise. Turning his stock is vital to his profit picture; and if some merchandise is turning too slowly, he will sacrifice his mark-up and price it so that it will move. The degree of success that the merchandise manager has in his overall operation lies in his ability to move merchandise, and this is inextricably linked to his skill in pricing. If he refused to ever take a mark-down, he would be in very serious trouble.

In the hands of an astute marketing manager, price reductions are handled with the fullest knowledge and understanding of what the short-term and the long-term results of each move are likely to be. The situation as regards a manufacturer is similar to those which apply to a retailer with the difference being one of degree rather than of basic conditions. In the case of a retailer, he is generally dealing with a much more volatile and rapidly moving situation. He is in direct touch with the consumer whereas a manufacturer is several steps away and any pricing maneuver takes longer to put into effect.

An additional factor for the manufacturer is the potential effect of price reduction on his brand in the marketplace; a consideration with which the retailer usually is not concerned. If a brand has too many price reductions applied to it over a given period of time, it tends to erode the brand's image in the trade and with the consumer. The brand then becomes known as one which is "footballed" around, and a permanently lower price level will be associated with it. In addition, the effect of a lower price level will generally lower the profit available to the retailer, so that he may eventually turn to other more profitable brands.

Price reductions, then, are vitally important in the marketing scheme of things; and they place as much demand for good sound judgment on the marketing manager as any other technique used in marketing.

Price Reduction as Consumer Incentive

Price reductions qualify as consumer incentives when the consumer is offered a reduced price on something of known value, which can be calculated as a known saving. The price reduction in itself then becomes an incentive to purchase; it is the extra promotional offer which will move her to purchase the product over its competitor.

A housewife is engaged in her principal job when she is shopping. There is nothing more important to her than to get value for her dollar. Her role as purchasing agent means that a bargain, in one form or another, is exactly what she is looking for; and therefore, when properly applied, price reductions are the most potent and effective consumer incentive that exists.

Instead of a straight price reduction, a deal may refer to an offer of free merchandise with a purchase or of reduced price on multiple purchases. In other words, a product deal implies some involvement of additional product or products with a saving in price. As we shall see, the deal may involve two related products or multiple purchases.

The way a deal or price reduction is planned and promoted offers the widest latitude for marketing skill and for creative imagination. Just as a successful product is promoted with imagination in its package, its advertising, and its display, the presentation as a special offer can be done with excitement and flair.

The simplest form of price reduction is the price-off, which is an offer imprinted right on the package. This form of offer is not only the simplest, but for most products the most effective because it is direct and uncomplicated. As deals and offers become more involved, complexities are added which tend to embroil the consumer in the mechanics of getting paid or in a decision about multiple purchase. While there are almost always valid reasons for making an offer more complicated, it must be realized that the simpler the deal is, the simpler it is for the consumer to act on it.

A common method of handling a price-off is to have the price offer printed right on the package. However, in many instances it is desirable to carry the offer to the consumer through advertising or direct mail. It is this consideration that has led to the popularity of the price-off coupon, on which is printed the denomination of the price reduction and the name of the product.

Coupons are also distributed in the product package itself. If a product is subject to a price-off or deal and a coupon is inserted inside the package in an attempt to stimulate a second sale, this second coupon is known as a bounce-back coupon.

Fig. 2.1 *This advertisement uses the magazine to promote deals on a line of four Almay cosmetic products. Sales prices vary from $2.50 to $4.75. With this type of advertising, follow-through in retail outlets is absolutely essential. Advertisement appeared in McCall's, February 1969. (Schiefflin and Company.)*

When two related products are couponed it is known as cross-couponing. An example of this method would be a coupon for a liquid dishwashing detergent carried in a powdered detergent box, both representing products of the same manufacturer.

Consumer Deals

A deal is a special offer related to purchase of more than one package of identical products at a special price. Common examples are:

- Two for the price of one
- Three for the price of two
- Buy one, get one free
- Buy one, get another for 1 cent

Product deal offers are often banded together on the store shelf. The band is imprinted with the deal information, the special price and the amount of savings involved. Another device commonly used is to have the consumer send in proof of purchase (label, box top, carton flap, etc.) and receive in the mail a coupon good for a free purchase.

When a deal involves sending in proof of purchase, the offer is often made in the form of cash instead of a coupon. ("We'll pay you 50 cents to try it.") These are called coin refund offers.

The Trade Impact of Consumer Promotions

Every consumer promotion has an effect not only on the consumer, but also on the trade. The relationship between the two is important in fulfilling the ultimate objectives of the promotion.

In many deals and price-off promotions, the trade effect is absolutely vital to the success of the promotion.

For example, in the case where a coupon campaign is run in a particular marketing area with the purpose of getting distribution in major retail outlets, the trade must stock the product on the shelves in order for a consumer to take advantage of the offer.

When a refund offer is made through newspapers or magazines on a product which already has been distributed, the effect of the promotion will involve primarily the consumer. The retail trade will enjoy additional sales from whatever extra sales are made.

The important thing here is to be sure that both the consumer and the trade are considered in the planning of a promotion.

Marketing Factors in Consumer Price Offers

The marketing situation and the gross profit of a product will determine whether a price-off or deal is indicated. In general, the direct price-off, whether on the product or via a coupon, will produce direct sales action faster than other forms of deals and offers. As the deal is rendered more complicated, fewer people will respond to the offer. For example, a send-away offer for 25 cents requires the consumer to send in a label from the product. This involves addressing and stamping an envelope, putting the label in it, and mailing it. Or taking another example, a multiple purchase which offers different sizes or related products involves a more complicated purchase decision for the consumer, with a corresponding hesitancy to act on it.

An analysis of the product and the market will reveal many decisive factors as to which type of offer to select.

A product's share of market has much to do with the strategy of employing price-offs. One with a substantial share (over 20 percent) of market may run the risk of "spinning its wheels" with a price-off promotion. A price-off may increase its share two or three percentage points, at the end of which time it will simply slip back to its former position—after the manufacturer has paid a substantial amount for the promotional costs.

A product which has a small (under 5 percent) share of market may have different problems in trying to use deals to expand its share of market. Trade acceptance is a definite problem; and unless a strong brand name has been established, consumer acceptance will be very low. On the other hand, if the product has a very small share, a deal is one way to introduce the brand to new users.

The consumer orientation of a product has much to do with the strategy of price promotions.

The first factor to be considered is how often the product is purchased. In other words, if you are successful in obtaining consumer purchase from new customers as a result of the deal, how quickly will they be back in the marketplace to repurchase?

The second factor to be considered is the percentage of con-

Fig. 2.2 *"You put together the 1969 Kraft Italian and a Hefty Bag, and we'll put together 50 cents for you." A cooperative promotion that helps sell both products through an interesting use of refund offer. (Kraftco and Mobil Chemical Company.)*

sumers who have tried the product. If there is a very high percentage who have never tried it, your deal can attract new users. On the other hand, if you have a high percentage of consumers who have used the product, you may attract them to repurchase during deal, only to lose them again afterwards. In this connection, one must be constantly aware that a substantial percentage of all bargain-conscious consumers will buy a deal regardless of product name, moving on to the next deal the next time they shop.

The fact that this bargain-conscious group is a factor for marketing men to consider is borne out by research sponsored by *This Week* magazine and conducted by Market Research Corporation of America. In this study, they used their National Consumer Panel and studied price-offs and coupons as well as retailers' specials. Their study was confined to light-duty liquid detergents, regular coffee, and margarine, products subject to heavy dealing. The buyers were classified by their proneness to deals. In this panel, 61 percent are light dealers, 22 percent are heavy deal buyers, and 17 percent are in the medium group. The following table shows the extent to which the three classes take advantage of deals.

The most significant finding was that heavy deal buyers, comprising one-fifth of all householders studied, accounted for *three-fifths* of all deal volume. At the same time, light deal buyers accounted for only 14 percent of the deal volume. This survey shows that marketers should be aware that their deal efforts tend to concentrate certain types of consumers.

Another study was conducted under the sponsorship of the Association of National Advertisers by Alfred Politz Research, Inc., with a national sample representing households which contained "one woman who is the principal grocery shopper."

This study, (see Table 2.1) was made to determine, among other things, the relative popularity of cents-off sales versus coupons and other forms of consumer incentives. In this instance, the desire of consumers to have the simplest, least complicated form of deal is apparent.

Class	Proportion of purchases made with deals, %*		
	Coffee	Margarine	Detergent
Heavy deal buyers	88	71	78
Medium deal buyers	50	34	40
Light deal buyers	8	6	6

* Market Research Corporation of America.

TABLE 2.1*

Offers studied	Liked best	2nd best	3rd best	Liked least	No opinion
Cents-off deals	61.3	19.0	10.4	2.8	6.5
Coupons	19.3	37.9	27.5	7.7	7.4
Premiums	11.4	30.9	41.6	8.4	7.7
Contests	2.3	4.3	11.4	73.9	8.3
Did not place any offer in this rank	5.7	7.9	9.1	7.2	
Total	100.0	100.0	100.0	100.0	

* Alfred Politz Research, Inc.

The type of product involved can have a lot of bearing on consumer price offers. Certain packaged brands involve a basic product with size variations and one or two taste or flavor variations. In other instances, a long line of different products, with variations in size, exist under one brand.

Many consumer deals are determined by a sales goal of broadening the base for a particular brand by promoting sizes or variations in product lines. Deal offers are used as a means of achieving various objectives.

For example, consider a food line which has fifteen different varieties with three or four varieties producing a major percentage of sales. In such cases, a deal is often used to promote trial usage of those items bought less frequently. In other cases, deals may be used to expose additional sizes on the shelf or counter not only for extra sales appeal, but also to gain more product exposure on the store shelf.

Deals and price-offs are also related to the price of a product. In the case of products with retail prices over $5, the retailers, rather than the manufacturers, initiate competitive pricing action.

Manufacturer's deals generally apply to products in the packaged goods area. These products include food, toiletries, health and beauty aids, household products, and the like.

For products which have limited distribution, a deal or offer is one way to "force" distribution. For example, a direct mail coupon promotion can create advance excitement to get the product on the shelf; or a two-for-one deal, backed by strong newspaper support, can be used to gain additional outlets.

If the purpose of a consumer promotion is to gain distribution, it is generally combined with some sort of allowance so that the retailer himself has an incentive to buy the product.

In packaged goods, the amount of sales volume affected by deals varies from product to product. Some products are very frequently subject to deals, for example, detergents, soaps, coffee, canned dog food, and toothpaste. Other product categories are not subject to deals nearly as frequently. However, to give a measure of the extent to which some of these categories are influenced by dealing, in some product categories which are frequently dealed, over 20 percent of total sales are regularly in deal merchandise.

During a given period in a deal promotion, well up to 40 percent of a heavily dealed brand's sales may be in deal merchandise.

The effectiveness of a promotional approach involving deals is made understandable when one realizes to what a great extent the U.S. consumer is deal-oriented. For example, a Direct Mail Advertising Association study showed that over 50 percent of respondents, representing a representative sample of the U.S. population, habitually save coupons. In another study, a *Food Field Reporter* survey showed that only 6 percent of those surveyed never take advantage of price-offs.

Establishing the Face Value of the Price-off

The rate of discount represents the relationship of the coupon face value to the retail selling price of the product. The discount rate can range from about 10 percent to a high of 100 percent. (Coupons are good for a free package of the product.) The average rate of discount is about 30 percent.

Establishing the face value of the coupon, or other price-off, is naturally of tremendous importance as far as success of the promotion is concerned. If the face value of the price-off is too low it will not generate the necessary consumer appeal. On the other hand if it is too high, promotional costs will be inordinately high and misredemption will be encouraged.

One further point is important to note. If a price-off coupon carried in a magazine or newspaper has a face value in excess of the cost of the publication, there is a temptation for mass misredemption of coupons as one can cash in the coupons for more than the price of the publication. Therefore, it is unwise to establish a coupon value with more than a few cents above the cost of the publication.

Breakdown of Coupon Distribution Methods

Nielsen reports over 20.3 billion coupons distributed in 1971, with distribution by media broken down as follows:

Newspaper. 50.5%
Magazines 14.2%
Sunday supplements. 16.8%
In/on Pack. 9.7%
Direct mail. 8.8%

Nielsen Clearing House, A. C. Nielsen Company

Rates of Return from Coupons by Mode of Distribution

The rates of return for various media follow fairly well-established patterns. Nielsen reported on 251 cases involving seventy-six grocery brands, including foods and nonfood (health and beauty aids were not included in this study). The face value of the coupons studied averaged 10 cents, and ranged from 5 to 25 cents.

Cumulative rates of return by mode of distribution over a twenty-four-month period were as follows:

REDEMPTION RATES BY MODE OF DISTRIBUTION

Mode of distribution	24-month redemption (cumulative)
Newspaper	3.7%
Direct mail	15.3%
Sunday supplement	3.9%
In/on Pack	18.4%
Magazine (on page)	4.3%
Magazine (Pop-up coupon)	9.4%

Nielsen Clearing House, A. C. Nielsen Company

Newspapers represent the most retail-oriented medium because of their broad reach and relatively low circulation costs.

Magazines and Sunday supplements have similar, but slightly higher, redemption rates. (However, placing a coupon on a pop-up card can almost double redemption rates at an average media cost increase of about 60 percent over a regular full color page.)

In-pack and on-pack coupons have a high rate of redemption because they are acquired right at the point-of-purchase. Obviously the cost of distributing coupons with the package is less of a factor than other forms of distribution. (There are some costs involved with special packaging and additional inventory control.) However, the effect of these offers is to confine themselves, for the most part, to existing users of the product.

Direct mail with its high redemption rate has gone down in popularity during the past decade or so, probably because of the large postal rate increase over the period. Most manufacturers use cooperative mailings, in which seven to ten participants share the cost. In this way costs can be held, for an individual coupon subscriber, to $18 to $20 per thousand as opposed to $90 or more for a solo mailing. While solo mailings will yield better redemption than cooperative mailings, the large increase in cost usually does not warrant the extra costs. Of course, in some instances, if a mailing is being planned anyway, a coupon can be used effectively to generate extra sales.

Redemption Rates by Mode of Distribution

The period of time needed to redeem coupons is an important factor which must be taken into account by marketing-planners. (See Table 2.2.)

Newspaper and Sunday supplement coupons are nearly all redeemed by the end of twelve months, while there is a substantial carryover into the second year for direct mail, magazines, and in/on pack coupons.

The redemption rates during the first twelve months are shown

TABLE 2.2   Redemption Rates by Media

Mode of distribution	First 12 months	Second 24 months	Remainder after 24 months	Total
Newspaper	3.4%	0.3%	0.1%	3.8%
Direct mail	12.0	3.3	0.6	15.9
Sunday supplement	3.7	0.2	0.1	4.0
In/on Pack	13.0	5.4	2.0	20.4
Magazine (on page)	3.5	0.8	0.3	4.6
Magazine (pop-up)	7.6	1.8	0.6	10.0

Nielsen Clearing House, A. C. Nielsen Co.

TABLE 2.3 Monthly Redemption Patterns*

Month	Newspaper	Cum	Sunday supp.	Cum	Direct mail	Cum	In/on pack	Cum	Magazine	Cum
1	3.0	3.0	3.6	3.6	1.0	1.0	0.5	0.5	1.1	1.1
2	15.2	18.2	10.9	14.5	6.1	7.1	2.6	3.1	4.7	5.8
3	16.3	34.5	18.1	32.6	11.0	18.1	7.0	10.1	7.9	13.7
4	16.1	50.6	16.0	48.6	12.7	30.8	8.2	18.3	10.7	24.4
5	12.9	63.5	13.1	61.7	11.7	42.5	8.0	26.3	9.5	33.9
6	7.1	70.6	8.8	70.5	8.8	51.3	7.7	34.0	8.9	42.8
7	5.4	76.0	8.5	79.0	6.8	58.1	7.2	41.2	7.5	50.3
8	4.2	80.2	3.9	82.9	5.0	63.1	5.9	47.1	6.8	57.1
9	3.6	83.8	2.6	85.5	4.2	67.3	5.3	52.4	6.1	63.2
10	2.2	86.0	2.5	88.0	3.3	70.6	4.0	56.4	5.4	68.6
11	1.7	87.7	2.3	90.3	2.6	73.2	3.7	60.1	4.2	72.8
12	1.3	89.0	2.1	92.4	2.5	75.7	3.7	63.8	3.1	75.9

*Nielsen Clearing House, A. C. Nielsen Co.

in Table 2.3. These figures are extremely important in budgeting coupon promotions. Note that they reflect the first month that coupons are received at Nielsen Clearing House. In most cases, about a month will elapse between coupon distribution and receipt at Nielsen.

It must be kept in mind that the figures given here are averages and that a substantial variation can occur, depending upon variables which will be discussed later in this chapter. The table below[1] shows the middle half of the cases studied in terms of redemption by mode of distribution.

Coupon Misredemption

One of the most difficult problems plaguing the users of coupons is misredemption, when housewives take coupons through the checkout counter and turn them in for cash without having purchased the product. In many cases, the clerks at the check-out

Mode of distribution	Total redemption	Middle-half range
Newspaper	3.8%	2.1–4.3%
Direct mail	15.9	12.0–19.4
Sunday supplements	4.0	2.4–4.5
In/on pack	20.4	7.9–21.2
Magazine (on-page)	4.6	2.5–5.3
Magazine (pop-up)	10.0	9.2–11.7

[1] Nielsen Clearing House, A. C. Nielsen Co.

counters do not pay attention, or do not wish to risk an argument with a customer.

The face value of the coupon naturally has much to do with the degree of misredemption— the higher the value, the greater the temptation to misredeem. In addition, there is a geographical factor involved, with certain areas tending to run higher than others.

Manufacturers have, of course, made determined efforts to stop this practice, not only through attempts to "educate" the consumer to redeem her coupons fairly, but also to try to have the retail chains take strong steps to insist on proper redemption at the check-out counter. In this connection, the retailers do have a stake in maintaining honest redemption practices; drastic reduction in coupon programs would mean that manufacturers' deals to the consumer would be eventually curtailed.

The percentage of misredeemed coupons ranges between 5 and 10 percent in most programs, with some rare instances going as high as 15 percent or over.

CONSUMER REFUND OFFERS

Coupon offers, product price-offs, and deals at the point-of-sale place the product in the hands of the customer at the moment of purchase.

In the coin refund offer the consumer buys the product at regular price, and then sends away for the refund accompanied by a proof of purchase. (An alternative to the coin offer is a check which is payable to the bearer.)

The refund offer cuts down on response drastically because the consumer must go to the trouble of filling in a card with her name and address, checking to make sure she has the proper proof of purchase, finding an envelope, and mailing it in order to get the refund.

Despite the built-in deterrents to consumer action, the consumer refund offer is, in many cases, preferable to direct coupon offers.

In the first place, if a large discount is desired, a high denomination coupon will encourage misredemption. In consumer refund offers, proofs of purchase are sent to the manufacturer so he is sure the sale was made. Thus, the face value of price-offs and coupon offers usually runs from 6 cents to 15 cents, while consumer refund offers run from 25 cents up. Secondly, when the marketing objective of a manufacturer involves multiple purchases (for example, getting trial usage of five or ten different flavors, or requiring the housewife to buy seven or eight units), a consumer refund offer makes possible a rather large offer. You get fewer people into the promotion but you will get them to invest more.

The methods of distribution for consumer refund offers are the same as for coupons, with redemption rates running much lower, as would be expected. In coin refund offers the average rate of redemption in newspapers and magazines generally runs between 1/2 to 3/4 percent, while offers at the point-of-sale (on package or on pads on the shelf) run around 2 percent.

In the case of the consumer refund offer, the redemption rate does not necessarily accurately reflect total product sold because some consumers who buy the product, intending to redeem the offer, never claim the refund. On the other hand, in some cases, consumers who have already bought the product anyway may decide to collect on the offer.

Naturally, the higher the value of the offer, the larger the percentage of women who will send in for the refund; and also, the higher the percentage of women who will be tempted to send in for the refund even though they already have the product.

Other factors affecting redemption rates are distribution of the product or products, complexity of consumer requirements, amount of discount represented by the refund, and retail price of the product.

Selecting the Method of Coupon Distribution

It is interesting to examine certain cost factors which reveal the net cost of a coupon promotion on a particular product. Let us assume that we wish to compare the promotional cost of a product A sold on the basis of a 10-cent price-off coupon in newspapers, magazines, and direct cooperative mailing (with five to seven noncompetitive products). In order to establish a common starting point for the comparison, let us assume we wish to achieve a redemption of 250,000 coupons for product A. Therefore we will figure out how many coupons we must distribute via each vehicle— newspaper, magazine, or direct mail—in order to achieve a return of 250,000 coupons. For this purpose, we will use the average rate of return for each medium in order to establish our comparison.

We also will use an average cost per thousand for each medium based on general experience.

The purpose of this example is to show how overall cost of a price-off promotion is figured out in establishing a projected cost structure as related to the results obtained in actual sale of product. Table 2-4 shows the way we figure the cost.

Effect of a Coupon Offer on Wholesale and Retail Trade

The success of a coupon offer often depends on the support of the wholesale and retail trade. One reason for the frequent use of newspapers for these offers is that retailers use newspapers as one of their primary media, because they know that newspapers produce immediate sales action.

When a coupon offer is effectively promoted to the trade, the results are of tremendous importance to the ultimate success of the promotion. The retailer, when he backs a product promotion, may order additional stock, give additional shelf facings, or otherwise give attention to the product at point of sale, which he would not have done otherwise. Naturally, this added emphasis on the product at retail is going to result in increased sales.

Advantages and Disadvantages of Various Types of Deals and Offers

So far we have investigated a number of different methods of mounting deals and price offers, and have studied the facts that pertain to them. Now let us compare these various methods, spelling out their advantages and disadvantages.

Price-off on Product

Advantages   Price-off on the product is direct communication at the point of sale in its simplest form. It tells the consumer immediately what she is getting.

There is no misredemption since there is no coupon. There is no cost of distribution to the manufacturer.

Disadvantages   The price-off on the product encourages, to the greatest degree, competitive price wars that cause profit problems in most product categories. In addition, a price-off simply gives a price reduction to regular customers who shop where the

**TABLE 2.4 Hypothetical Cost Analysis
(Product A—10¢ Price-off Coupon)**

Medium	No. coupons redeemed	% coupons redeemed	No. coupons distributed	Cost of distribution Per 1,000	Cost of distribution Total	Cost of redemption at 13¢ per coupon*	Total cost
Cooperative direct mail (with 7 or 8 different products)	250,000	16	1,562,500	$18	$28,875	$32,500	$61,375
Newspaper	250,000	3.8	6,575,000	$ 3	$19,725	$32,500	$52,225
Magazine	250,000	4.6	5,400,000	$ 6	$32,400	$32,500	$64,900

*Face value of coupon 10¢, store handling 3¢.

71

product has distribution, and therefore there is little opportunity to gain new customers.

Combination Pack Deals

Advantages   The combination pack has a lot of attraction in certain situations. It can be used to offer the consumer multiple product at a savings (two for 49 cents, buy three—get one free, etc.). It may make it possible to gain additional space on the shelf.

It gets multiple purchase of product, and the promotional cost is spread over several units. There is no cost distribution to the manufacturer. Generally, the offer is communicated quickly, as in the case of the product price-off, so that the consumer's buying decision is made quite quickly.

Disadvantages   There is no exposure to consumers except where distribution already exists. The multiple-pack offers a problem to many retailers because it tends to be bulky, and shelf space is at a premium. As in the case of product price-offs, it may lead directly to competitive price reductions, with profit reduction for all sellers in the product category.

Coupon In/On Product

Advantages   You offer a price reduction on the *next* sale instead of this sale. This not only spreads the price reduction over two units, but also assures that a large percentage of purchasers resulting from the promotion will be repurchasers. There is no cost of distribution to the manufacturer.

Disadvantages   The offer is confined to consumers in stores where you have distribution. Allowance must be made for a certain amount of misredemption. The offer is not quite as appealing (10-cent coupon inside) as the straight price reduction ("10 cents off") to the bargain-conscious type of consumer, who wants the saving now.

Coupon–Newspaper

Advantages   A newspaper advertisement makes possible a description of the product to new consumers and old users alike, and gives them an incentive to buy through offering a coupon. The retail trade will respond to newspapers, especially if the ad is timed to run on the best day of the week for them. For example,

Fig. 2.3 *Typical cooperative mailing containing ten price-off coupons. (General Foods Corporation, Kellogg Company, Anderson Clayton Company, The Mennen Company, Warner-Lambert Company, Popular Science Magazine.)*

in the food stores Thursdays and Fridays are generally the time of the week for greatest advertising.

A coupon offer will also generally tend to increase the readership of newspaper advertisements, thereby encouraging greater readership, and reducing the cost per thousand readers.

Disadvantage   The redemption (median 3.8 percent) on coupon offers in newspapers runs quite low compared to other means of distribution. Therefore, after allowing for misredemption one must buy proportionately more circulation in order to move a given amount of product.

The demographic profile of readers of most newspapers tends to have lower income and less education. Hence it does not fit certain product categories.

Coupon–Magazines

Advantages   Magazines enable the marketer to place his coupon into the hands of an audience which is generally in higher income, and which is better educated than average.

Redemption rates are higher than newspapers (4.6 percent average) with pop-up coupons going over 10 percent. However, pop-up card coupons increase cost per thousand substantially, and should be used only when the additional cost is warranted by the objectives of the promotion itself.

Disadvantages   Using magazines for coupon offers does not offer nearly as high redemption as direct mail. Therefore, where the highest return on a given circulation is desired, magazines have limitations.

For a manufacturer interested in reaching an extremely broad audience, magazines do have their limitations—no single magazine reaches more than 15 million homes out of 60 million in the U.S.

Coupons–Direct Mail

Advantages   Direct mail offers the greatest flexibility in reaching selected audiences with coupons. In the computerized mailing lists available from mass retailers, the manufacturer can select the audience which represents his best prospect from a large number of characteristics including car and home ownership, age and number of children, education, occupation, and many others. In addition solo mailings offer pinpointed localization—block by block, if desired.

Direct mail offers the highest rate of return of all advertising media, and the timing of direct mail couponing can be closely controlled. It can be set up on an area by area basis if so desired.

Disadvantages   The disadvantages of direct mail couponing are chiefly related to the high cost of direct mail as a method of distribution. This factor has to be regarded in the view of the marketing objective, as previously discussed.

If maximum returns per dollar invested are desired regardless of total exposure of the coupon offer and product message to "non-redeemers," then direct mail is usually the best performer.

PLANNING THE DEAL PROMOTION
FOR YOUR PRODUCT

The deal promotion is designed to achieve certain marketing objectives. It is set up in logical steps leading to a selection of one promotion which will most effectively (i.e., at lowest cost ratio) accomplish these objectives.

Some of the marketing considerations that are brought to bear in the selection process are as follows:

Sales and Distribution

- Need for broader distribution
- Need to reduce factory inventory
- Need to create excitement (action) at the retail level at low cost
- Need to give manufacturer/distributor salesmen a promotion to sell (because no new products are available now)
- Need to introduce an improved product
- Want to improve market share

Consumer

- Want to gain new users for our brand
- Want to get trial of three new flavors being introduced
- Want to get past purchasers to try new product
- Want to get consumers to stock up on our product

In planning the deal promotion you will analyze the relative importance of the various elements that will make up the promotion. When properly evaluated, they will determine your promotional mix and lead the way to a logical decision.

Here are some of the factors you will take into account:

1. Importance of advertising impressions	vs.	Importance of direct sales (redemptions)
2. Importance of consumer action	vs.	Importance of retail action
3. Importance of new users	vs.	Importance of regular users
4. Importance of single product	vs.	Importance of entire product line
5. Amount of discount	vs.	Promotional funds

As each of these factors is weighed, it will affect one or more phases of the program.

Under Variable No. 1—Advertising versus Direct Sales   If advertising impressions are more important, a newspaper or magazine coupon or consumer refund will be the solution indicated. If, however, each dollar spent on the promotion must work toward direct sales, a price-off label, product deal, in-product coupon, or direct mail coupon will probably be selected.

Under Variable No. 2—Consumer Action versus Retail Action   If the brand is strong enough at retail, then most of the emphasis of the promotion will be directed at the consumer. If, on the other hand, the brand lacks retail support, the greater part of the emphasis may be directed at the retail channels in a drive for distribution, shelf position, or display, depending upon where weaknesses or opportunities exist.

As the importance of the retailer increases, the tendency to use a cents-off label or on-product coupon increases, since the retailer will respond more readily to action which is happening right in his store. Naturally, if the retailer is the most important factor, consideration will also be given to promotional tactics aimed directly at him. On the other hand, if advertising budgets and media plans are already approved and the deal is primarily aimed at the consumer, a magazine or newspaper price-off or refund deal may be clearly preferable.

Under Variable No. 3—New Users versus Regular Users   The promoter is considering the question of *which* type of consumer he wants to reach. As we have discussed before, if his deal is directed primarily toward winning back his regular customer, a cents-off label or in/on product coupon may provide a relatively good solution with minimal distribution cost. If, on the other hand, new users are sought, it is vital to clearly define the profile of these new users so that a logical selection of the distribution method can be made. If a generally higher income, better educated woman is sought, magazines may be the answer. If a much more detailed consumer profile is desired, solo direct mail may be chosen.

Variable No. 4—Single Product versus Entire Product Line   This refers to the scope of the promotion relative to product or products promoted. If a single product in a single size is the subject of the deal, a large amount of flexibility will be possible in the selection of the promotional deal. But if two or more products are to be promoted, a combination deal or consumer refund offer may be programmed.

Variable No. 5—Amount of Discount versus Promotional Funds   This relates to the amount which is spent on the deal itself as opposed to the money spent in promoting the deal. Here the decision is to establish the point at which a price reduction is effective, but beyond which it no longer has any great effect in attracting purchasers. In other words, if there is only a marginal difference in redemption rate between a 10-cent coupon offered and a 15-cent coupon offered, the 15-cent offer will needlessly waste 5 cents for each item sold, 5 cents which could have been used to promote the offer (5 cents represents $50 per 1,000).

At the same time, if the price-off is too small, the cost per unit of the promotion can become exorbitantly high, and market goals in terms of sales will not be reached. In general, it is better to establish too great a discount, and to overspend in promoting your offer, because the most expensive promotion is the promotion that fails to generate sales.

In order to illustrate the way in which the decision-making process works, let us review a couple of hypothetical product problem/solution situations.

Hypothetical Case No. 1—Product C
Woman's Shampoo

Product C is a woman's shampoo. It has been on the market for many years and once enjoyed over 25 percent share of market, but its market position has been gradually eroded to 10 percent. Its distribution is 90 percent in food stores, which represents 75 percent of all shampoo sales.

On most food store shelves one or more of the 3.5-ounce medium size (55 cents retail) are shown, and one or more of the 7-ounce large size (99 cents retail) are shown. However, the 11.5-ounce family size ($1.19 retail) has very spotty distribution.

It has been proposed that a 20-cent price-off on the label of the 11.5-ounce family size would enable the brand to get shelf facings in a large number of stores, if backed by a case allowance to the retailer. The rationale behind this proposal is that the price reduction on the larger size would appeal to the bargain-oriented woman with a larger than average family. The proposer also argues that this bargain-oriented woman would tend to keep buying the larger size after the deal because of the economy built into the regular price.

Several questions should be asked about this proposal. First, what percent share of the total shampoo market does the 11.5-ounce size occupy? If the answer is 20 percent or more, the promotion may have a chance. If it is less than 5 percent, the consumer buying patterns would appear to be against the promotion being successful.

Second, will the retail food trade accept this promotion? A trade deal should probably be included with the consumer deal to make it more appealing. In addition, the sales force should probably be provided with a presentation which would show the retailer the volume and profit potential for him in this promotion. Incidentally, in a manufacturer's price-off promotion, the retail profit margin on the deal merchandise is usually increased so that the retailer gets the same profit per unit as he gets on regular merchandise.

Third, in what percent of food stores will the 11.5-ounce size get on to the shelf, and what will it mean in terms of extra sales volume? This extra sales volume should be balanced against the cost of the deal.

Cost analysis—product C

Three-month deal

11.5-oz. size 20¢ off 240,000 units . . . . $	48,000
Retail case allowance at $2.00 per case	40,000
Retailers profit protection at 6¢ per unit	14,400
Total cost of promotion . . . . $	102,400
Total retail sales, annual volume product C pre-deal. . . . . $	10,000,000
Retail sales 11.5-oz. size pre-deal 10% of total	1,000,000

```
Manufacturer's sales in 11.5-oz. size pre-deal. . . . . . . . . .      650,000
Manufacturer's sales increased volume product C . . . . . .      650,000
Product C retail sales annual increased volume . . . . . . . .    1,000,000
Assume total retail shampoo (all brands) market annual
   sales . . . . . . . . . . . . . . . . . . . . . . . . . . . . . . . . . . .  100,000,000
Product C pre-deal share 10% . . . . . . . . . . . . . . . . . . . .   10,000,000
Product C post-deal share 11%. . . . . . . . . . . . . . . . . . . .   11,000,000
```

Product C has been brought to industry average of 20 percent of volume in 11.5-ounce family size, representing $2 million in annual sales, of which $1 million is increased volume.

Hypothetical Case No. 2—Product A Liquid Soup

Product A is a premium-priced soup which has had a successful introduction into the intensely competitive liquid-soup market and is now in its third year since introduction. The total liquid-soup market is $500 million at retail; and product A has 4 percent share, or $20 million. However, as premium-priced soups have only 10 percent of the total liquid-soup market, product A does have 40 percent of this category and is well ahead of other competitors in the field. Product A has 75 percent distribution in food stores. While this factor is of concern, those responsible for the brand's future are more concerned about the fact that in the great majority of stores six or fewer of the fourteen flavors available are stocked.

The product group responsible is seeking a promotion which will accomplish two major objectives:

1. Encourage retailers to stock, on the average, three additional flavors they are not now stocking.

2. Give regular customers an incentive to try the flavors which they have not yet tried, at the same time attracting new users to the brand.

Advertising budgets and media plans are fairly well established, and a proposal has been made that for a two-month period magazine advertising be devoted to a consumer refund offer whereby $1 would be sent to anyone who sent in eight labels from eight different flavors of product A. Total magazine circulation involved over the period will be approximately 10 million.

Here are the factors which will be discussed in selecting a promotion:

First, retail cooperation in stocking additional flavors is vitally important because if the promotion is not successful in this area, the consumers will be unable to fulfill the offer and will be frustrated and annoyed. It would be assumed, therefore, that this promotion must have substantial lead time to allow the sales force to sell it to the trade; and furthermore, it would appear that retail trade incentives would be logical to help gain retail acceptance.

Secondly, the immediate response of consumers to the promotion (due to low redemption rate from coin refund offers), will be less important to sales than the consumer effect caused by exposure to additional facings on the shelf.

Finally, this promotion must be discussed in the light of the risks involved. After some retailers have been informed of the consumer refund offer, it is not possible to withdraw it. However, if it is not successful in its retail objectives, serious consumer dissatisfaction will result. A localized test of the program in one or two markets would probably be a wise course of action in this instance.

Cost analysis—product A liquid soup offer

```
10,000,000 circulation, 1/2 of 1% redeemed
  (50,000 at $1 each). . . . . . . . . . . . . . . . . . . . . . . . . . . . . . . $50,000
Cost of handling and postage 25¢ × 50,000  . . . . . . . . . . . . .   12,500
  Total cost of offer   . . . . . . . . . . . . . . . . . . . . . . . . . . . . . $62,500

Product labels sent in on refund offer (8 × 50,000) . . . .   400,000 units
Retail price of product moved (25¢ × 400,000) . . . . . . . $100,000
```

If the total result of the promotion were to increase the average flavors offered on shelf from six to eight, the potential for increased sales would be measured in terms of increased volume and share of market for the brand. Assuming that the two additional flavors contributed an additional 10 percent to product A sales, the annual volume of product A would rise from $20 million to $22 million annually. The cost of the consumer offer ($62,500) would be added to the trade offer ($2 case allowance) to be evaluated against the gain in store produced.

3

SAMPLING — TRIERS ARE POTENTIAL BUYERS

Sampling is a consumer offer in which the product itself is the primary incentive. It is a means of getting a consumer to try a product free, or at a minimal price, on the premise that product usage will lead to product purchase.

The sample is sent or given to prospects; a secondary incentive often being to further promote product purchase. This extra incentive may be a price-off, sweepstakes, or a premium.

Basically, sampling depends upon the nature of the product for its success. If a product has immediately perceptible advantages, and a relatively high frequency of purchase, some form of sampling may be very effective. If, on the other hand, a product is just a "me too" variety, sampling is not likely to be very effective. For this reason, products which have an immediately perceived taste, feel, or smell respond readily to sampling.

Forms of Sampling Programs—Mass, Selective, and Prescreened

There are three forms of sampling programs. The first is mass sampling in which virtually all the people in a given area are exposed to the product. This type of sampling would be accomplished by a sample offer in *Reader's Digest,* a street corner campaign in which cigarette samples are given out by pretty girls, or a mass direct mail campaign in which a small packet of the product is included.

The second form of sampling is selective sampling in which the audience exposed to the sample is highly selective either through the medium used, the special location in which the sample is distributed, or by a process of self-selection in which sample recipients are those who respond to an offer.

The third form of sampling program is known as prescreened. In this fairly recent development, a research technique is used to determine whether or not a particular group are users of a product or brand. The samples are then directed only to those who are not users of the product or brand, so that sampling investment is not directed at the product's own regular customers. Obviously, this technique is exclusive and, therefore, pertains only to certain special situations.

Methods of Delivering Samples

Direct sampling—the product is sent or given directly to consumers

In direct sampling, a small quantity of product is given out by personnel on the street or in public places, or sent by mail to consumers. For this type of sampling to be successful, many of the consumers must try the product and subsequently purchase it.

Mail sampling can be used in mass, or it can be quite selective. In door-to-door selling, extensive use is made of sampling. Samples are used as good-will builders or to "thank" regular customers for their orders.

Send-away offer—the product sample is offered in magazines or direct mail

If a product offered is dependent upon a reader's order, the amount of product exposure is greatly reduced as opposed to cases where the product is given away to all the people in a particular group. However, this method requires sufficient interest in the product for a reader to send for it. Accordingly, there will be a very high degree of actual usage of product.

When a product will appeal to only a relatively few people, as opposed to cases where a product is used by almost everyone, having the readers request a sample obviously helps to prevent wasting samples on people who are not interested.

Products Which Respond to Sampling

A product which is new, a product which is improved, a product which is unique, a service which has something faster or better to offer—all these can respond to sampling in a dramatic way.

Sampling is a form of incentive which derives its effectiveness from being news. If you can honestly say that you have a product that does sell itself, then a sampling plan should be considered.

Properly planned and executed a sampling program will thrive on word-of-mouth advertising—those who try it and like it will talk about it. And, if it is a question of taste or smell, those who do not like it will also talk about it, which is fine as long as there are enough people in the "likers" column.

There are various categories of products which will respond most readily to sampling, and they have fairly definite characteristics.

Frequency of purchase

A product which is purchased frequently is a particularly good candidate for sampling because if a consumer becomes a regular user, the investment in sampling is more rapidly amortized against product sales than in the case of slow-moving products.

Consumer perception of product

The faster the consumer perceives a product's attributes, the better potential it has for sampling. Products which taste or smell, beauty or health products, products whose advantages quickly demonstrate themselves to the user—all are potentially suited for sampling.

Extent of product usage by consumers

If a product has easily demonstrated benefits but is generally used by only a small percentage of potential customers, sampling can provide an excellent way to increase the number of regular customers. Therefore, an existing product which needs new users has potential for sampling as good as a new, improved product. Consider, for example, a diet food which is used regularly by 2 percent of all households, with only 5 percent of households ever having tried it. A sampling program could be set up which would be directed to households with the same demographic characteristics (age, income, number of children, education, etc.) as those of the regular users. The potential number of additional regular users to be attracted would be extremely high in this sampling program.

Product distribution and sampling

A product which is in powdered form, or a product which is small and light, is ideal for sampling because the most common means of delivering a sample is through the mail.

However, products which are heavy or bulky, products which require freezing, or liquid products tend to pose budgeting problems in mail-out programs.

Physical form of the product

As is the case with couponing, product distribution is a vital factor in considering a sampling program. In sampling, it becomes even more important because the investment in each consumer is generally much higher than in couponing. This is due to two factors:

1. The cost of the sample itself as compared to the face value of a price-off coupon
2. The cost of delivering a sample to the consumer as opposed to the cost of delivering a coupon

If a product has only limited distribution, a high percentage of those who wish to buy (having tried the product and liked it) will find that they are unable to locate the product in the stores. Thus, the relatively high investment in these individuals who cannot buy means a serious waste of promotional funds.

At the same time, sampling can become a means of obtaining distribution. In this situation, the sales force must persuade the retailer that sampling will create consumer demand.

These two variables in distribution must be carefully balanced in planning the sampling program. In the first place, having a certain proportion of people frustrated by not finding the product in stores is usually unavoidable. The question is what percentage of stores with out-of-stock can be tolerated.

In the second place, a selling program can be set up which calls for a distribution drive before samples are sent out. Ideally, this will result in the placement of product on shelves just as the triers are finishing their samples and becoming potential buyers.

SEND-OUT SAMPLES

Samples should be sent to the home only when an extremely high percentage of those who receive them are potential users. This is because of the high costs involved and the necessity for maximum conversion of recipients to triers and triers to buyers. The receipt of a sample, unfortunately, does not guarantee that the recipient is actually going to try the product; and the trial of a product obviously does not guarantee that the trier is going to become a purchaser.

In determining whether or not to mail a sample into the home, an accurate demographic profile of the potential user is essential to establish whether or not sampling will be economically profitable.

For example, a baby food manufacturer can mail a sample of baby cereal to all mothers with babies who are six months old, since all babies go into solid food at about the same time. In this situation, sample usage would be very high, as well as the conversion from triers to buyers. The basic reason for this is simply that an extremely selective list, which contains 100 percent of interested prospects, is available.

However, another type of product which has a well-defined consumer profile may have appeal to only a portion of those who fall within this profile. For example, a hand cream especially formulated for women with problem hands may have its best prospects among housewives who are between thirty and forty with more than three children and with a household income between $6,000 and $12,000.

While this hand care product has a well-defined consumer, for whom a direct mail list can be easily developed, the difficulty is that only 20 percent of all women have real problem hands, and another 20 percent have some slight problem. It is not possible to identify those women who perceive they do have problems, so that 60 percent of all samples would be delivered to women who are not prospects for this particular product.

In this case, the logical decision would be to use some form of sample-ordering technique to let the best prospects screen themselves. A direct mail sample offer or a magazine advertisement featuring a sample would provide one answer; use of a pre-screening program to select women who do have problem hands would provide another answer.

The degree of interest that a sample recipient has in a product has a tremendous bearing on the success or failure of the sampling program. In the case of the baby food, there is a very high interest factor because the baby is mother's major concern at this particular time. In the case of the hand cream, the product represents a very high interest product to those women who have real problem hands because their hands hurt and they are trying to find relief.

When a product has a low interest factor, there is a risk that a very high percentage of recipients will simply not get around to trying the product. A certain toothpaste, for example, was sampled in a small trial size. Research studies showed that over 40 percent of samples sent out were found unopened on medicine cabinet shelves, three months after being received. The small sample size was considered one factor in the high incidence of nonuse. The average housewife felt that she would prefer to use up the existing tube of toothpaste and to save the sample for a weekend trip, or for an overnight guest. This situation does not necessarily mean that this sampling was uneconomical. It simply illustrates that only 60 percent of the mailing was used by the recipients in the first three months; and, therefore, the sample would have to pay off on the basis of those in the 60-percent category who actually tried the sample.

Reaching Nonuser Prospects Through Prescreening

If your product has a very small penetration of the market, so that the great majority of homes reached are nonusers, your chances of creating new users are obviously excellent. If, however, you have a large number of customers in the market, it is desirable to reach competitors' customers with your sample, while screening out those who do not use this type of product.

To accomplish this objective, several sampling companies have developed programs which can deliver, through research techniques, selected lists of product users who are also customers for competitive products.

Prescreening involves telephone interviews in a large number of product categories to determine user patterns, as well as the degree to which these products are desired.

The results of the telephone interviews are fed into a computer which selects prospects to receive samples of several products. A variety of samples is then sent out to selected households and nonusers in one large package.

Costs of this program run about 23 cents to 40 cents per product including interviewing and sample delivery, but not including the sample itself. When it is considered that these samples are directed only to families which are not currently users of the brand but are prime prospects, these programs offer a strong attraction to products which are susceptible to sampling and have a fairly well-established franchise in the marketplace.

The Sample Product—Size and Packaging

The size of the product sample is extremely important. A sample package which is too large will provide free product for too long, taking the recipient out of the market while increasing the sampling cost. A sample package which is too small may provide too little product for a convincing trial. If a product has a distinct taste factor which is immediately perceived, a very small sample may work very well; or if it has any other immediately recognizable attributes, a small sample can work very well.

If, however, a product needs to be used over a period of time to have its merits appreciated, the supply must be sufficient to "make the sale." Such products as beauty or health products often require several usings in order to be evaluated.

The sample package must be carefully designed so that it provides quick information on the product's benefits and, if possible, arouses curiosity and a desire to try the product right away.

If it is a solo mailing, the sample package must be designed so that it can be mailed out without damage to the product. The sample package should also be identical in lettering, color combination, and overall design to the product package itself, so that the receiver identifies the sample with the product in the store.

Cooperative Sample Mailing versus Solo Sample Mailing

In sampling, there are more differences between solo mailing and cooperative mailing than in couponing.

A solo mailing will cost 15 cents to 35 cents or more after product, package, and all mailing costs have been absorbed. A cooperative mailing, by contrast, can cost as little as 4 cents to 5 cents.

However, the solo mailing will produce a much higher incidence of use by recipients than a cooperative mailing, because it is only a single item and not packed in with eight or ten other items.

Many products will not adapt themselves to cooperative mailings since they require a usable sample package which can be enclosed in a small paper or plastic envelope along with eight or ten coupons. The product, therefore, must be one which can be tried by using a small quantity and will usually represent only one use or application.

Powdered foods, or powdered cosmetic products, are often limited to this type of sampling. Liquids or pastes can also be applicable provided they can be effectively sealed in impervious plastic packages.

Solo mailings enable a sampler to place a package containing multiple applications or portions in the hands of a prospective buyer.

Therefore, for products which require several uses to demonstrate their attributes the solo form of sampling, with its greater expense factor, can be far more effective in the final analysis. After all, the final result required is to develop a customer who will be a repeat purchaser, to make the sampling program pay for itself.

Examples of products which are suited to the two forms of mailings:

Fig. 3.1 *Cooperative mailing sample is ⅜ ounce of D-Zerta Low Calorie Gelatin Dessert in paper envelope. Makes four servings. Sample comes with 10-cent price-off coupon. (General Foods Corporation.)*

Cooperative	*Solo*
Immediate taste reaction	Taste must be tried several times
One trial proves efficacy	Needs a trial period
Adapts to small, slim	Requires a tube, bottle, or
package	aerosol container

Specialized Forms of Direct Sampling

Package plans for sample delivery

There are several forms of cooperative, direct sampling available for reaching special groups such as high school and college students, new mothers, families which have just moved, or military personnel.

These samples are delivered much more inexpensively than if they were given out individually, and they are usually distributed direct to the home or residence of the recipient.

For example, in some localities, a firm called Welcome Wagon Inc., offers a service whereby a basket containing various products is brought to new residents in a neighborhood. Selected local residents bring the basket by car to these homes; and by a personal visit, they acquaint the housewife with information about local services, schools, and so forth.

A second service which Welcome Wagon often provides is to new mothers in the community—giving them various products for the baby and giving them information about local diaper services and other information of interest to new mothers.

Another form of sampling which is directed at several specialized audiences is run by Gift-Pax. This concern gathers a box of eight or ten samples and then delivers them to specific groups such as college students, new mothers, newlyweds, military personnel, or other specialized groups.

Gift-Pax boxes are delivered to college students on campus, to new mothers through the nursing staff at hospitals, and to newlyweds at marriage license bureaus.

The college program is directed at 4,250,000 college students. The new mother program reaches 3,300,000, and the newlywed program reaches 1,200,000. Another similar program is called Campus Pac and is directed at 1 million high school students and 1,200,000 college students. The students are sold the Campus Pac box for a nominal fee or are given it with a purchase.

The advantages of these programs are that they cost much less than solo direct mail or hand delivery and they provide assurances that the samples are actually delivered.

In addition, the student will tend to put more valuation on a whole box of samples than he would on any single sample.

Fig. 3.2 *Gift Pax packages like this one are distributed to special groups—brides, new mothers, or students, enabling marketing people to sample these groups on a cooperative basis. (Gift Pax, Inc.)*

For manufacturers who have health and beauty aid products, or similar items, this type of specialized sample distribution can provide a means of reaching their best, young prospects at a relatively low cost.

In-Store Sampling Programs

One of the most commonly used forms of sampling, when a new food or cosmetic product is being launched, is to use sales people especially hired to do the work. This type of sampling becomes a good-will builder and a promotional technique attracting attention, while actually involving people with product trial. The type of store (supermarket cosmetic counter or mass merchandise outlet) will provide the prospects most prone to purchase the product being promoted.

Door-to-Door Distribution

For bulky products, especially in the cleaning products category, door-to-door sampling by neighborhood areas can be employed, either on the basis of leaving the sample at the door or on the basis of delivering the sample if someone answers the door.

This type of sampling can blanket an area with product samples but has the drawback of requiring reliable, fairly inexpensive help to deliver sample products to the desired recipients. Accordingly, considerable amount of waste can be involved in this type of program if the local operation is not carefully supervised.

SAMPLE ORDER PROGRAMS

Delivery of a sample to a group of prospects, by whatever means, does not sort out those people within the group who are particularly interested in the product.

Despite the selectivity which can be achieved in direct sampling by age, income, type of occupation, size of family, neighborhood or city locations, there is the important variable of individual want or need which is *not* taken into account in this direct sampling method. How many of these people really want a diet drink? How many of these housewives do have problem hands? How many of these teenagers do have a skin problem?

One simple way to select those interested is to make them send for an order — perhaps to send in a small amount of money to further justify their desire to try the product. Using the sample order system, the manufacturer can be reasonably sure that his sample will be sent to a person who has a basic interest in the benefits the product has to offer.

An immediate temptation in weighing direct sampling against a sample order program would be to come to the conclusion that the sample order method is far more efficient and therefore is the answer to most marketing situations in which a sampling program would apply.

However, sample ordering does not offer mass exposure of the product because there are a great many potential users who would fail to act upon a sample offer. The sample order method, then, gives selectivity within prospect groups; but it cannot provide a total exposure of product to the selected group, as in the case of direct sampling.

To simplify this situation, take, for example, a comparison

to show the difference. Product A is a toothpaste which appeals to an adult taste—its potential prospects are all consumers who use toothpaste. It has a very distinct taste and is therefore ideal for sampling because a consumer, after one trial, either likes it very much or dislikes it.

One method of sampling is through a 25-cent trial offer in mass-circulation magazines. The other method is through a mailed sample. For purposes of comparison, assume that magazine circulation is 15 million and that 15 million samples are mailed out.

In the case of the magazine offer, 5 percent, or 750,000, of the readers send in for the sample. Of those who receive the sample, 85 percent try it; the other 15 percent forget to use it. This means only 640,000, or 4.3 percent of the target audience, actually try the product.

In the case of the direct mail sampling, assume that 75 percent of those who receive the sample try it. This means that 11,250,000 people will try the product.

Now, let us say that of those sampled, consumer research has shown that 50 percent like the taste to the extent that they intend to purchase the toothpaste.

Therefore, when the magazine offer is used, 50 percent of 640,000 triers, or 320,000, will buy the product; when the direct mail sampling is used, 50 percent of 11,250,000, or 5,675,000, will buy the product.

This example illustrates the effectiveness of direct sampling as opposed to sample order programs in cases where all members of a target audience are prospects and where a distinct product characteristic is inherent in the sampled item.

When only a relatively small percentage of the target audience will be attracted to the product, however, direct sampling becomes inordinately expensive in terms of purchasers produced and the sample order method can provide a better means of reaching interested prospects.

Offering Samples in the Retail Store

A method of using a sample offer to get prospects to the retail counter, as opposed to mailing a sample to the reader, has advantages for Dorothy Gray cosmetics.

Algene, a skin cream, has properties which are immediately evident to a user and is therefore ideal for sampling. The Dorothy Gray people can see definite benefits, however, to offering the sample in the retail store:

- The reader must have contact with a sales person to pick up her sample
- Thus, she is exposed to a sales message on the product
- The reader must find out where her Dorothy Gray dealer is so she knows where to buy Algene after she has used her sample
- The cost of handling and marketing is avoided

This technique of offering samples is confined to products which control their own retail counters as well as have all the other attributes necessary for successful sampling.

Direct Mail Sample Offers

Cooperative direct mail operations represent a very effective method of carrying the sample offer. Return on circulation, as is the case in coupon redemption, is much higher in direct mail than it is in magazines. Magazine offers will pull from 2 to 12 percent, depending upon the form of advertisement, whether an insert card is used, and other variables. Direct mail offers will pull from 5 to 25 percent.

Direct mail not only pulls a high rate of response but also enables the promoter to reach an extremely selective target audience with his sample offer.

For the most part, sample order offers are carried in cooperative mailings because of the saving involved by having partners to share the cost of the project.

For the purpose of reaching certain specialized audiences, however, there are various specialized cooperative mailing programs available, some of which are extremely successful.

An excellent example of this type of vehicle is Mailbag, which has several cooperative mailings targeted at the teen-age and college audiences.

Mailbag is sent out in the form of a large envelope and contains various direct sales offers, brochures, and actual samples or sample offers. Sample offers, to this audience, are the most frequently used incentive because they get product trial efficiently and relatively inexpensively. Many manufacturers have a big stake in getting their products used at the school and college level, both in terms of their immediate market and in terms of the future buying habits of this consumer group.

Mailbag reaches college and junior and senior high school groups, with each envelope containing ten to twenty pieces. Response is excellent, running from 10 percent to 25 percent depending upon the product and the offer.

Cost for Mailbag runs at about $35 per thousand, including printing of coupons.

A good example of a single product sample offer is the Arrid Extra Dry antiperspirant spray piece which was carried in the college women's Mailbag. A dime is required for a $1 retail size, which will provide sufficient product for a trial period to demonstrate the product benefits.

Another form of sampling strategy is exemplified by the Jergens "5 for 1" offer in which they charge $1 for a product line of five skin care products. Here the manufacturer is able to improve his "batting average" by giving the trier a range of choices. Where he misses on one product, he can expect to catch on with another. With a certain percentage of the sampled group, he can expect to end up with regular users of two or three of the products sampled.

Charging for sample order offers

The great majority of sample offers require a handling charge. There are several good reasons for this:

1. There is a relatively small difference in percentage of return in a minimal charge offer as opposed to a free offer.

2. The handling charge is of real benefit to a promoter in reducing the promotional budget (25 cents represents $250 per thousand).

3. The psychological effect upon the recipients—if they have paid for a sample—is that they are much more prone to use it than if they received it free.

CONSUMER PURCHASE AND REPURCHASE PATTERNS

Intensity of consumer interest in a product will determine the percentage of triers in any consumer group, and the percentage of consumers who are satisfied with the product after sample trial will determine the extent to which it is purchased.

These variables are not absolutes, but their various dimensions can be established in broad outlines by marketing men who know their products and who are able to use consumer research programs intelligently.

For, after all, the success of a sampling program depends upon getting prospects to try the product and having tried it, to buy it again and again. For one product this means one type of sampling program, for another a very different one.

Many products have a very narrow band of appeal even within a particular type of audience. (For example, women with problem hands). In these situations, heavy users may comprise as little as 20 percent of a selected audience yet use 80 percent of the total product consumed.

The job of the marketer is to delineate consumer buying patterns before finally determining his exact sampling program.

If he can reach a particular group with a mass sampling program and can achieve a 50 percent purchaser conversion rate among them, his course of action points toward mass sampling.

If he has a relatively small segment with a particular group, his sampling program points toward a selective sample-order program of some type.

And somewhere in between these two programs lies the opportunity to use other types of incentive programs to help achieve his objectives.

One of the most serious potential pitfalls in establishing an analysis of purchaser behavior in a sampling program is to base the evaluation on first time purchasers.

When a product has a rapid family use-up rate, it is often possible to examine repurchase rate, so that a better idea may be obtained as to the final percentage of triers who become regular purchasers.

Fig. 3.3 *The reader of* House Beautiful *who is in the market for carpet can send in 50 cents for a swatch of Bigelow—an ingenious form of sampling. It doesn't take many wall-to-wall jobs to make this sample pay for itself. Advertisement appeared in* House Beautiful, *September 1971. (Bigelow-Sanford, Inc.)*

If a product really does not have distinctive advantages, or is not really new, the sampling investment can be completely wasted after the first phase of the program is over.

OTHER CONSUMER INCENTIVES AS SAMPLING DEVICES

To the marketing man, who thinks in terms of objectives, a sampling program may be a direct sample delivery or a sample offer; or the same purpose may be served in a somewhat different manner by making product purchase more desirable through other incentives.

The point here is that if a promotional program involves a product which demonstrates itself, and which has never been tried by a large percentage of prospects, then the principles of sampling apply regardless of whether it is purchased at a reduced price or as a result of a sweepstakes.

The question to be answered, then, is as follows: "When product trial is the answer for increased share of market, what form of incentive program is going to be most effective in achieving product trial at the lowest cost?"

In some cases, sample delivery will be the most effective method; but the expense factor may rule it out. In other cases, sample order offers will be the answer; but it may be that the relatively few of those exposed to the offer who ultimately become purchasers will indicate that such an approach will fail to produce purchasers in large enough numbers.

A middle ground offer can be reached through price-off, coupon, premium, or sweepstakes—or combination of these—which will give incentive to buy and will give the untried product a chance to demonstrate itself.

To illustrate how this can work, let us refer to the example of a toothpaste, product A used on page 93, which compares direct sampling with a magazine sample offer. Circulation here was 15 million. Direct sampling produced 5,675,000 purchasers, while the sample offer produced only 320,000 purchasers.

Now let us suppose 15 million 10-cent price-off coupons with a special self-liquidator premium offer were sent out in a cooperative mailing. Let us assume a redemption rate of 15 percent. This coupon program will produce 2,250,000 purchasers, which is a very substantial number (although only about 40 percent of that produced by direct sampling) at a good cost-per-purchaser ratio.

Incidentally, the sample offer looks very weak as a vehicle when compared to the results produced by the solo direct sampling or the coupon program. As discussed before, however, it is necessary to consider the 15 million advertising impressions achieved in this program to fully evaluate results here.

Here are the cost factors analyzed between the three forms of programs translated in terms of cost per purchaser produced.

Cost analysis—product A toothpaste

Total circulation: 15,000,000
Direct sampling: samples mailed direct
   Cost per sample mailed 33¢ × 15,000,000 . . . . $5,000,000
Number of purchasers produced: 5,675,000
   (75% try product; 50% of triers buy the product)
   Cost per purchaser produced = 88¢

10¢ coupon: 15,000,000 coupons mailed
15,000,000 coupons × 15% redemption = 2,250,000
  purchasers
Costs:
  Cost of mailing at $20 per thousand
    15,000,000 . . . . $ 300,000
  Cost of redemption:
    2,250,000 × 13¢ (10¢ coupon + 3¢ cost of handling) . . .   292,500
    Cost per purchaser produced = 26.3¢ $ 592,500

Magazine Sample Offer:
Cost of space: 15,000,000 × $6.00 per 1,000 . . . . $ 90,000
750,000 samples sent out 33¢ each (offset by 25¢ handling
  cost) = 8¢ each   60,000
  (640,000 try product A; 320,000 buy product A) . . . . $ 150,000
  Cost per purchaser produced = 47¢

Discussion

The cost per purchaser produced in the direct sampling and the magazine offer is based, you will recall, upon a 50 percent rate of conversion among triers. If the repurchase rate among purchasers in the 10-cent coupon program is the same rate, only 1,125,000 will become repurchasers of brand A.

In the case of direct sampling, therefore, a regular purchaser group has been established among a trier group in excess of 6 million while the coupon program has produced only 1,125,000 who will become regular purchasers.

Even so, the coupon has produced purchasers at a much lower cost ratio than either of the other methods.

Direct sampling . . . . $0.88 per purchaser
10¢ coupon . . . . 0.23 per purchaser
Magazine offer . . . . 0.47 per purchaser

It becomes apparent, then, that each form of sampling will have certain applications which will be carefully analyzed with the marketing situation to determine when it is to be used.

Direct sampling, when applied to a relatively new product, gives an immediate response on a mass scale to a new product. This method can, at very substantial unit cost per purchaser, gain a very rapid position in the marketplace.

Coupon or price-off programs can help a product which has not been tried by a large segment of the audience reached. They can contribute new purchasers at an economical rate. However, these methods cannot capture as many purchasers as the direct sampling method.

Magazine or direct mail trial offers are limited in terms of the response factor; and the exposure of product message to the group who does not respond must be taken into consideration as an important positive factor in the analysis of these programs.

Within the actualities of the marketplace, the products which can be launched with an extensive direct sampling program are, by necessity, very limited. If every phase of the program is not exactly right, such broad scale programs can be a financial disaster. It must be established through market research and test marketing that the product can answer the basic wants of the consumer to make the program work.

The reason that price-off coupons have become so popular as a sampling device is because price-off coupons can achieve limited mass exposure of a product which needs new triers.

In a solo direct sampling program, in which a sample is sent to the home, a price-off coupon to encourage purchase is almost always worth considering. After all, with a substantial investment in such a program, a price-off coupon will help to raise the percentage of purchasers at a slight extra cost.

Use of Premiums or Contests as Sampling Incentive Vehicles

Just as price-off coupons can be used to achieve similar objectives as a direct sampling program, so can premiums and contests be used to achieve these ends. However, as a promotional technique, their effect is not strong enough to produce immediate mass sampling for most products.

Premiums are more often than not used as a secondary promotional vehicle. With a price-off coupon, for example, a good self-liquidating premium or a sweepstakes can often bring in a few additional purchasers which will help to increase response and cut down on the cost per purchaser.

HYPOTHETICAL CASES

Hypothetical Case No. 1—Cooperative Sampling— Product K Powdered Soup

Product K, a leading powdered soup, is about to introduce a new flavor. Having a substantial share of this market and having national distribution, product K's consumer profile is large family units with a low to medium income.

In order to launch the new soup, a cooperative mailing seems to be a very logical solution because:

1. Cooperative mailings reach a mass audience at low cost.
2. A very high percentage of consumers reached will be potential users.
3. The product can be packed in a paper envelope of small size and inserted in the envelope. The small size sample will be sufficient to make a cup of the product for trial usage.

Having established the reasons for using a cooperative mailing, product K marketers proceed to establish projected costs and purchasing patterns:

```
Cooperative mailing to 20,000,000 households at $44 per
  1,000. ................................................ $   440,000
Cost of samples at 2¢ each = $20 per 1,000 × 20 MM  ....     400,000
    Total cost of sampling. ............................. $   840,000
Number of triers (50% of 20,000,000) = 10,000,000
50% of triers purchase product 20¢ × 5,000,000 ......... $1,000,000
1,000,000 purchasers become regular users—average family
    with 3 children using 2 packages of this flavor per
    month—monthly sales. .............................. $   400,000
At end of one year retail sales of new flavor:
Initial sales ..........................................$ 1,000,000
Regular purchasers (400,000 × 12) ..................... 4,800,000
    Total retail sales ................................$ 5,800,000
```

The manufacturer's sales dollars are 65 percent of $5,800,000 or $3,770,000 produced at a promotion expense of $840,000.

Discussion

Product K added $3,770,000 of sales in the new flavor. However, if product K's new flavor just took sales away from the established flavors, then the launching of a new flavor was a costly mistake. On the other hand, if the new flavor resulted in greater usage among existing customers, or resulted in the addition of new customers, then it would be considered successful on the basis of increased market share, sales, and profits for product K.

Hypothetical Case No. 2—Free Trial Offer— Product H Hair Conditioner

In this instance, a leading hair care manufacturer has developed a hair conditioner, product H, which is particularly effective in adding body to the hair. However, only about 40 percent of women really want the particular benefits which this product offers.

A solution to this problem is to advertise the product in several leading general and women's magazines using a full page color ad plus an insert card as an order form to be mailed in with 25 cents to cover handling for a free sample of the product.

The sample size offered will be sufficient for two treatments and will be packed in a plastic bottle to eliminate any danger of breakage in the mail.

Here are the cost factors and purchase patterns as projected for this sampling program. Product H offer carried in one general and two mass women's magazines with a circulation of 34 million.

Cost per 1,000 including order card = $10 per 1,000 × 34,000,000.	$ 340,000
Percentage of those ordering 7% (high interest product, plus effect of a special card)	
Number of readers who order.	2,380,000
Cost of mailing samples (12¢ each × 2,380,000 samples) . . .	$ 285,600
Cost of samples at 12¢ each	285,600
Cost of addressing and handling at 10¢ each	238,000
	$ 809,200
Less 25¢ handling charges received 2,380,000 × 25¢.	576,000
Net cost of sample and distribution.	$ 233,200
Add advertising cost	340,000
Cost of advertising and sampling	$ 573,200

The purchase pattern is as follows:

Sales—1st purchasers:
40% purchase product H after using at $1.15 average retail
  price 2,380,000 × 40% × $1.15 . . . . $1,094,800
20% become regular users: purchase 2 products in year of
  introduction—20% × 2,380,000 = 476,000 regular
  users—purchase 2 × $1.15 or $2.30 in year.   1,094,800
    Total sales 1st year. $2,189,600

Discussion

A sampling and advertising cost of $573,200 has resulted in sales of $2,189,600 at retail or $1,422,240 in the manufacturer's sales dollars. The sampling cost here probably used up all available profit on the brand for the year. However, a core of regular users has been established who will presumably keep using product H and who will tell their friends about it.

    This sampling program solved several problems. In the first place, a solo direct mailing would have been prohibitive as only 40 percent of all women had a definite need for the product. Because the product came in ten colors, it was necessary for the reader to indicate which color she wanted. Hence, a second major reason for using a sample ordering device.

4

SWEEPSTAKES AND CONTESTS—
THE CHANCE TO WIN

Contests and sweepstakes are those consumer incentives which depend upon the chance to win to motivate people. Several hundred national contests and sweepstakes and many times that number of regional or local chance-to-win promotions are run annually. The number of individual entries runs into the tens of millions, and a recent survey estimated that the value of prizes offered in one year amounts to over $300 million.[1]

Sweepstakes offer housewives, and other consumers, excitement, requiring minimal effort, by offering a chance to win prizes. Contests require some effort but are often fun for the participant or a challenge to their ingenuity.

Choosing a sweepstakes or a contest as opposed to a premium or a price-off deal is generally dictated by the fact that chance-to-win promotions have an aura of excitement about them compared

[1] *Incentive Marketing Facts*, Bill Brothers Publishing Corporation, New York, N.Y., 1968.

to other promotional forms. At the same time, they are relatively inexpensive as the cost of prizes is spread over a large number of entrants, only a few of whom will win.

Contests and sweepstakes are often used in combination with other consumer promotions, most commonly price-off coupons. They are usually planned to have an effect on both the trade and the consumer. They stimulate the involvement of retail stores by giving them a reason to put up displays or, otherwise, give the product a more prominent position than it would regularly have. At the consumer level, they stimulate store traffic, encourage product purchase, or create brand name awareness (through greater exposure of product).

The Difference between Contests and Sweepstakes

If a chance-to-win promotion can be classed as a lottery, it is illegal under federal postal regulations and most state laws.

In order to be classed as a lottery, a game of chance must have three elements present: prize(s), chance, and consideration (i.e., you are required to buy something in order to enter). Any *one* of those three elements must be eliminated if the promotion is not to be classed as a lottery.

In the case of contests, the element of chance is eliminated, as the contestants must perform some action which involves an element of skill. The promoter may, therefore, require a purchase of the product, in the case of a contest, as he will then have only two elements: prize and consideration.

In the case of a sweepstakes, the element of consideration (requirement of purchase) is eliminated (hence, the frequently seen advisory, "No purchase required"). Thus, only the elements of prize and chance are included in a sweepstakes.

In contests, the skill element may involve a guessing exercise (how many beans in the jar?), a creative exercise (complete the jingle), or expression of opinion (in twenty-five words or less, tell why you prefer brand X), or any other assignment which the entrant must perform and which will be individually judged according to a prescribed set of rules.

Since contests demand more consumer involvement than sweepstakes, they produce far fewer entrants. However, in cases where proof of purchase is a requirement, or when a greater degree of attention on the part of the entrant is considered important, a contest may be the best way to accomplish the promotional objective.

Sweepstakes outnumber contests by four or five to one because they attract five to ten times more entrants. In addition, a proof of purchase may be requested in a sweepstakes as long as an alternative (product name written on a plain piece of paper) is offered to the entrant. In the average sweepstakes, 50 to 60 percent of entrants send in actual proof of purchase.

The Prize Structure in Contests and Sweepstakes

Regardless of the size of the promotion, most contests and sweepstakes offer a combination of a large grand prize, or prizes, plus a number of smaller prizes in various categories or groupings.

In selecting prizes, keep in mind that while a way-out prize may sound very imaginative, it will not pull in many entrants if only a few people really want it. This is why there is great similarity in prize structures offered.

Early in your planning, you will have to decide whether to offer cash, trips, or merchandise, or a combination of all three. Cash has the virtue of being wanted by everyone. Merchandise and trips enable you to offer more value because you can buy these items from the incentive companies at substantially below the retail cost.

A study by Premium Advertising Association of America of 265 sweepstakes programs gives a good idea of the way in which sweepstakes promoters divide their prize selections.

Prize Categories for 265 Sweepstakes Programs

By prize classification, here is how the leading prizes ranked.[2]

Cash	23.1%
Automobiles	14.4
Cameras	5.2
TV sets	4.4
Trips	4.2
Home electronics	3.7
Books	3.3
Others	41.7
Total	100.0%

[2] Premium Advertising Association of America.

The number of prizes awarded was reported on in 143 sweep-stakes.[3]

Range of number of prizes	Number of sweep-stakes in category
1–500	50
501–1,000	16
1001–1,500	30
1501–3,500	23
3501–6,000	12
6001–10,000	2
over 10,000	10

As far as prize categories were concerned most of these sweep-stakes studied confined themselves to four categories or less. The tabulation was as follows:[4]

1st and 2nd prizes only	23
1st, 2nd, and 3rd prizes	26
1st, 2nd, 3rd, and 4th prizes	17
1st, 2nd, 3rd, 4th, and 5th prizes	15
Total	81

6 prize groups	7
7 prize groups	8
8 prize groups	7
9 prize groups	7
Over 10 prize groups	2
Total	31

One reason for the preference for fewer groupings is that the more groups of prizes offered, the greater the possibility of con-fusing the consumer.

The retail value of prize structures studied was as follows:[5]

Under $99,999	32%
$100,000–$250,000	32
$250,000–$2,050,000	36
Total	100%

In this study, over one-third of the top prizes were multiple prizes involving merchandise, trips, and/or cash.

Examples:

[3] Ibid.
[4] Ibid.
[5] Ibid.

- Trip to Paris and Rome for two, a $5,000 wardrobe, a beauty treatment at a famous beauty salon and $10,000 cash.
- $10,000 to pay off mortgage, $5,000 for tuitions, house full of furniture, and automobile and family weekend at a famous hotel.

These multiple top prize awards are aimed at making the sweepstakes so attractive that a great many entrants will be brought into the contest even though they know that their chances of winning are remote.

Quite often, however, in the case of multiple prizes, especially when they include glamorous trips, it is desirable to offer a cash alternative for the entire top prize so that people who cannot take the trip will not be discouraged from entering.

Typical examples of this type of multiple top prize:

- Trip to NFL Championship game plus $200 or $500 cash.
- Trip to Cape Kennedy for family of six plus $7,500 or $9,999 cash.

Guidelines for Setting Up the Prize Structure

In setting up the prize structure, the type of prizes offered, as well as the relationship between the grand prize or prizes, the secondary prizes, and the minor prizes, must be considered.

It is important to appeal as strongly as possible to the target audience for the product so that you are automatically appealing to your best prospects. Thus, for a woman's beauty product, prizes are based on beauty and fashion; for a man's razor, sports; for an airline, trips and travel accessories, and so forth.

The grand prize

The grand prize is the attention getter, which urges a reader or TV viewer to look into further details about the promotion. The portion of the budget that should be allocated to the grand prize will run from 10 percent to 20 percent, allowing room for additional prizes in the other categories.

Grand prizes are often trips because of their inherent glamour (with cash prize alternative as mentioned earlier). Automobiles are also particularly favored as grand prizes, although in large sweepstakes they turn up as second prizes as well. A large amount of cash is often used as the primary top award.

Secondary prizes

The second prize category serves as a reinforcement or support to the grand prize, often being a less expensive version of the same general category of prize. Typically, a single grand prize will be backed up by two to ten secondary prizes.

Minor prizes

The number of minor prizes generally runs from 100 to over 100,000 based upon budget, as revealed in the PAAA study. When budget permits, broadening the base of the minor prizes is a potent force in attracting entrants.

Minor prizes are almost always merchandise, as inexpensive items can be purchased in quantity at considerable savings.

Guidelines for Preparing Sweepstakes and Contest Rules

There are two basic reasons why rules are important in setting up a consumer giveaway prize promotion. First, it is essential to make absolutely clear to the entrant what she is supposed to do to participate. Secondly, the sponsor of the game must be certain that his promotion fulfills all legal requirements.

In many cases, directions for consumer participation are printed separately from the legal rules, so that the consumer does not have to read every word in the legal requirements (although her attention should be referred to detailed legal rules if printed elsewhere in the promotional presentation).

There are a number of essential elements that must be included in drawing up a complete set of rules. Incidentally, in every chance-to-win promotion, specific legal counsel regarding the rules is a "must" to be sure all necessary legal aspects have been covered. One oversight in drawing up or in properly disseminating the rules can lead to very unpleasant legal consequences.

Description of consumer participation

The first element in putting down the rules is to tell the entrant what to do in the simplest terms:

Contest   Fill in entry blank below with your name and address. Complete statement "I like product A . . . ." in twenty-five words or less. Mail to Box XYZ. Mail with box top of product A.

Entry blank sweepstakes   Fill in entry blank below with your name and address. Mail to Box XYZ. (Describe proof of purchase or facsimile requirement.)

Lucky number sweepstakes   You may have already won—Compare the number of your card with winning number on product A display. If you have a winning number, fill in your name and address and mail this card by registered mail to Box XYZ.

Game sweepstakes   Obtain a game piece every time you visit our store. Affix game piece to corresponding spot on your game card. If you get five game pieces in a row, you are a winner. Take your winning card to our store for verification and awarding of specific prize.

Qualification of entrants—eligible and ineligible

The sponsor of a sweepstakes or contest may limit the requirement for participation in any way he sees fit, as long as all within a classification are eligible. Thus, an automobile company can confine its promotion to all licensed drivers; a cigarette company can confine it to all entrants over twenty-one years of age. Rules should describe clearly all those who are eligible.

In order to remove any suspicion of favoritism on the part of the sponsors, members of the sponsoring company and its advertising or promotion agencies are almost invariably barred from eligibility.

Purchase requirements

Description of proof of purchase, or facsimile, necessary to accompany entry blank must be covered in detail (e.g., "Mail entry with bottom panel from carton of product A or with 3 x 5 inch sheet of paper on which you have printed words, 'product A' in plain block letters.").

Frequency of entry

Notify consumer how often he can enter (e.g., "only one entry per person (or household)" or "enter as often as you like").

Information on expiration dates, date of drawing, and winner's notification dates

In sweepstakes or contests, the rules should specify the expiration date. Where entry blanks are involved, a cut-off date usually refers to a postmark date on the mailed entry. Date of drawing or completion of judging is usually also specified, as well as date by which winners will be notified.

Legal protection statement

In order to protect the sponsor from any possible legal complication, the rules usually state, "Void where prohibited by law."

In cases of sweepstakes and games, "No purchase required" must be included in the rules, in bold type.

CONTESTS

In today's marketing, contests represent a specialized promotional tool for most marketers. They are very important in cases where it is desired to get entrants much more involved in a given product or service than possible with the mass appeal of sweepstakes.

Generally speaking, while contests follow the basic principles established for setting up prize structures (i.e., grand prize, secondary prize, and minor prize categories), the total amount of the prize structure is usually much more modest since the contest relies on a combination of interests and desire on the part of the entrant to win the prizes offered. In addition, a contest has fewer entrants against which to budget the prizes offered.

Cost of handling

In setting up a consumer contest, handling and judging costs of a substantial nature may be encountered, unlike the situation in a sweepstakes where winners are selected at random.

In some contests where there are only a *few* correct answers, a basic handling charge is necessary because each entry must be individually inspected. This service is most effectively provided by a contest-handling organization.

However, in contests where talent or skill are involved, a much more costly judging process is required. In instances where naming of a product, recipes, sentence completion, or jingle completion are desired, independent judging organizations are available to screen the great mass of entries on the basis of certain established ground rules such as originality, aptness, imagination, and so forth. After this screening, those entries selected can be turned over to expert independent judges for final selection.

In other cases which involve original talent such as musical composition, poetry, package design, art, table setting, or essay writing, it may be necessary to line up competent judges who will review every entry. Needless to say, the more complex and demanding the contest assignment is, the fewer the number of entries. So, to some extent, the problem tends to take care of itself.

However, it is absolutely essential that detailed planning of the handling of contest entries and judging be carefully considered and carried out with the help of a professional organization before the contest gets underway.

Marketing Objectives of Contests

Contests are aimed at accomplishing marketing objectives for a product. Therefore, their functions must be analyzed in the light of these objectives. Some of the most common of these are outlined here.

Promoting product benefits

A common objective of a contest is to get entrants sufficiently involved with a product that they will become aware of its benefits. For example, a recipe contest requires most entrants to try out the product themselves so that they can properly compete. Or, in a sentence completion contest ("Why I like this product in twenty-five words or less."), the entrant cannot write an effective entry without having been thoroughly exposed to the product.

In another way, a guessing game can point out product benefits. For example, in a "Mixer Life Test" conducted by Iona Manufacturing Company, shoppers had to guess how long an Iona Mixer on store display would run, based on the assumption that every seven hours the mixer ran would be worth one year of use in the home. This contest dramatically demonstrated the durability of the mixer.[6]

Gaining information about new uses
for the product

In a recipe contest, the consumer is not only exposed to product benefits, but also gives the manufacturer new ideas about cooking with the product. A few of these recipes will give him new ideas with which to promote his product in the future.

[6] *Consumer Contests,* Premium Advertising Association of America, 1968.

Using the same approach, many other products, which have a variety of different uses, employ contests to get new ideas. For example, Aluminum Company of America has run several contests in which prizes are given for suggesting new uses for Alcoa Wrap.

Getting ideas for product names or slogans

In many instances, products have been named or slogans developed through contests. While the entrants are being informed about a manufacturer's product, the manufacturer receives a side benefit by obtaining many ideas for names or slogans which, by the rules of the contest, are owned by him.

Promoting the product name
with consumer contests

Many contests promote a product name by skill contests, in which a provocative question attracts attention to the product. Contests may be based on outcome of major sports events, guessing who will win elections, or what the vote will be on any topical subjects interesting to a large number of people at a particular time. For example, a Buffalo meat packer ran a promotion from December 10th to the 24th in 2,500 supermarket and grocery stores on "Name the Score" of the Buffalo Bill Championship game to be played December 26th.

Another version of a guessing contest is to choose a subject of particular interest to your best customers. For example, a New Jersey ski equipment distributor ran a contest in which participants were asked to guess the total snowfall in Kitzbühel, Austria, and St. Moritz, Switzerland, between August 1st and December 31st. Naturally, this contest received good publicity in the ski press.

Gaining favorable publicity for
company or product

A contest or talent hunt can create favorable publicity, especially where youth-oriented products are concerned. For example, Jantzen bathing suits ran a "Smile Girl" contest in thirty market areas. Winners competed in the national finals.[7]

A skill contest for high school and college girls, built around the product, is well exemplified by Lenox China. This company runs an annual table setting contest which is promoted through

[7] Ibid.

home economic courses in schools. Local winners are brought to New York for finals.

Schaefer Beer ran a talent hunt for musical youths. Winners' submissions became part of Schaefer's advertising campaign.

Probably the great-grandmother of them all is the Pillsbury Bake-off. In a typical Bake-off $100,000 in cash and appliances is awarded to 100 finalists chosen from all over the country. Each finalist receives a G.E. range, and the top winner gets $25,000 in cash.

Recipes are developed by contestants all over the country and screened by local areas to produce the 100 finalists, who are brought into New York. During the "Bake-off" they are gathered into the grand ballroom of a hotel where they actually bake their own recipes on 100 G.E. ranges. Then their work is judged, and the winners are chosen.[8]

This contest provides all the factors which are contained in a well-concerted contest effort—involvement by a large number of participants, excellent publicity coverage involving good will for the company, and a good number of promotable recipes for Pillsbury.

In another youth-oriented contest, Union Carbide's Linde Stars Division attracted attention to its products with a "great jewelry" design contest open to high school students. A $1,000 college scholarship was the first prize.

Here again the contest was used to gain promotable ideas, jewelry designs, for the product while getting an important age group to learn and gain knowledge about a product.[9]

Obtaining product exposure to a mass audience

It is obvious that relatively few people actually participate in many of the contests we have discussed. However, there are contests which do attract a great number of participants, only a few of which actually send in their entry blanks.

An example of this type of contest was Post Cereal's cartoon coloring contest. This contest, for children under thirteen, was carried on 50 million cereal cartons. Their assignment was to complete and color a cartoon on the package. There were five separate divisions, each with a different cartoon. Each division offered

[8] Ibid.
[9] Ibid.

2,005 prizes: 5 first prizes of Stallwin bikes; 400 prizes of Mattel power shop for boys, dolls for girls; 600 third prizes of linoprinters; and 1,000 U-R Room toy cars.[10]

Obtaining product exposure to a selective audience

In other situations, contests can reach a highly selective audience. For example, Scott Paper Company's business papers used a contest to get a product story told to a selective audience — businessmen. In this case, the company, which is very well known for its consumer products, wished to promote its relatively unknown business products. The solution was the "Great American Memo Contest," a contest which appealed strictly to businessmen (i.e., users of the product) who were involved in the daily business ritual of memo writing. The contestants were invited to write the funniest, zaniest memos they could; and the top prize was $2,000 plus, as the copy says, "another one of those idiot plaques." The copy in the advertisement is sophisticated and tongue-in-cheek. The advertisement appeared in *Newsweek* and specialized magazines directed to a business audience.

Getting demonstration of a new product

In another humorous contest, Scripto promoted trial use of its new Graffiti pen, capitalizing on the urge of people to decorate advertising posters with embellishments. The contest awarded prizes to those who did the best job of marking up a girl's photograph with a Scripto nylon tip pen. This contest accomplished two important objectives for Scripto.

First, the new pen called for demonstration to sell itself. In this contest, entrants had to use the product to enter; and at the same time, the contest was fun. Secondly, the contest provided an excellent vehicle to gain store display, because retailers were aware that the product demonstrations would lead to sales.

There were 3,053 prizes in the Scripto contest, ranging from a poncho to a grand prize of a Camaro convertible. The Scripto people could have conducted a sweepstakes in this case, but the contest gives them the added benefit of a built-in consumer demonstration which would probably sell more products (many of those who enter

[10] Ibid.

will buy the pen for 49 cents). In addition, would-be entrants would ask retailers where the Scripto contest display was, encouraging him to put the display on his counter.

SWEEPSTAKES

There are three types of sweepstakes which are available to marketing management.

The first is the entry blank sweepstakes, in which an entrant obtains an entry blank through a magazine or newspaper, direct mail, in a store, or other place of business. He sends his entry blank to a central address, with proof of purchase (label, box top, etc.) or facsimile card.

An expiration date is established, and on that date, all entry blanks are drawn at random to select the winners.

This type of entry blank sweepstakes is used when consumer purchase of product is an important consideration.

Lucky number sweepstakes

The lucky number sweepstakes is conducted by inserting numbered cards, some of which have already been selected at random as prize winners, in a magazine or direct mail.

Among the cards distributed, there are a certain *predetermined* number of winners.

The entrant may take his card to a retail store to compare his number or symbol with the winning list or symbol on display at the store or on a product, or he may send his card into headquarters to be compared to the winners' list.

Games

Games are actually another form of sweepstakes. They have a built-in continuity factor which encourages the consumer to visit a supermarket or filling station numerous times because the more often she participates, the better her chance to win.

Most games are played with a master card to which individual game pieces are fastened or affixed. Certain combinations of game pieces are winners, and the prizes are varied as in other sweepstakes with grand prizes, secondary prizes, and minor prizes. Only frequently visited retailers such as supermarkets or filling stations use games since they are based on a continuity feature—the more often a person enters, the greater his chance of winning. The purpose of the game is to draw the consumer away from competition by giving her a chance to win a prize.

Games are sweepstakes in that they do not require purchase; they involve only chance and prizes and not consideration. Therefore, they are not classed as lotteries.

Marketing Objectives of Sweepstakes

Of all forms of consumer incentives, the sweepstakes is one of the most difficult to use effectively because there are many intangibles involved; and the creative aspects—theme, choice of prizes, advertising presentation—are much more complex than with price-offs or premiums.

There are many variables which enter into the decision of whether or not to select a sweepstakes in the first place, and how to plan and execute it successfully in the second place. The considerations involved in these decisions can be analyzed provided there are clear-cut objectives established at the outset.

Generally speaking, the objectives for sweepstakes can be related to the type of product involved. Products which are sold through high-traffic outlets such as food and drug stores are primarily interested in obtaining displays, greater shelf space, and greater brand awareness. Products which are sold through low-traffic retailers such as automotive and furniture are interested in creating additional store traffic and stimulating their dealers to display their product.

A survey, reported in *Sales Management* magazine, was taken of 151 national advertisers who conducted sweepstakes. The difference between the high-traffic product and the low-traffic product is clearly shown in this comparison in Table 4.1.

In neither category is direct accomplishment of product purchase given as an important accomplishment for a sweepstakes because sweepstakes sell product primarily through the stimulation of retailers, dealers, or company personnel. The direct requirement for purchase is, when used, only a secondary objective. This does not mean that a manufacturer will not put in the purchase stipulation where it is possible to do so, but it does mean that most sweepstakes cannot be evaluated solely on product sold to entrants.

TABLE 4.1*

Most important accomplishment	High-traffic products, %	Low-traffic products, %
Secured display space in dealer outlets	31	12
Improved brand awareness	27	10
Stimulated company sales force	17	10
Stimulated dealers to greater sales effort	8	14
Introduced new product	1	8
Increased store traffic	. . .	14
Miscellaneous	10	32

*Sales Management Magazine, October 15, 1968.

To put it another way, in most sweepstakes, far more product will be sold to those who are attracted to a display or to the product on the shelf but do not enter the sweepstakes, than will be sold to participants in the sweepstakes.

Product exposure gained through sweepstakes

Let us refer to high-traffic frequently purchased products for which food, drug, variety stores, and mass merchandisers represent the major distribution outlets. There is a tremendous competition to achieve product prominence on shelf and in display. In looking over the various consumer incentives, a sweepstakes offers one of the most attractive alternatives to gaining some type of product exposure. However, a lucky number sweepstakes, which is based upon posting winning numbers on a display of product in the supermarket, may result in getting displays in only a small percentage of total stores. For the would-be participant who is looking for the sweepstakes display, this situation can result in a very negative attitude on the part of the potential customer.

It is important therefore to make sure that this type of sweepstakes is advertised to the consumer and aggressively promoted to the retailer.

Send-in lucky number coupon

In some sweepstakes, the point-of-sale activity is not considered to be as important as enabling the consumer to participate, imme-

Fig. 4.1 *Hood's Dairies of New England use an ingenious approach to draw attention to their 125th anniversary. Each winner gets 125 items as part of his or her prize, and there are lots of winners — 2,081 in all! Advertisement appeared in* Boston Globe, *May 4, 1971. (H. P. Hood, Inc.)*

diately involving her with the selling story of the advertisement or the direct mail offer. In these cases, the consumer enters by mailing her entry blank into sweepstakes headquarters.

The send-in entry is often used in cases where distribution is spotty for a relatively new product or when new uses of an old product are highlighted in the ad, making an additional reason to purchase product. In these cases, the proof of purchase request is more important than in cases where retail display is primary.

Building traffic through sweepstakes

For "big ticket" products (relatively high unit price), the use of sweepstakes has quite a different set of objectives. Typical of these products are automobiles and accessories, home furnishings, TV and hi-fi sets, and the like. For this group, providing traffic in retail outlets becomes a primary function of the sweepstakes. In addition, there is another group of products, which are not "big ticket" items but which are sold through franchised outlets or selective dealerships, to whom creating traffic is the primary function of a sweepstakes.

An important legal point relates to the definition of "consideration" in connection with traffic-building promotions. Federal regulations, and most state regulations, do not classify "consideration" in a sweepstakes as a visit to a store. For this reason, a sweepstakes can require a store visit as part of the conditions for entering. Indeed, most rules permit demonstration of the product as an entrance requirement. Requiring a product demonstration encourages retail salesmen to suggest a demonstration to entrants, when otherwise they might fail to do so.

Once the low-traffic dealership has the sweepstakes traffic in his showroom or store, it is up to him to convert as many entrants as possible into customers.

Incidentally, it is often desirable to give the product promoted as the major prize or prizes because those who are attracted to enter the sweepstakes will be better-than-average prospects for the product. As soon as they have checked their number at the dealership, they know whether or not they have won anything; and at that point, they can be exposed to a sales talk.

It is a fact of life that the large majority of those who enter traffic-building sweepstakes are, as one would expect, principally

Fig. 4.2 *Nabisco promotes its entire line of snack crackers and cheese process spreads in a sweepstakes with a prize structure based on a $50,000 purse. Advertisement appeared in* Family Circle, *June 1971. (Nabisco, Inc.)*

Fig. 4.3 *Sweepstakes is used as a dealer-locater, traffic builder to help gain new customers. Entrants must visit "Martinizing" store to enter. Advertisement appeared in* Family Circle, *June 1969. (Martin Sales, Inc.)*

interested in the prizes. Therefore, in promoting a traffic-building sweepstakes, it is important not to give the dealers or the sales force the impression that every other individual who comes into the store will be a customer. In most sweepstakes of this type, a longer range view must be taken. For many manufacturers, it is important that thousands of people see their merchandise or try it out. For others, it is important that thousands of people find out where their retail outlets are so that when they are in the market for the product or service they know where the retailer is located.

The Martinizing Dry Cleaning franchise is a good example of a dealer-locating and traffic-building sweepstakes. The Martinizing franchise offers dry cleaning service using a special process. In order to enter this sweepstakes, the customer has to locate the outlet and enter there. In this case, the planners chose an entry blank sweepstakes in favor of a lucky number version. It is likely that a relatively high percentage of entrants will give the local Martinizing outlet some dry cleaning business because if they are going to visit the dry cleaner to enter the sweepstakes many would take some dry cleaning along. Therefore, the Martinizing sweepstakes not only will expose many thousands of new customers to the retail outlets, but also will bring in many who try the service, many who will become regular customers.

Using sweepstakes to aid in direct selling

Direct selling, primarily presented through magazine and direct mail, makes very heavy use of sweepstakes in order to encourage the participation of customers. There are certain categories of product or service which make use of this technique. They can be classified as follows:

Record clubs
Book clubs
Credit cards promoting specific merchandise including gas companies, banks, and travel and entertainment cards
Magazine circulation promotions

The sweepstakes enables a participant to enter regardless of whether or not he accepts the offer or purchases the item. However, it is obvious that a high percentage of those who enter the sweepstakes will take advantage of the offer.

Many credit card concerns utilize their lists to sell merchandise to their card holders. These are direct mail promotions which are either contained within the monthly billing or are separate mailings. When sweepstakes are involved, the separate mailing is almost always used because the billing itself should demand primary attention from the card holder; and therefore, the sweepstakes cannot be properly promoted within the mailing.

In a credit card sweepstakes promotion, the same principle is generally used as with record and book clubs. The recipient is instructed that he can participate in the sweepstakes whether or not he orders the merchandise.

Choosing the Advertising Media for Sweepstakes

Many of the considerations which were discussed in the chapter on price-offs and deals also apply to sweepstakes. Direct mail is the most expensive medium for sweepstakes advertising but will produce the highest degree of participation; newspapers are the least expensive media but will produce the lowest rate of return. Magazines fall in the middle category with cost per thousand running in between the other two media.

Promoting a sweepstakes solely on a product package or through store displays is seldom practical because there is insufficient space available and because contests and sweepstakes must be run with fixed deadlines.

Radio and TV can be used to promote sweepstakes as support media but, for the most part, a sweepstakes needs the printed page to get its complete message across—prizes, rules, and product message and so on.

In magazines, using the pop-up card as entry blank is an effective way to promote a sweepstakes if there is a sufficient budget. The card is easily detached from the magazine and is carried to the store or mailed in to sweepstakes headquarters.

Hypothetical Case No. 1—Product S Color TV Line

Product S is a color TV line of products which have approximately 10 percent share of market. The line is primarily sold through appliance dealers and TV repair shops. Those dealers who carry the line generally sell one or two other lines; but the manufacturer tries to get the dealers to concentrate 35 to 50 percent of their purchases with him. Total number of dealers is 4,000.

This announcement is both an offer to give away stock and a solicitation to buy our delicious frozen foods.

Win 5 shares of every stock on the Dow Jones Industrial List.

Enter the Morton Blue Chip Bonanza.

Grand Reward: A portfolio of 5 shares of every stock on the Dow Jones Industrial List.

Two 2nd Rewards: 2 portfolios of 3 shares of every stock on the Dow Jones Industrial List.

Ten 3rd Rewards: 10 portfolios of 1 share of every stock on the Dow Jones Industrial List.

Five Hundred 4th Rewards: A Blue Chip Bonanza coupon booklet redeemable for $5.00 worth of Morton Pot Pies and Casseroles.

This offering sponsored by:

Morton MACARONI & CHEESE   **Morton** CHICKEN POT PIE

Morton BEEF POT PIE   **Morton** SPAGHETTI & MEAT

Morton TURKEY POT PIE   **Morton** TUNA POT PIE

To enter, just send the entry form below together with the ingredients panel from a Morton Pot Pie, Morton Spaghetti & Meat or Morton Macaroni & Cheese package, or the words "Morton Pot Pies" hand printed on a 3" x 5" piece of paper. Winners will be selected in a random drawing. All prizes will be awarded.

OFFICIAL RULES—NO PURCHASE NECESSARY
(1) Print your name and address on an official entry blank, or on a plain 3" x 5" sheet of paper, and mail to Morton Blue Chip Bonanza, Old Chelsea Station, P.O. Box 469, New York, New York 10011. (2) Each entry must be accompanied by an ingredients panel from any Morton Pot Pie, Macaroni & Cheese or Spaghetti & Meat package, or the words "MORTON POT PIES" hand printed in block letters on a plain 3" x 5" piece of paper. (3) Enter as often as you like. Each entry must be mailed separately, postmarked by June 15, 1971, and received no later than June 30, 1971. (4) Winners will be selected in a random drawing conducted by Blue Ribbon Promotions, an independent judging organization, whose decisions are final. Only one prize to a family. No cash substitutions. Liability for taxes is the sole responsibility of the individual winners. (5) Contest open to all residents of the United States except employees and their relatives of ITT Continental Baking Co., its advertising agencies and Blue Ribbon Promotions, Inc. (6) Contest void in state of Washington and wherever prohibited or restricted by state or local regulations. (Residents of Missouri enclose no proof-of-purchase or substitute therefor.)

Morton Blue Chip Bonanza
Old Chelsea Station, Box 469
New York, New York 10011

ENTRY FORM

Name _____
PLEASE PRINT
Address _____
City _____
State _____ Zip _____
MUST BE INCLUDED

Fig. 4.4 *Morton's Foods offers stock—five shares of every stock on the Dow Jones Industrial List to promote their pot pies and casseroles. Advertisement appeared in* Family Circle, *March 1971. (Morton Foods, Div. of ITT and Continental Baking Co.)*

The marketing management has added three new models to the product S line and plans to promote them heavily to the retail trade through a series of distributor/dealer meetings, at which it is hoped many retailers will place orders for the new merchandise.

Now, the marketing team wishes to develop a consumer/dealer promotion which will create store traffic and help the dealers move their new merchandise to consumers.

Several premiums are discussed as traffic builders; but the majority of product S dealers are away from major shopping centers or main streets, and it is felt that the winning appeal of sweepstakes would have more success in attracting participants.

Accordingly, a sweepstakes drawing promotion is developed. Entrants go to the dealerships to fill out official entry blanks, which will be sent by the entrant to contest headquarters.

The participation in the sweepstakes will be offered to all dealers who place a minimum order with their distributor at the meeting. The meetings take place in November, and the sweepstakes is scheduled to run during the month of April.

Sweepstakes plan

The sweepstakes is scheduled to appear in early April in general magazines having circulation of 14 million. In addition, a cooperative direct mail program on the sweepstakes is offered, in which the manufacturer and distributor share half the cost with the retailer.

The prize structure is as follows:

```
20 trips for 2 to Hawaii at $2,000 each................. $40,000
1,000 cameras at $15 each...........................   15,000
     Total value of prize structure...................... $65,000
```

Cost analysis—product S sweepstakes

```
Magazine advertising 14,000,000 at $7 per 1,000 .......... $ 98,000
Direct mail program (3,000,000 mailers at $65 per
   1,000) = $195,000 × 25% manufacturer's share..........   48,750
     Total cost of advertising the sweepstakes............. $146,750
```

However, in this case, where the product S retailers are off the beaten track, a low percentage of actual participants is expected.

Here is how this figures out:

```
% of magazine readers who enter at product S
  dealerships 14,000,000 × 2%. . . . . . . . . . . . . . . . . . . . . . 280,000
% of direct mail readers who enter at product S
  dealerships 3,000,000 × 4%. . . . . . . . . . . . . . . . . . . . . . 120,000
    Total store traffic . . . . . . . . . . . . . . . . . . . . . . . . . . . 400,000
```

We are now ready to establish the cost for each participant produced at the retail store as a result of this sweepstakes. It works out to 50 cents each.

Now let us assume that of the entire dealer body 1,500 out of the 4,000 dealers participated. We now must analyze what the dealers' return was in terms of his costs and his sales.

The average dealer received traffic of 266 people (400,000 traffic divided by 1,500 dealers). Let us assume he sold product S to ten people, or one in twenty-six. Assume his average retail price is $225. He will have sold $2,250 for an investment in direct mail of $65. Naturally, these figures are averages, so some dealers will have sold many times the average and others will have sold only one or two sets.

The manufacturer of product S has planned this sweepstakes to help dealers move product S to the consumer during a particular promotional period.

Here is how this works out:

```
1,500 dealers sold an average of 10 sets each . . . . . . . .    15,000 sets
15,000 × average manufacturers cost . . . . . . . . . . . . . $2,625,000
Cost of promotion . . . . . . . . . . . . . . . . . . . . . . . . . .    $201,750
```

Discussion

The immediate sales from this sweepstakes promotion are not the only factor in determining the results of the investment.

There are two important additional factors which must be considered.

1. *Advertising Impressions.* The magazine circulation reached 14 million and a readership several times that number. If the sweepstakes advertisement was properly planned, the product message was delivered to many millions who never acted upon the sweepstakes. Of these readers, 98 percent of whom did *not* respond to the sweepstakes, a certain percentage would be in the

market for a color TV in April or May. Hence, a certain number of additional sales will be generated from the investment.

2. *Dealer Promotional Activity*. The dealers, in addition to putting up sweepstakes display material and the lucky number list, will naturally be encouraged to display product S, since they have purchased the new items as a result of the promotion. This activity will mean that they will have not only displayed the product S prominently, but also will encourage their sales people to feature it in their sales contacts.

Hypothetical Case No. 2 — Product C Toothpaste

Product C is an established brand of toothpaste with 5 percent share of the market which produces a sales volume at retail of $15 million (approximately $10 million in manufacturer's sales).

In the face of very heavy competition from many new products in the market, this brand has been losing distribution and market share. While some of these new brands will not succeed, they are selling with very liberal trade discounts and conducting very aggressive couponing and sampling programs which tend to take regular users away from product C, at least temporarily. While couponing or price-offs were considered, a decision has been made to run a sweepstakes.

In view of the amount of couponing and price dealing in the toothpaste market, it is felt by the product C management group that further dealing will be an expensive way to "buy" consumer sales; and furthermore, it is considered likely that such sales gains will be taken advantage of by the bargain-conscious consumers who will buy the competitive price-off the next time they are in the market.

It is felt that a sweepstakes may be able to help in two important objectives for product C and lead to more lasting sales gains.

Marketing objective for sweepstakes product C

The objectives for product C's sweepstakes are:

1. Give sales force a promotion to help them to improve distribution from 66 percent to the 75-percent range.

2. Give sales force a promotion to help them to gain additional facings on the shelf for the brand.

It is felt that the sweepstakes will be more important in its effect on sales force and retail trade than it will be upon the consumer. As a part of this sweepstakes promotion, there will be a sales contest with very substantial prizes, and there will also be a trade allowance to help the sales force sell additional stocks of the product.

The sweepstakes plan   The sweepstakes will require an entrant to send in an entry blank from the magazine advertisement with an end flap from the carton, or a 3 x 5-inch card with the product C name on it. In stores where product C does not have distribution, there will be consumer inquiries asking for product C. This in itself will exert some pressure on chain store management to stock the brand.

The sweepstakes will appear in magazines having 14 million circulation.

Here is the prize structure:

	Totals
Grand prize at $25,000	$ 25,000
25 prizes at 1,000	25,000
1,000 prizes at 25	25,000
Total 1,026 prizes	$75,000

Analysis of hypothetical case No. 2 — product C

This sweepstakes has been promoted to the consumer through 14 million circulation and to the sales force and the trade.

The reinforcement of brand name is through consumer advertising expenditure. However, the major objectives have been established as related to sales force and the retail trade.

Using the sweepstakes promotion, the sales force will be able to gain an additional distribution in food stores, representing an increase of 5 percent from 66 percent to 72 percent.

In existing retail outlets, the sales force will be able to achieve extra shelf facings in 10 percent of outlets, representing 20 percent of sales volume. (The sales force has concentrated their promotional efforts in larger volume outlets.) Let us assume that the combination of these two objectives has resulted in a 10 percent increase in sales.

Costs of promotion

Advertising — 14 MM circulation at $8 per M $112,000
Cost of prizes   75,000
Trade promotion   50,000

Total $237,000

A 10 percent increase in sales represents to product C $1 million in manufacturer's dollars annually, which would represent $600,000 at 60 percent margin of gross profit. Against this must be balanced an expenditure of $237,000. If this gain in volume represents a share which can be maintained, this might be considered a promotional expenditure which was profitable.

5

SALES INCENTIVE PLANS, CONTESTS, SWEEPSTAKES, AND AWARDS

A large number of promoters of consumer and industrial products have found that they can profitably increase their sales by supplementing their regular sales compensation plans with sales incentives—extra rewards in the form of cash, merchandise, trips, or prestige awards such as plaques, testimonial letters, or special clubs.

The extent and importance of these plans are shown by the fact that the dollar volume estimated for sales incentives was $924.1 million for 1970, as compared to $1,350.4 million for total consumer premiums, $770 million for trading stamps, and $488.2 million for dealer premiums.[1] Furthermore, sales incentives have been growing faster than other segments of the incentive field, having increased over 50 percent since 1967 when they accounted for $600 million.

[1] *Incentive Marketing Facts*, Bill Brothers Publishing Corporation, New York, N.Y., November 1970.

131

The use of sales incentives permits management to place special emphasis on particular objectives, to create excitement and interest, and to intensify competition among sales people. The results of an incentive program are usually immediately apparent. Furthermore, the sales incentive plan is easily and inexpensively communicated to a relatively small group of salesmen as compared to the comparatively difficult and costly job of communicating facts about a consumer incentive to the general public.

Incidentally, the use of the word "salesmen" as used in this chapter must be understood in its very broadest connotation— meaning anybody who has any contact with or influence upon the selling process. While direct sales personnel are, perforce, the main recipients of sales incentives, in many plans nonselling personnel are included in order to get as many employees as possible involved in the plan. Only incentive plans which are used to motivate company and wholesaler salesmen are discussed in this chapter. Retailer programs are covered in the next chapter, as are programs which reward retailers or wholesalers with merchandise or trips in exchange for merchandise orders.

Determining Objectives

While many users of sales incentives set up the rewards on the basis of paying off for increased sales as an overall dollar-for-dollar basis, it is usually desirable to plan on specific objectives set up to be accomplished within a given span of time. Here are some of the more frequently used objectives for sales incentives:

Product or service objectives

Sales incentives are often applied to certain segments of a complete line of products or services.

For example:

Introduce a new product line
Sell slow-moving items
Sell seasonal items
Promote higher unit items
Promote a profitable group of products
Sell a particular type of bank service or insurance policy
Promote specialty items

Distribution objectives

In many cases, instead of stressing a specific product or service, sales incentives are applied to distribution objectives.

For example:

Get better territory coverage
Open new accounts — retail or wholesale
Reactivate old accounts
Develop new prospects
Get broader distribution
Obtain greater sales volume per call

Promotional objectives

When a consumer promotion is being launched, sales incentives are often used to give it added impetus.

For example:

Overcome a seasonal sales slump
Sell the promoted items or a promotional deal
Gain a more profitable balance of sales
Get displays in major accounts
Obtain local retail or wholesale advertising support
Ease a high inventory situation

Sales training objectives

Sometimes sales incentives are used as a tool for sales training, either to train the salesmen or to encourage them to train retail or wholesale salesmen.

For example:

Answer a product quiz in order to qualify for incentives
Set up sales training meetings with dealers
Develop new sales skills

Of respondents replying to *Incentive Marketing Facts* questionnaire, 12.3 percent reported that they used a sales training feature in their incentive plans.[2]

[2] *Incentive Marketing Facts,* Bill Brothers Publishing Corporation, New York, N.Y., November 1970.

General objectives

In some situations, sales incentives may be primarily instituted for general purposes; for example, to boost morale to respond to a similar plan being conducted by the competition, or to lower selling costs.

The relative importance of various objectives is shown in a survey which was conducted by the Sales and Marketing International among 323 firms representing a wide spectrum of manufacturing and service companies.

TABLE 5.1　Objectives of Sales Incentives for Your Own Sales Force*

Objective	Most important	
	Number	*Percent*
Total	323	100.0
Increase overall sales	217	67.2
Find new customers	133	41.2
Promote special items	70	21.7
Obtain greater volume per call	89	27.6
Overcome seasonal sales slump	66	20.4
Introduce a new product, line or service	51	15.8
Get better territory coverage	58	18.0
Stop or slow a sales decline	33	10.2
Get better balance of sales	36	11.1
Get renewal of business with former customers	29	9.0
Develop new sales skills	23	7.1
Ease an unfavorable inventory position	27	8.4
Improve sales service to customers	24	7.4
Sell higher quality products	24	7.4
Build better product displays	17	5.3
Do self-training	14	4.3
Lower selling costs	13	4.0
Reduce selling time	7	2.2
Get better sales reports	2	0.6
Other	17	5.3

*Contests, Prizes and Awards for Sales Motivation, Sales and Marketing Executives International, New York, N.Y., 1968.

DECIDING UPON THE PARTICIPANTS

A sales incentive program can involve only one group, for example, manufacturer's direct sales representatives. However, there are various ways in which a sales incentive plan can be broadened to include other types of participants.

Sales incentive plans broadened by levels of distribution

A sales incentive plan can be broadened by including various levels of sales responsibility within the organization and then can be carried through to the wholesale level, management or selling personnel, and finally to the retail level (treated separately in the next chapter).

The levels of selling responsibility generally considered are:

Divisional Sales Managers
Regional Sales Managers
District Sales Managers
Sales Force
Wholesaler/Distribution Management
Wholesaler/Distributor Salesmen

The decision whether to broaden a plan to include other levels within the company sales organization will depend, of course, on budget considerations. However, it will also depend upon the type of salesmen and sales management involved. In one situation, middle sales management is considered an important part of the overall company management and would not be happy to be included in an incentive plan. In other sales forces, the middle sales management is considered as the field officers of the sales force and are just as susceptible to motivation as the individual salesmen on the "firing line." In the SME study,[3] 29.9 percent of all respondents reported sales management participated in their sales incentive plans.

The decision to include wholesalers in sales incentive plans or to make them the major recipients for the plan will depend, again, on the structure of the selling operation. A setup in which

[3] *Contests, Prizes and Awards for Sales Motivation*, Sales and Marketing Executives International, New York, N.Y., 1968.

products are sold by route salesmen who are essentially delivering merchandise to retail stores would be treated quite differently from one in which each wholesaler salesman was responsible for selling several hundred thousand dollars worth of products per year. Here, the decision has to be made as to whether or not the program will be offered to a particular group, and also as to the form of program which will be offered.

Broadening a sales incentive program by including nonselling employees

In many situations, a question will arise whether or not to include service personnel, general management, warehouse personnel, or other nondirect employees in a sales incentive plan.

One problem here is the budget. If the sales incentives are spread too thinly, there is not sufficient reward to properly motivate the people involved. Another problem is related to the method of scoring. Nonselling employees generally receive awards on a team basis in which individual effort is not recognized. Naturally, some personal motivation has to be sacrificed here.

However, as we shall see, there are means of involving non-selling employees in sales incentives which are effective and affordable.

In the SME study, 14.3 percent of the programs involved service personnel, 13.7 percent involved branch management, 7.8 percent involved office order handling staff, and 3.7 percent involved general management.[4]

There are one or two typical situations in which the involvement of nonselling personnel becomes extremely desirable.

One example is service personnel who have very frequent direct contact with the customers on the telephone. In this case, the service personnel often know the customers on a first-name basis, talk to them every day, and have almost as close a relationship with them as the salesman does. When a sales incentive plan is put into effect, it is very difficult not to include these service personnel who can use a certain amount of suggestive selling, and

[4] *Incentive Marketing Facts*, Bill Brothers Publishing Corporation, New York, N.Y., November 1970.

who also are liable to become extremely upset if they are not included in such a plan.

Another typical situation is represented by a bank plan. In this situation, there are contact personnel such as tellers; and there are other personnel who have very little direct contact with customers; but who can exercise a definite effect upon prospective customers—their friends, neighbors, and relatives who can be influenced to become customers of the bank. In the case of a bank or other large service institution, therefore, it is generally considered desirable to obtain the broadest involvement of personnel. In these programs, teams representing one branch or another, or various departments, are usually organized to establish a competitive spirit during the sales incentive drive.

Broadening the sales incentive plan to include the family

A rather warm controversy has developed on the subject of whether or not to include wives in sales incentive plans. The consensus seems to support the idea, while cautioning against taking a heavy-handed approach which can arouse resentment on the part of the salesman or his family.

In general, the feeling seems to prevail that if a company is making extra rewards—especially merchandise or trips—available to a salesman, why shouldn't the wife and family become participants; and, at the same time, encourage the salesman to his best efforts on a day-to-day basis? *Incentive Marketing Facts'* survey indicated that the salesmen's wives were involved in approximately two-thirds of the respondents' programs.

The type of sales force and people exposed to the program will, to some degree, determine the extent of involvement of salesmen's wives. Good judgment and common sense must be exercised, obviously, to determine how to promote the program to the salesmen's wives, and the extent to which they are approached directly.

FORMS OF SALES INCENTIVES

There are various forms of incentive plans generally used in developing motivational programs for sales organizations.

However, the most widely used and most effective type is

called a sales incentive plan; as opposed to a contest, a sweep-stakes, or honor award program.

The sales incentive plan

The sales incentive plan is set up to bestow on *all* participants who achieve certain sales performance goals *rewards* over and above their regular sales compensation. The plans are based either on straight dollar or unit sales performance, or upon certain achievements related to a sales quota. Rewards can be either in cash, merchandise, or trips—or a combination of these. From the budget point of view, a sales incentive plan poses some difficulty; because the exact amount paid out in incentives will be determined by the amount of sales increases produced. Management must be prepared to realize that projected budget levels may be exceeded if the program produces greater sales than anticipated.

A typical sales incentive plan is illustrated by the Lehn-Fink Industrial Products Division of Sterling Drug Co. This incentive plan was based on S&H green stamps, cash prizes, and trips.

> Since profits in our industry are made primarily on the sale of 55-gallon drums of a product, we offered one S&H book for every combination of 55 gallons of a new product sold. The program was conducted with 350 Lehn-Fink salesmen. Bonus books were offered to field, regional, and national winners based on total gallons sold. Two top national winners won a trip to New York, with visits to corporate headquarters, and dinners out, a Broadway play, and a luncheon in their honor.[5]

This sales incentive plan contains the basic features of all well-conceived plans; namely, the average and below average salesman can win something, while top performers are rewarded for outstanding results.

The sales contest

The sales contest is an incentive plan in which a certain group of prizes is set up for those who achieve the best performance as spelled out by the ground rules. Naturally, those who are the top performers generally win. The difficulty here is that the average or below average groups know in advance that they

[5] *Advertising and Sales Promotion Magazine*, May 1969.

won't win, and therefore fail to put out their best efforts—or indeed any extra effort at all.

Contests, however, are effective in situations where a team effort is desired. In this case, the contest is used to award the districts, divisions, departments, or branches which do the best selling job.

Sales incentive plans often have team contests added to them so that both types are combined into one program. Incidentally, many people misname sales incentive plans, calling them "sales contests," which is quite confusing. The key difference is the participants compete for a fixed set of prizes in a contest, as opposed to a sales incentive plan in which everyone who attains the objectives assigned is entitled to certain specified awards.

In an American Motors sales incentive plan, involving their dealers, a contest feature for American Motors zone managers and district managers illustrates how this element is used to spark competition among the factory sales force, who in turn must be responsible for selling the program to their dealers.

> Zone managers and assistants participated in an auto-racing contest, dividing the promotion period into six 10-day events successively named Daytona, Sebring, Lime Rock, Mid-Ohio, Meadowdale, and Riverside. Rankings for the six periods were averaged at the end; the two top-ranking zone managers became hosts for a Vienna–Paris trip, the next two for a Vienna–Madrid trip, and the next eight for San Juan. Thus twelve of the twenty-three managers won trips in any event.[6]

Sweepstakes

Sweepstakes are a form of sales incentive frequently used as supplementary activities, although they can also be used to form the entire basis of an incentive program. They are not used more often because those who participate in a sales effort, and who are working hard to achieve results, do not like the element of chance being present in the gaining of rewards.

A good example of a sweepstakes device used to accomplish a simple sales goal was employed by F&F Laboratories, Inc., a Chicago-based manufacturer of nonprescription drugs and candy.

[6] *Incentive Marketing Facts*, Bill Brothers Publishing Corporation, New York, N.Y., 1970.

The objective was to motivate jobbers to place orders. Here is how it worked:

> The terms of the [sweepstakes] were straightforward and simple. We mailed order cards for our lozenges and candies, [along with] different colored lead pencils, to jobbers we had done business with in the past [and to jobbers] we hadn't [done business with].
>
> Before we mailed the cards and pencils, we chose a particular color, which was kept secret even from our own salesmen. If the jobber got a pencil corresponding to this particular color and [wrote] an order with it, he won $100 and got his money back on the order he placed.
>
> The "lucky color" [sweepstakes] was highly successful. There was a marked increase in sales to wholesale jobbers during the promotion. In addition, we added a sizable number of jobbers who have stayed with us since the [promotion] ended.[7]

Another example of the use of sweepstakes to stir up excitement in a sales incentive program is illustrated in Bankers Trusts' "Big Difference" bank-wide incentive program. It involved 8,000 bank employees in an E.F. MacDonald prize point program, lasted 16 weeks, and included the bank's officers as well as contact and noncontact employees.

> To spark installment loan business, the "Win Mink or Music" sweepstakes was run during May. Employees gained one entry ticket for every new customer in that category. A special drawing was held for a mink coat or a stereo console.
>
> In June, the "Town and Country" sweepstakes shifted the accent to the Bankers Card/advance checking service. Every approved application earned an employee an entry in a drawing for 3 days and nights at an upstate resort or in a midtown New York hotel.[8]

PRIZES

There are three basic types of prizes offered as sales incentives: cash, merchandise, and trips. Each of these has its own particular attributes as a motivational force.

In the Sales and Marketing International survey, the respon-

[7] *Incentive Marketing Facts*, Bill Brothers Publishing Corporation, New York, N.Y., October 1970.

[8] *Incentive Marketing Facts*, Bill Brothers Publishing Corporation, New York, N.Y., November 1970.

Fig. 5.1 *A self mailer is used to promote the Bankers Trust "Win Mink or Music" sweepstakes. The back fold was used to explain the rules of the sweepstakes for contact and noncontact employees. The first fold was used for the mailing address. (Bankers Trust Company.)*

dents were asked which types of awards they used in their sales incentive plans. Here are the results:

Category*	Percent
Merchandise.	57.5
Cash	47.2
Trips.	39.1
Combination of cash, merchandise, honor awards, trips.	32.6
Honor, i.e., pins, titles, trophies, etc.	29.8
Stocks, bonds, etc.	6.2
Vacations with pay.	5.3
Other.	3.7

* Contests, Prizes and Awards for Sales Motivation, Sales and Marketing Executives International, New York, N.Y., 1968.

When it comes to the amount spent in each category, these figures are shown in the survey of incentive users conducted by *Incentive Marketing Facts:*[9]

INCENTIVE EXPENDITURES
(% of total purchasers reported)

Merchandise awards	58.7
Travel	24.4
Sweepstakes prizes	15.4
Honor awards.	1.5

Cash is the simplest type of prize. It needs no explanation; and, therefore, for very short programs or as a bonus feature, is used regularly. However, the salesman gets the cash in his weekly pay check and it is difficult to glamorize. Unless a very large amount is offered, it is difficult to promote.

For this reason, many sales incentive planners do not favor cash as the principal prize award for the major incentive plans.

Cash can be used, however, with imagination. For example, one sales manager had a sales force of a dozen salesmen. He was extremely anxious to get these men to open new distributors using a new sales presentation he had turned over to them at the sales meeting. Each man had rehearsed the presentation, but he wanted to give them a fast and urgent reason to successfully use the presentation right away. After the formal meeting was over, he dis-

[9] *Incentive Marketing Facts,* Bill Brothers Publishing Corporation, New York, N.Y., November 1970.

Fig. 5.2 *Cover of the convention folder for NCR's Hundred Point Club Convention. Each January, the qualifying salesmen who have achieved at least 100 percent of their quota enjoy a four-day trip to such locations as Honolulu or Hollywood-by-the-Sea, Florida. (The National Cash Register Company.)*

missed the staff people, and then, alone with his men, he pulled a dozen $100 bills out of his pocket. He tore the bills in half, giving one half to each man and keeping one half himself in an envelope marked with the man's name. He told them as soon as they had opened a new distributor, he would send them the remaining half of their $100 bill. Within ten days, he had sent out all the bills. In addition, this quick and drastic way to get his men started resulted in a tremendously successful follow-through in getting a distributor organization started.

Merchandise

Merchandise is the most frequently used category of prize rewards because of its motivational power, its promotability, and its flexibility. A merchandise prize worth only $2 or $3 can be promoted effectively, while the same amount in cash seems negligible. Merchandise prizes for the wife or family make it possible to offer a wide variety of tangible rewards which are wanted and desired. And merchandise prizes can be offered in a tremendous variety of ways, from programs which offer certain selected items to catalog programs which can offer 3,000 to 4,000 items.

In general, the longer lasting, more important programs tend to use a multigift catalog approach such as is available through the incentive divisions of trading stamp companies, or through other organizations in the incentive business. These organizations all have elaborate full-color catalogs which feature thousands of items of merchandise running in retail value from a dollar or so all the way to mink coats and living room furniture. Much of this merchandise is in the incentive organizations inventory. The other items are guaranteed to be in stock by the prime manufacturer.

The incentive organizations also provide a complete service to help set up an incentive program. Most of their representatives are thoroughly experienced in incentive plans. In addition, they make available at cost mailing pieces which can be adapted to each particular program. Probably most important of all, the incentive companies handle the fulfillment of prizes, making sure that they are shipped promptly and assuming responsibility for any complaints from the reward winners.

Another desirable feature of the incentive prize catalogs is that they are received in the salesman's home, available for the whole family to scrutinize and enabling them to select, in advance, the prizes they would like to win.

All of these factors have great appeal to many incentive programmers. However, for short-term, low-budget plans a simpler approach to prizes is often more desirable. (Also, the large catalogs cost approximately 85 cents and can become a big cost factor when promotional money is limited.)

In these shorter, lower cost plans, the prize offerings are often confined to a single line of merchandise (cameras or sportswear, for example). Then, too, a more advantageous buy can often be made by dealing directly with the premium department of a manufacturer rather than with a large prize house.

An example of this approach would be to employ one manufacturer who sells shirts, blazers, and ties. He would provide an eight- or ten-page catalog and could handle the prize fulfillment with certificates sent in by those running the sales incentive plan.

Still another option is to deal with a premium representative or supplier who assembles merchandise selections on various value "plateaus" — $5, $10, $25, $50, etc. On each plateau, there are eight or ten items which offer a variety of choice at that particular price level. As each salesman achieves a certain sales performance level, he is able to choose any one gift from that particular plateau. This type of plan offers a form of step-up incentive — where a man has attained enough sales or points to reach the $10 plateau but sees that with a little extra effort he can get to the $25 plateau.

According to *Incentive Marketing Facts'* survey, 37.2 percent of firms use a catalog service firm, 13.1 percent use a single manufacturer's catalog, and 47.7 percent buy items individually. In general, the programs set up as longer term, major efforts are inclined to use the catalog prize houses because they offer a wide range of merchandise. For smaller programs, a planner is more inclined to purchase direct in order to get more favorable prices.

Trips

Trips are used to give glamour and excitement to sales incentive plans. They are sometimes used as an extra reward to the top producers or as prizes in sweepstakes, which are used to add excitement and extra motivation to a sales incentive plan. The fact that they are used so frequently in these plans indicates that they are extremely effective in stimulating response from participants.

As in the case of merchandise, trips offer a great deal of flexibility as an incentive reward. They can range all the way from a weekend for two in a nearby city or resort to a fully paid trip around the world. However, the greatest number of trips are those to the glamor spots in the United States: Hawaii, Florida, Las Vegas, California; and outside the United States: Mexico, the Caribbean, South America, Europe.

Most trip awards involve group travel so that those participating can enjoy being with the other winners, so that company management can meet with them, and because there are substantial savings in group travel arrangements. Automotive companies, business equipment companies, and insurance underwriters are all big users of travel incentives.

Honor awards

Honor awards are reported as accounting for only 1.5 percent of the amount spent for incentive merchandise in the Sales Incentive Facts Survey. However, this figure does not, in any way, indicate their tremendous importance as a tool in making sales incentive plans work. The recognition that the salesman receives from his fellow salesmen, company management, and his family is a potent force, indeed, motivating him to try harder.

The most successful plans combine honor awards with trips, cash, or merchandise, so that the material rewards as well as the psychic rewards are both included.

The Sales and Marketing Executives International Survey reports on the type and kind of honor awards used most often by this representative group of sales incentive users:[10]

Titles—"Salesman of the Month," etc.	62.3%
Congratulations from high officials.	58.5%
Publicity in house publications	57.8%
Trophies	56.1%
Recognition for wives of successful salesmen	41.9%
Certificates, diplomas, etc..	37.7%
Pins	28.4%
Rings	10.0%
Other	16.6%

As we can see from this table, there are several aspects to honor awards; and there is quite a degree of duplication among them. Actually, this is logical because these aspects cover three areas.

1. Titles, organizations, or clubs:
   President's Club
   Winners' Circle
   Salesmen of the Year
   100 Million Club
2. The honor awards themselves:
   Trophies
   Rings
   Lapel pins
   Plaques
   Certificates

[10] *Contests, Prizes and Awards for Sales Motivation*, Sales and Marketing Executives International, New York, N.Y., 1968.

3. The means of communication:
   Sales meetings
   Publicity in house organs
   Letters from management to salesmen or their wives
   Sales letters

All of these, in one form or another, are apt to be used in a successful honor award program.

TIMING AND DURATION OF SALES INCENTIVE PLANS

One feature common to all sales incentive plans is the time factor. As they represent a form of promotion which calls for "something extra," they must have a beginning and an end—otherwise the "extra" would become a built-in part of the salesmen's compensation.

A sales incentive plan, which involves a large number of sales people on different levels and has a wide variety of prizes, takes a tremendous amount of planning and a good deal of promotional expense. It is really not worth the time and money involved for a major program to run for only a month or so. *Incentive Marketing Facts'* survey reports that the average major program runs 19.6 weeks. Some programs run to a full year, but the most frequently encountered time frame for major programs is two to six months.

There are, however, many variations on sales incentive plans. When the objectives are limited and the prizes are kept simple, a minor sales incentive plan can be as short as a week or less. Let us take a typical minor program or "quickie." Assume that the sales manager has a sales force of 100 men who are selling direct to 4,000 dealers. He has a warehouse stock of product A, which he wants to move; so he sends telegrams to all the men telling them that each man who sells a gross of product A to each of 10 dealers, in the next two weeks, will get a prize of $100. Here is a plan which has simple rules, uses cash for prizes, and accomplishes its purpose in a very short time. According to the *Incentive Marketing Facts'* survey, minor programs run to an average of 6.2 weeks, and the range runs from 2 weeks to 3 months for the majority of minor campaigns.

The starting dates for sales incentive plans peak in January and February, then drop back to a lower level through the spring and summer months, and increase in September and October, reflecting fall programs which are announced as the summer months draw to a close. December, due to holiday activity, is a low point for starting incentive programs.

Scoring Methods

The method of scoring in sales incentive plans is of extreme importance. If the scoring method is not set up properly, the incentive plan cannot produce results. Every precaution must be taken to ensure that the system is fair and that it really motivates a majority of those in the sales force. The result of an improper scoring plan may reward top producers for sales they would have made anyway, while failing to motivate the average or below average men.

The simplest scoring methods reward salesmen for direct dollar or unit sales. For some sales forces, where the sales per man are evenly balanced, this method works very well. However, in many situations, within a sales force there are wide variations between territories. These variations can be caused by the differences between high volume and lower volume territories in relatively lower population areas covering much greater geographical area. On the other hand, the differences may be caused by the variations between experienced men and relative newcomers; or it may be a combination of both factors.

The most popular method of setting up scoring systems is to establish individual quotas for each territory so that each man is, in effect, competing against himself. These quotas can be based on last year's performance or upon a sales potential based on each particular territory's share of industry sales adjusted for geographical differences.

In the *Incentive Marketing Facts'* survey[11], 22.8 percent of incentive users were awarded prizes on the basis of unit sales, 35.4 percent on the basis of dollar sales, and 41.8 percent on individual quotas.

Among those using the quota system in their sales incentive plans, the majority of the companies in the *IMF* study began crediting their men with awards at 93 percent of quota, although some gave partial credits as low as 50 to 60 percent of quota. There are

[11] *Incentive Marketing Facts*, Bill Brothers Publishing Corporation, New York, N.Y., November 1970.

also quite a few plans which do not begin crediting for awards until the 100 percent quota level has been achieved.

Most sales managements try to set up their programs so that rewards can be attained by the average salesman with a reasonable effort. Yet, most sales managers feel that they do not wish to reward a routine effort with extra compensation. If 50 percent of the sales force achieves rewards, then the rest of the men realize that with a certain amount of extra effort they could have participated in the prizes. In some sales incentive plans, which involve a high calibre of sales personnel, however, as high a percentage as 80 percent gain a prize-winning position. And in some programs which involve an entire sales force, everyone involved wins something, regardless of how small it may be.

The table below[12] shows the Sales and Marketing Executives International Survey results as to the percentage of eligible salesmen who actually win some award.

ELIGIBLE SALESMEN WINNING A PRIZE	Percent
Less than 10%	10.0
10 to 24%	22.1
25 to 49%	24.3
50 to 74%	20.9
75 to 99%	13.4
100%	9.3

Scoring methods—points or stamps for prize merchandise

Incentive plans which are based on merchandise prizes usually employ a point system or trading stamps as a means for determining the requirements to win a prize. There are several good reasons for using these methods of scoring as opposed to cash.

In the first place, if cash values are used as a basis of comparison, the participants can "shop" many items in discount stores. If they find a similar item for less money they are unhappy about it, feeling either that they are working too hard to get these prizes or that someone is getting away with something. Points and trading stamps deemphasize price comparisons.

In the second place, 1,200 stamps seems like more than $3, and 600 points seems like more than $3. Even though the partici-

[12] *Contests, Prizes and Awards for Sales Motivation*, Sales and Marketing Executives International, New York, N.Y., 1968.

pants really do know the approximate retail value of most of the prizes offered, the psychology of the larger number of stamps or points makes the items seem to be worth more. This is especially important in cases where quite a few participants will win merchandise worth less than $5. Those who win the lower-priced prizes are often the most difficult to motivate, as we have pointed out before. They are the below average performers, and anything which serves to enhance the value of the prizes which they win is especially desirable.

When stamps are used, the trading stamp catalog can often be used just as it is, because the pages of the catalog show the value of each item. In a point system, a separate list is included with the catalog which lists the items by number together with their point value. Points are usually set up on the basis of 1/2 cent per point or 1 cent per point.

If it is desirable to have the merchandise look more valuable, the 1/2 cent basis can be used. However, some planners feel that having a $75 prize list for 15,000 points looks ridiculous and prefer to use the lower basis, or 7,500 points.

As far as the sales incentive planner is concerned, he can choose between any one of these three methods, but he certainly would be advised to use some scoring system like this in a merchandise prize program.

Scoring extras

Once the basic scoring system has been established, a great number of methods are at the disposal of the planners to create additional excitement and motivation during the period the plan is running. It is well to remember that the average major plan runs 19.6 weeks —almost 6 months—and if various special activities are not used, even the best conceived plan can settle down into a familiar, routine, everyday affair.

There are several special scoring devices which are commonly used to serve this purpose.

Bonuses

During the course of a typical sales incentive plan, excitement is created by offering carefully planned bonus offers which will serve to accomplish particular objectives. The basic scoring system should be, at this point, clearly understood by all participants. These bonuses are, therefore, planned to work within the framework of the incentive plan. In order to achieve maximum dramatic impact, they are announced as they occur, without prior notification to the participants.

Bonuses are used to accomplish a great variety of objectives. They can be used to sell specific products, to promote product introductions, to promote continuity in sales performance, or to sell an entire line. They can be used to promote selling to dealers, opening new dealerships or reactivating old ones; they can be used to get display of product or to launch promotions; they can be used to promote sales training or recruiting of new customers or salesmen.

Sprints

A sprint is a form of bonus which is used on a temporary basis to spur quick action. For example, one type of sprint provides extra points to those who attain a certain rate of performance during the initial week or two of the promotion. This type of sprint is called a "fast start" bonus. The fast start is particularly desirable in cases where a sales incentive plan is being launched for the first time, since it works to encourage all those in the participating group to "get into the act" and start enjoying the extra rewards which the incentive plan can bring them. Usually a fast start sprint doubles the normal rewards for the initial period, although providing a 50 percent bonus may be sufficient.

In addition to a fast start sprint, three to six additional sprint events are normally run during the course of a six-month program. These sprints are often based on special objectives, which direct the participant's efforts to selected products or special tasks such as display placement, certain types of retail calls, and the like.

Product-oriented bonuses

Probably the most common use of bonuses is to place special emphasis on certain products or groups of products during a major sales incentive drive. Royal Typewriters' use of a special two-month extra bonus on its electric machines provides a good example of this type of extra incentive.

The Royal Typewriter sales incentive program, which is a full-year plan, demonstrates a typical use of this type of sprint.

> Such special campaigns are fairly frequent at Royal; this year the company has had them on each of three product lines. These are short term efforts, usually two months,[13] with special objectives tied to particular products. Catalog prize points are the usual payoff.
>
> Typical of such sprints was the "Sales Blazers" campaign conducted in January and February to focus sales attention on three electric typewriter models. Sales emphasis at Royal is, of course, heavily on electrics where the key sales potential and the big growth potential are. Special prices were announced on the 440, 550, and 660 models—with an extra bonus of 500 prize points per machine for the salesman. At a cost of 1/2 cent per point the bonus is not great, but it helps build excitement. "Sales Blazers" bulletins show samples of the incentives offered—four from 5,500 to 21,500 points were shown in one January bulletin; names and point earnings of the leaders were also shown.[14]

The product-oriented bonus can take many forms. It can, for example, be used to reward sales people for continuity of performance in which they get increasing rewards for consistent sales effort. Another facet of the Royal Typewriter program illustrates this form of bonus.

> If a year seems like a long incentive program, Royal's MAD Club will look even longer; it runs up to 100 months. MAD stands for a "Machine-a-Day," and it is based on a dollar amount set for a month's sales. Anyone achieving the level the first month receives a ring signifying membership in the Club. The next plateau is 15 months, when he gets his choice from a broadside of awards; at 25 months, there is a broadside of more expensive items; at 50 months, a still more valuable group to choose from, and an opportunity to visit the plant; after 100 months the most expensive group of items is achieved, and a handsome plaque goes to the winner.[15]

Another form of bonus based on a balanced selling performance is used in cases where it is desirable to sell an entire

---

[13] In shorter programs, running four to six months, a sprint will generally run from two to four weeks.

[14] *Incentive Marketing Facts*, Bill Brothers Publishing Corporation, New York, N.Y., November 1970.

[15] *Incentive Marketing Facts*, Bill Brothers Publishing Corporation, New York, N.Y., November 1970.

line. Southern Union Gas Company of Dallas is in the appliance business in an important way. They used their incentive plan bonuses not only to encourage balanced selling, but also to provide extra rewards for those who attain their sales quotas the fastest.

> The program is designed to encourage early results by a sliding scale of "qualification" dates. Thus, the appliance salesman, if he sells his qualifying quota of twenty each of six appliances by a certain date, wins a $200 bonus. Then, if by the end of the twenty-sixth pay period he sells thirty of each, his bonus is $400; forty units of each, $800; fifty units of each, $1,250. If he sells sixty units in each category, he can take his choice of a Chevrolet Camaro, $2,500 in Southern Union stock, or a seven day trip to Europe for two. The later in the year he qualifies, the lower the bonus; so that by September, the big prizes have shrunk to His n' Her Hondas, $1,000 in stock, and a trip to Nassau. September is the last month in which the salesman can qualify.[16]

Bonuses based on sales-call performance

Sometimes it is desirable to base bonus awards on the performance of salesmen in terms of sales-calls instead of product sales.

In one situation, sales management will be looking for new accounts. Especially in cases where an introductory sale can lead to repeat sales, this type of a drive can result in continuing sales over a period of time.

In other situations, sales management may be looking for reactivation of existing accounts which have not been cultivated for a period of time.

In either case, the incentive bonus will probably be tied to a minimum order on each sales call, designed to place a certain amount of stock in the retailer's inventory.

A typical example was a plan run for Carlsberg Beer, ". . .to secure new accounts, [it was] directed at distributors. The winner won a three-week trip for two plus $500 expense money. Five others won Omega gold watches."[17]

---

[16] *Incentive Marketing Facts,* Bill Brothers Publishing Corporation, New York, N.Y., November 1970.
[17] *Sales Incentive Promotions,* Premium Advertising Association of America, Inc., New York, N.Y., 1967.

Fig. 5.3 *Southern Union Gas of Dallas used shares of its own stock as prizes in its incentive plan. This is the presentation folder's cover. (Southern Union Gas Company.)*

Bonuses to get display of product

Especially in the case of packaged goods—supermarket or drug store products—special displays have an immediate, verified effect upon sales. In these situations, bonus points are often offered for performance in getting displays set up.

Aluminum Company of America's "Soft Drink Display Contest" illustrates the display-oriented approach for bonus prizes.

> Each off-shelf display had to consist of at least ten cases of easy-open aluminum cans of one or more brands of soft drinks . . . display had to be up for an entire week including two weekends between June 26th and September 11th . . . salesman photographed the display and sent [the photograph] in with his special entry blank . . . 226 prizes — 113 for bottler salesmen, 113 for retailers . . . top prizes, Pontiac Firebirds . . . 4 second [prizes] RCA . . . TVs . . . 20 third [prizes] RCA stereo[s] . . . 200 fourth [prizes] Revere camera outfits . . .[18]

Bonuses based on sales training objectives

A bonus award can be used as a means to make sure that salesmen understand the selling points and customer benefits of a particular product or line of products. In these situations, the salesman is generally asked to fill in a questionnaire which he sends in to qualify for a bonus. This technique would generally be used where there is a very large sales force and minimal personal contact with the men, or in cases where distributor or broker salesmen have a great many different items to sell and there is a need to attract their attention to one particular product.

Bonuses based on quota performance

Sometimes a sales incentive plan increases the incentive bonuses based upon the extent to which the sales quota is exceeded. The Royal Typewriter program illustrates this approach.

> By April and May another sprint campaign was underway; this one, tied to quota performance on all office typewriters, featured "Six Great Ways to Win." It was called the "Royal Swing into Spring." The [six] great ways to win:
>
> 1. Sell 105 percent of April quota for 2,000 points
> 2. Sell 105 percent of May quota for 2,000 points
> 3. An extra 2,000 points for 105 percent of both months' quotas
> 4. "Double or Nothing" — bet your April points on making your May quota and win 12,000 points total

[18] *Sales Incentive Promotions*, Premium Advertising Associates of America, Inc., New York, N.Y., 1967.

5. 400 more points for every $100 of commercial business over 105 percent of quota (including dealer wholesale)
6. "Open Season on IBM"—an extra 1,000 points for every IBM typewriter traded in during the Plus Performers program[19]

Sweepstakes used as bonuses

One of the most effective devices used in developing additional excitement and motivation in a sales incentive plan is the use of a sweepstakes, in which the special performance requirements provide chances to win prizes. Sweepstakes provide a less expensive way to apply bonuses than direct bonuses which are paid to all those who achieve certain goals. They can be used in a great many ways to keep the interest in a sales incentive plan active and to give extra awards to participants. Sweepstakes can act to motivate below average producers, as well as the top performers. For example, if every sale represents a chance to win, then the man who makes only two sales can still win, although he only has one-fifth of the chances that the man who has made ten sales has. Still, the two-sale man does not necessarily know how many chances the others have; and, therefore, the motivation continues as long as he feels that he has a chance to win.

An effective use of sweepstakes is illustrated by the Bankers Trust Company, as part of their "Big Difference" all-employee incentive plan.

Point values were given to all bank services. Combining the elements of selling skill and chance, participants were competing for tickets in a grand prize drawing as well as for individual prizes from the catalog. The grand prizes, consisting of six trips for two, were based on total prize point achievement. For each 5,000 prize points, an individual got one ballot in the drawing for a trip to Bermuda or Nassau. For 10,000 prize points, he was also entered in the drawing for a Caribbean cruise or a Mexican holiday. For 20,000 points, he merited a chance in the Hawaiian holiday drawing.

The point totals were cumulative—meaning that anyone scoring 20,000 points would have four entries in the Bermuda/Nassau drawing, two tickets in the Caribbean cruise/Mexican holiday drawing, and one ballot in the Hawaiian holiday drawing.[20]

[19] *Incentive Marketing Facts*, Bill Brothers Publishing Corporation, New York, N.Y., November 1970.
[20] *Incentive Marketing Facts*, Bill Brothers Publishing Corporation, New York, N.Y., 1970.

Importance of simplicity and clear communications

It is important to emphasize that the ground rules for a sales incentive plan should be as simple as possible. Many a plan which has been well-conceived in its objective, theme, and promotion has failed because the participants could not understand the rules. There is a temptation in the planning stages to start adding exclusions, extra changes, elaborate formulas, etc., until the rules become as difficult to understand as the long form of the U.S. income tax. No matter how great the rewards, the average salesman is not going to be motivated if he really cannot figure out what is in it for him.

Furthermore, the communication of the ground rules in sales meetings and written communications should be carefully prepared for clarity and simplicity. An excellent idea, if possible, is to present the communication (speech, sales letter, mailing piece, etc.) to some of those who will be participants; and then, listen to their questions to see if there are any ambiguities or complexities. After working on a sales incentive project for a while, one tends to become so familiar with the details that things which appear clear to the planning team are not at all clear to someone who is seeing the plan for the first time.

If this initial job of presentation has been done well, it is much easier to put on special sprints or bonus awards as the program progresses. Now, everyone involved will understand exactly how the plan works.

Another aspect of clear communication is to be sure that you rely upon every means of communication open to you. Do not just rely upon the first presentation of the plan, but follow up with detailed written rules, and, if necessary, additional smaller meetings which permit question and answer sessions. In cases where a large sales force is gathered in one meeting room, it can often be broken up into separate regional or district groups. At these smaller meetings, the quotas or projected sales goals can be discussed with each man.

PROMOTING SALES INCENTIVES

Regardless of the mechanics of the sales incentive program (the participants, the quotas, the prizes, the scoring methods, and the bonuses) the success of it depends, to a large degree, upon promoting the promotion. This aspect of a sales incentive program involves the theme, the introduction or kick-off, and continuing activities which promote the program to participants, including ways to inform them of their progress toward achieving their goals. In a complex program, the planners will be concerned with various types of participants, direct and indirect; or in different sales levels, such as manufacturer's salesmen, wholesalers or distributors and their salesmen. Promotion to each group should be handled separately, as their extent of participation will vary according to their type of involvement. In effect, this means that most sales incentive programs must be "sold" to all participants in order to have the investment pay off. In *Incentive Marketing Facts'* survey,[21] the cost of prizes (merchandise, travel, and awards) came to 4.1 percent of sales while the cost of promotion (printing, mailings, meetings) came to 1.7 percent, representing 41 percent of the total expense of incentive plans, which was 5.8 percent of sales. (Incidentally, the average sales incentive program was reported, in this same survey, to have achieved a 23 percent sales increase at the cost of 5.8 percent of sales in the sales incentive plan.) These figures demonstrate that the respondents to this survey, the majority of them being experienced incentive program operators, realize the necessity for this amount of promotional expenditure to ensure the success of their programs.

THEMES

Establishing a theme for a sales incentive program gives it an identity with which it can be promoted. The theme forms the basis on which all the promotional activities will be built.

Developing a theme for the sales incentive program is a project that should, therefore, be given considerable attention. Some of the factors that enter into theme selection are:

Relationship to the objectives of the program
Development of excitement, competition, action, or fun
Identification with the product, service, or company
Reference to the prizes or trips

It is generally not possible to reflect all these attributes.

[21] *Incentive Marketing Facts*, Bill Brothers Publishing Corporation, New York, N.Y., 1970.

The theme, like on the headline in an advertisement, should communicate as quickly and effectively as possible. Therefore, the most important element in the sales incentive program is to convey the importance and the excitement of the promotion to the participants.

Themes related to the objectives of the program

Themes are often developed which relate to the objectives of the program, or to the scoring system involved. Typical examples of these are:

> Profit Prophet
> Winnerama
> Quota Makers
> You're the Top
> Big Build-up
> Sales Showdown
> Sellstakes

This type of theme leads into an explanation of the ground rules and an immediate explanation of the rewards to be attained. However, themes can often be more effective when related to some form of activity which poses a challenge to the participants.

Themes which are based on excitement, competition, action, or fun

Themes are often based on sports, games, politics, international intrigue, space exploration, parties, or any other human activity involved with excitement and action. Some examples:

> Tee Off
> Big Game Hunt
> World Series
> Mountain Climber
> Spotlight on Sports
> Sales Safari
> Marathon
> The People's Choice
> Five-Alarm Fire
> Sales Agent 009
> Be a Buccaneer

The theme can combine reference to the activity and to the objectives which are desired:

Bring 'Em Back Alive (reference to new dealer drive)
Be a Touchdown Hero (point-scoring set up in football
  terms)
Line Drive (baseball theme refers to product line selling)
Treasure Island (pirate theme relates to search for treasure,
  i.e., prize awards)

Themes which identify the product or company

Often a humorous reference to the product or company can be built right into the theme, for example:

Open Season on Sales (outdoor sports equipment)
Cook up a Sale (ranges or cooking equipment)
Be a Key Man (locks and safes)
Farming for Futures (farm equipment)

Naturally, many themes bring in the actual name of the product or company when the theme is used.

A theme which would otherwise seem corny becomes much more meaningful and effective if it refers directly to the product or the product's use.

A theme which reflects the company name or product also gives the participants the feeling that the program was designed particularly for them, and therefore gives it greater importance in their eyes.

Themes which refer to the prizes or trips offered

There are many incentive programs in which the prizes or trips are of such importance that they are used as the major element in the theme. This is especially common with programs in which winners go on a major trip or win large prizes. Examples of these themes are:

Trips

Canadian Caper
Roman Holiday
Greek Sailaway

Springtime in Paris
Mystery Weekend
Mexican Fiesta

Prizes

Treasure Trove
Prize Magic
Hit the Prize Route
Winner Wonderland

Once a theme has been established, all facets of the incentive promotion should be related to it. In many cases, a special piece of artwork is created for the theme. This logotype is then used in all forms of promotion of the incentive program.

THE INTRODUCTION

The introductory period represents a vitally important time in the life of a sales incentive program. If the introductory promotion captures the attention of, and creates anticipation among, those who are going to be involved, it has a good opportunity to be successful. If the introduction is played down, or if the sales people are confused by its presentation, an otherwise well-planned program may end in failure, or in producing sales increases far below those anticipated. Fortunately, most incentive planners are well aware of the necessity for a combination of showmanship and sound presentation of the facts in a sales incentive introduction.

The principal means used to introduce sales incentive programs are sales meetings, sales presentations, and mailings. Each promotional technique has its particular place in the introduction. The degree of its use will depend upon the type of program, the number of participants, and the levels of distribution involved.

Kick-off meetings

There is no substitute for a good sales meeting to introduce a sales incentive plan. The sales meeting makes possible a dramatic presentation of the theme and the program, as well as personal involvement on the part of the group. Enthusiasm is contagious, and those who are involved become excited and stimulate others. There is also an opportunity to cover all details of the program thoroughly

Fig. 5.4 *An excellent series of mailings was used to promote Honeywell Computer's "Pace-setters/Pacemakers" Conference at El Conquistador Club in Puerto Rico. More than 1,200 award winning sales and systems representatives joined "The Achievers—Los Campeones" at the conference. (Honeywell Company.)*

with the participants so that sales management can be sure that the program is completely understood.

Sales meetings are used by 71.3 percent respondents of the Sales Marketing Executives International's survey[22] of three

---

[22] *Contests, Prizes and Awards for Sales Motivation*, Sales and Marketing Executives International, New York, N.Y., 1968.

hundred companies who use sales incentives. In some cases, there are huge national meetings to which thousands of salesmen, distributors, or wholesalers are invited. Here the meeting, more often than not, covers new product introductions and advertising and promotion programs, as well as sales incentive plans. In other cases, medium-sized regional meetings or small local meetings are set up. In many situations, the smaller regional meetings are used as a follow-up to a major national meeting, to carry the promotion to the distributor or wholesale salesmen.

Investors Diversified Services, Inc., of Minneapolis, provides a good illustration of the use of kick-off meetings for incentive plans. In this case, prize points in a merchandise catalog are an integral part of the plan.

> There is a kick-off meeting for each division, which is an integral part of the entire campaign. This conclave is planned and paid for by the divisional manager and, at his option, is a breakfast, luncheon, or dinner session.
>
> These scheduled meetings·provide a framework, . . . by getting the salesmen of a division together. In a metropolitan division, the men are in and out of the division with fair frequency . . . but there are divisions where a salesman could be 400 miles from divisional offices and his visits there are necessarily infrequent.[23]

Sales meetings, therefore, serve the purpose of giving the group a psychological identity; of stimulating a healthy competitive atmosphere; and of imparting a sense of participation in a group endeavor.

In planning a kick-off meeting, whether it is a large national one involving thousands of people or a small local affair, it is essential that close attention be paid to every detail. The program itself should be geared to the group. Scripts and visual presentations should be carefully prepared to provide information about the sales incentive program in a clear, but exciting fashion. Humor and showmanship should be used to keep up interest and arouse enthusiasm.

---

[23] *Incentive Marketing Facts*, Bill Brothers Publishing Corporation, New York, N.Y., 1970.

Sales presentations

In many cases, those who attend the kick-off meeting(s) will have to carry the introductory story to wholesalers or their salesmen. In other cases, regional or district managers will have to present the story to individuals or small groups of salesmen, wholesalers, etc.

For this purpose, a large presentation book is often prepared with products for program material which can be left with the participant. In some cases, a supply of the books will be given out so that the entire book can be left with a wholesaler, who can in turn use it to present the program to his sales people.

A more elaborate sales presentation might involve a flip chart presentation prepared to use in covering the program with a small group. This could be an additional element, used in conjunction with the program book mentioned above.

Introductory mailings

Mailings are an important way of introducing sales incentive plans. Where sales meetings are scheduled, mailings are used to reach people who cannot attend these meetings. They are also used as teasers, to build excitement before the sales meeting. In programs where sales meetings are not included in the plans, the mailings often must carry the entire message to the participants.

Mailings also represent an essential means of communicating with groups of people who are not active participants. Examples of such groups might be salesmen's wives and families, jobbers' or distributors' salesmen, or insurance agent's sales force.

Teasers

Mailings become an integral part of most sales incentive programs, and one of the most important roles that they play is in the introductory phase. After all, the interest and attention of the participants are the element that is necessary to encourage involvement of each group. Teaser mailings serve to tell them that something unusual, dramatic, and challenging is going to be coming their way.

The teaser mailing usually is limited to the theme of the incentive program and gives strong hints of the fact that exciting opportunities lie in the immediate future.

A good example of an imaginative teaser mailing is illustrated in a sales incentive plan for the Famous Artist's School in Westport, Connecticut. In this program, diamonds from Tiffany's, in New York, were the key prizes.

Before the details of the plan were spelled out, the salesmen's wives were sent a teaser mailing to which a fake diamond ring was attached. The copy (somewhat shortened here) read:

> *This is a fake diamond ring . . .*
> Sometimes it's called paste . . .
> It's worthless
> *BUT . . . suppose it were the real thing? . . .*
> *It Could Be The Real Thing*
> *This is what the Diamonds and Dollars Contest is all about.*
> Your husband has the power to help you possess a beautiful diamond . . . by Tiffany.[24]

Another example of a teaser approach is shown by a mailing used by the Sealy Mattress Company in a sales incentive plan involving 300 salesmen. The theme was "the Grand Prix of Selling." There were a series of teaser mailings. The first was a small plastic race car powered by a balloon which furnished "jet propulsion" when inflated. The balloon was imprinted "Win with Sealy Posturepedic."

> An accompanying flyer read:
> "Step up the pace." The enclosed car is a simple example of jet propulsion. The more lung power you generate, the faster it rolls. And in Sealy's Grand Prix of Selling, the more power you aim at your dealers, the faster you pile up contest laps for awards. What's the Posturepedic power? It's a product story without equal in bedding merchandise. Pour it on and you can be a winner in the big race of sales champions. Step on it.
> The next mailing brought a plastic mileage minder to be clipped to the salesmen's automobile visor. It carried the imprinted slogan "Sleeping on a Sealy is like sleeping on a cloud." The flyer explained how the mileage meter could help to keep accurate records and save cash. It urged the salesman to "pull ahead of the pack" and "go for the highest percentage over quota. The bigger the increase, the bigger the honors. When you race under the Sealy flag, you race to win."[25]

---

[24] *Advertising and Sales Promotion Magazine*, February 1967.
[25] *Advertising and Sales Promotion Magazine*, August 1968.

Mailings to wives and families

In 39.1 percent of all sales incentive programs reported on in the Sales and Marketing Executives International survey,[26] prize catalogs were used. In a very large percentage of these programs, the prize catalog is sent to the home. This mailing, with the accompanying literature announcing the program, becomes the major introductory piece of the sales incentive plan. It provides the roster of prizes offered, well-presented in full color together with a list of the points needed to obtain each item. A program developed by Davol Rubber Company illustrates the use of a mailing program to reach the wives of distributor salesmen.

> Promotional literature was sent directly to the ladies in their homes . . . [The program called] "Your Chance of a Wifetime to Get Beautiful Gorham Silver." The full color brochure displayed the handsome pieces available, listed each one's retail values, and explained, "All it takes is a little encouragement . . . to your husband, that is. He's a hardworking salesman. Every day he faces a tough bunch of customers, and a tough bunch of competitors. After that, he faces a tough sales manager (that's me).
>
> "Every once in a while, one of our manufacturers offers a reward that makes it worthwhile to maintain that extra effort. This Davol silver deal is a beaut. Just look inside and see for yourself.
>
> "It's easy to get; your husband has the tally card. All he has to do is sell Davol. Of course, he has to get by all the tough guys and that's where you come in . . . with a little encouragement."
>
> To add a personal note, each brochure was signed by the local distributor sales manager.[27]

The Davol mailing piece represents an excellent psychological approach to wives. It plays up the salesman, her husband, as a guy who has a tough job to do and who needs a little encouragement. At the same time, it lets her sell herself on the prize awards available. By building up the salesman in his wife's eyes, this mailing piece also helps to gain his approval of enlisting his wife's support in the incentive program.

[26] *Contests, Prizes and Awards in Sales Motivation*, Sales and Marketing Executives International, New York, N.Y., 1968.

[27] *Incentive Marketing Facts*, Bill Brothers Publishing Corporation, New York, N.Y., April 1970.

CONTINUING PROMOTION

Introductory mailings serve an important purpose in generating excitement and in stimulating enthusiasm among wives, families, and support personnel. However, the role of mailings in continued support of a sales incentive program is equally important, indeed, it often becomes crucial. No matter how successful the introduction, sustaining interest and active motivation is vital to eventual success.

The continuing mailings serve three major purposes in most incentive plans:

1. Keep participants keyed up and aware of the rewards to be won if they reach the assigned goals.

2. Serve as a vehicle to announce special bonuses, and sprints, which are announced from time to time to stir up extra effort and to accomplish special objectives.

3. Keep salesmen advised of their progress—showing them where they stand at this point in the sales incentive program.

This excellent example of a well-run direct mail effort was used in support of an Admiral Corporation promotion to stimulate sales of new model radios, tape recorders, and stereo units.

Salesmen and sales managers were introduced to the program via a "Think Mink . . . Think Admiral" portfolio of furs which was sent to each man's home. The ten-page, four-color brochure detailed the fur fashions, which ranged from mink berets to full-length coats, and from fur-trimmed sweaters to fun furs.

Wives as the ultimate winners were wooed with letters and mink baubles to keep them thinking mink, and keep their husbands thinking Admiral. One of the most important mailings was a letter requesting height, weight, and dress size. Before her husband had won anything, this woman was psychologically wearing the cape or coat of her choice.

For each radio and tape recorder sold, a salesman earned 50 cents in Mink Money. Each phonograph was worth $1; component stereo, $1.50; and console stereo, $3. Tallies were taken monthly and sent to Admiral. Mink Money certificates were then sent directly to the salesman at his home as a constant inducement to sell more. Although certificates were redeemable at any time, what women would settle for a boa when she could reach for a cape or coat? Or such was the strategy of Admiral.

For the Think Mink promotion, ten mailings, approximately

one every two weeks, were sent to Admiral salesmen's wives. Each one was accompanied by a mink-adorned item—a cocktail stirrer, a golf tee, key chain, etc. They were designed to keep interest high and to continue to play on Mrs. Salesman's ability to motivate her husband. One mailing was designed to keep the winners winning more. "Even if he has already earned the stole, jacket, or coat you've had your eye on," the copy read, "wouldn't it be exciting to have another lovely fur? There's still time, with just a little added effort, to be faced with that lovely dilemma this Christmas of "which fur shall I wear today?"[28]

The Admiral mailing program worked well to keep enthusiasm high and to keep participants advised as to where they stood in the winning of prizes. It represents an excellent example of the use of direct mail as part of a successful sales incentive plan.

The thrust of the Admiral mailing program was primarily to keep excitement high and was based mainly upon keeping the interest of the wives in the major prizes, minks.

Other mailing programs, especially those which promote plans based on sales quota achievement, involve regular weekly or semi-weekly mailings, which notify the men of how they stand in their progress toward attaining their goals and what they need in terms of sales to gain the points needed to win.

Additional methods

One of the most important vehicles used in promoting sales incentive plans is the company bulletin, newspaper, or magazine which publishes the standings of all participants. Naturally, the performance of winners becomes a matter of record made public before this entire group. Those who are in the lead have a chance for publicity, and those who are lagging are provided with even more of an incentive to catch up and get into the winning category. In general, the names of winners are published, as opposed to publishing the standings of all participants. If all standings were published, those who are at the lower end of the ladder might tend to become discouraged, and the publicity could serve to create lower motivation instead of spurring nonwinners to greater activity.

A chart which reports on individual standings is very common

---

[28] *Incentive Marketing Facts,* Bill Brothers Publishing Corporation, New York, N.Y., 1970.

when all participants are working out of the same office. Usually it shows the day-to-day performance of all the participants. Again, the regular reporting of progress serves to spur the salesmen on to greater efforts, so that they can win more and gain more prestige.

Team efforts

Many plans, which reward individuals with prizes or trips, are set up to recognize team efforts, as well. In these cases, the group performance is used to reinforce individual efforts. If appropriate, team members may be encouraged to assist each other in making more sales; and the sense of identification within the groups can serve to foster an atmosphere of healthy competition between teams.

Midland Life Insurance Company of Columbus, Ohio, runs incentive plans, for its agents, which serve as a good example of this approach.

> By far, our most popular contest is the annual Gridiron Classic. This is a four-week contest between general agents. It's played like a football game. The agencies are divided into teams, each carrying the name of a general agent, and each named after a local football team. For example, the Charles Yeager Agency at Warsaw, Indiana, is named after the Purdue Boilermakers; the Harris Agency at Atlanta, Georgia, is named after the Atlanta Bulldogs; and so on. The teams are paired off so that each plays another agency of [the same] approximate size. Each week different agencies square off. The total agency business produced during the week determines the winning team [of the week].
>
> The object is to win all four games, ending up with a perfect season. By matching agencies by size, each team has a chance to win all four games. All teams with a perfect season receive publicity, recognition, and a trophy to display in the agency office.[29]

An unusual use of the team approach was used by the Agricultural Division of American Cyanamid in their sales incentive plan promoting products used in the animal health field.

> Since the announcement of the program, Cyanamid has merchandised it intensely to the salesmen. One major reminder is a quarterly inter-district competition. The districts are paired off, and the

---

[29] *Incentive Marketing Facts*, Bill Brothers Publishing Corporation, New York, N.Y., September 1971.

team which has the greatest percentage increase for the quarter is the winner. The two teams meet for dinner. The winners get steak. The losers [get] beans. One member of a losing team [said], "I didn't think you guys would actually give us beans, but by God, our team isn't going to eat them anymore! From now on, we're steak eaters."

The men, and their wives, receive periodic mailings. . . . [For example] everyone received a can of beans with a warning to make sure they didn't have to eat them at the quarterly dinner. Other mailers have included . . . place mats which say, "Let's eat steak on these."[30]

There are, then, many variations on how the team concept can be utilized to add extra motivation and excitement to incentive plans. In bank plans, or others where quite a few noncontact people are involved who have only a small influence on sales, the team concept is used to help generate more interest and enthusiasm, because these nonselling people can get the feeling that they are part of a group which is competing.

FOLLOW-THROUGH PROMOTION

The follow-through promotion, after a sales incentive program is completed, is of utmost importance. It is used to congratulate the winners and recognize their efforts. It is used to wish "better luck next time" to the "also-rans." The honor awards, special meetings, or trips, and publicity in company publications or the local press are all part of the follow-through promotion.

The Sales and Marketing Executives survey reported on follow-through techniques:[31]

Hold sales meetings for awarding prizes to winners. 67.9%
Send letters of congratulations to winners. 43.3%
Inform salesmen of helpful sales techniques learned during
   the [sales incentive plan] 21.2%
Run "follow-up" [programs]. 5.6%
Other 5.9%
Nothing. 6.2%

[30] *Incentive Marketing Facts*, Bill Brothers Publishing Corporation, New York, N.Y., 1970.

[31] *Contests, Prizes and Awards for Sales Motivation*, Sales and Marketing Executives International, New York, N.Y., 1968.

The recognition of winners and awarding of prizes at sales meetings is particularly effective because it combines the approval of management, as well as appealing to the pride of the winners (and hopefully creating a strong desire in nonwinners to be there next year). The planners often set up their sales incentive plan schedule so that the plan ends shortly before a major sales meeting is to be held.

In the absence of a sales meeting, letters from management, recognition of winners in company publications, and recognition to wives are also promotional techniques to be considered.

The important objective of follow-through promotion is to build morale by not only coming up with the prizes but also by giving the winners the attention and thanks they deserve for their hard work.

HYPOTHETICAL CASE HISTORIES

Several hypothetical case histories will serve to illustrate the economics and mechanics of sales incentive plans. One involves a carpet manufacturer typical of big ticket products; another a soft drink manufacturer representing packaged goods; and the third, a bank to show how a sales incentive plan is used to promote services.

Hypothetical Case History No. 1—Product C

A carpet manufacturer has sales of $50 million annually (manufacturer's selling price). He sells his product nationally through 100 distributors. His sales goal for the first six months is a 20 percent increase over the year before. To help achieve this goal, he decides to set up a sales incentive plan which will involve both his company salesmen, twenty-five men, and his distributors and their salesmen. His 100 distributors have an average of 5 salesmen each.

He decides to peg his scoring system for both company salesmen and distributor salesmen on a quota based on last year's first six months' sales. He plans to set up a prize budget based on 2.5 percent of the anticipated sales increase. (2.5 percent times $5 million yields $125,000.) To this amount, he adds another $50,000 to promote the sales incentive plan. Total cost will be brought to $175,000 or 3.5 percent of the sales increase.

For the twenty-five company salesmen, he sets aside $1,000 per man or $25,000 in prizes.

For the 500 distributor salesmen, he sets aside $200 per man or $100,000 in prizes.

As his major objective is to increase sales 20 percent over the year before, he sets up his scoring system to start paying a modest reward at 80 percent, so that a salesman can realize he is beginning to get rewards at this level. At 100 percent he will pay a slightly greater reward; then at 120 percent he will pay a large bonus, with additional increments for each 10 percent increase thereafter. Here is the average company salesmen's scoring chart.

AVERAGE COMPANY SALESMAN SIX MONTHS SALES:

Previous year. $1,000,000
This year's quota $1,200,000

Sales	Quota	Points (.01 each)	
$ 800,000	80%	10,000	
$1,000,000	100%	25,000	85,000
$1,200,000	120%	50,000	
$1,300,000	130%	25,000	
$1,400,000	140%	25,000	

When he attains quota at $1,200,000, the average salesman will have earned 85,000 points which are worth 1 cent each or $850. Each 10 percent additional earns him another 25,000 points or $250.

This scoring system rewards the salesman with a total of $350 in prizes for hitting last year's quota but gives him another $500 for reaching 120 percent. Then, for additional increments, he gets $250 for each 10 percent.

Incidentally, 85,000 points used at 120 percent of quota leaves 15,000 points per man to be used for district sales managers, who will also participate in the plan.

15,000 points × 100 = 1,500,000 points or $15,000. Assuming there are ten district managers, this will allow for a total of $1,500 for each of them to participate in the program. Naturally, their motivation is an important key in their salesmen's motivation.

The distributor salesman works on the same basis except that the prize values are lower. There are a total of 500 distributor salesmen who must contribute a total increase of $5 million in the first six months in manufacturer's sales dollars. This amounts to an increase of $10,000 per man.

Their total sales last year in the first six months were $25 million, so that their sales quota, after a 20 percent increase, comes to $30 million for the first six months, or $60,000 per man.

Here are the figures for the average distributor's salesmen:

Sales	Quota	Points (.01 each)	
$40,000	80%	2,000	
$50,000	100%	5,000	17,000
$60,000	120%	10,000	
$70,000	130%	5,000	
$80,000	140%	5,000	10,000

Thus, the distributor salesmen's prizes are set up on the same basic principle as the company salesmen at one-fifth the level of compensation. At 120 percent of quota, he has earned $170 in prizes.

While this plan will be proposed to the distributor, it will be up to him to decide whether or not to adopt it or to set up a different plan which might apply better to his own situation. This reflects the fact that he is an independent marketer, and also that he is required to pay for 50 percent of the prizes won in his plan. It is up to him to make whatever plan he adopts work. It is, however, very important for the distributor to share in the costs of the incentive plan so that he has a financial involvement in its success.

If all of his men attain 120 percent and he uses the company plan, the distributor will have given out 85 percent of the points allotted to him. This will leave $1,500 worth of prizes to use in motivating *his* sales manager. As in the case of the company district managers, the distributor's sales manager will be an important factor in motivating the distributor salesmen.

Let us assume that the actual six months sales increase was 30 percent. It will be interesting to see how much money was put out in prize money, and what the total incentive plan cost as compared to the 20 percent increase projected when the planning was started.

Total 130 percent of quota:

Prize total for average salesmen, 110,000 points × 25 . . . . . . $ 27,500
Prize total for average district manager, 2,000 points × 10 . . .   2,000

$ 29,500

Prize total for average distributor salesman,
22,000 points × 500 . . . . $110,000
Prize total for distributor sales managers,
2,000 points × 100   20,000

$130,000

The costs of promoting the sales incentive plan remained at $50,000. Total prize cost was $159,500 plus $50,000 promotion for a grand total of $209,500.

Total sales increase projected at 20% $5,000,000
Actual sales increase $7,500,000

The percentage of cost of the sales increase comes out to 2.8 percent of the sales increase as compared to 3.5 percent projected at 120 percent of quota.

Incidentally, the distributors will pay $65,000, representing 50 percent of their share of the prizes. This brings the actual company cost of the program down to 1.9 percent of the sales increase, which compares with 2.5 percent at 120 percent of quota.

Hypothetical Case No. 2—Soft Drink Product P

This case involves a soft drink manufacturer who sells his product (syrup) through 200 bottlers. He wants to meet his competition with an effective sales incentive plan, which is directed essentially at the bottler's route salesmen. The route salesmen are an important key because they are the men who have daily contact with the retailers, primarily supermarkets.

One of the most important ways to develop increased business is to get special case displays of the product at the end of the aisle, or in other areas away from the soft drink section of the supermarket. This sales incentive plan has been set up to try to get these displays.

This manufacturer's sales are $50 million annually. The biggest months of the year are June and July, which traditionally represent 25 percent of the year's sales for him. Therefore, the two months accounted for $12,500,000 in the past year. The manufacturer is looking for a 20 percent increase as a result of this plan, or additional sales of $2,500,000 (20 percent $\times$ $12,500,000). It is in these two months that he schedules his sales incentive plan.

The merchandise prizes are to be selected by the winners from catalogs which are sent to the bottlers for distribution to the men.

The sales incentive plan for the men is set up to reward the men for case displays and for making quota, 20 percent increase over last year's sales. If a man cannot make quota, he can win by getting case displays. Here is the way the plan is set up.

The typical bottler's route salesman who makes quota and gets eight case displays, or one display per week during the eight-week promotion in June and July, will be allotted prize merchandise worth $40 or 800 points (points are worth 1/2 cent). The points are allocated as follows:

```
For making quota (120% of last year) . . . . . . . 400 points
For getting special displays (8 × 50 points) . . . 400 points
   Total . . . . . . . . . . . . . . . . . . . . . . . . . . . . 800 points (worth $40)
```

The average bottler has 10 route men, and there are 200 bottlers. So this represents $40 per man for 2,000 men if the program is successful. In addition to the route men, the program allows each bottler $100 or 2,000 points to award to merchandising men or supervisors at his discretion. Here is the way the cost projection for the sales incentive plan works out:

200 BOTTLERS

```
10 route salesmen × $40. . . . . . . . . . . . . . . . . . . . . . . . . . . . $400
Supervisory and merchandising men  . . . . . . . . . . . . . . . . . .  100

   Total . . . . . . . . . . . . . . . . . . . . . . . . . . . . . . . . . . . . . $500
200 bottlers × $500  . . . . . . . . . . . . . . . . . . . . . . . . . . . . . $100,000
Promotional costs. . . . . . . . . . . . . . . . . . . . . . . . . . . . . . .   20,000

                                                                               $120,000
Bottlers share is 50% of prize merchandise . . . . . . . . . . . . .   50,000

Net cost to manufacturer. . . . . . . . . . . . . . . . . . . . . . . . . . $ 70,000
```

This works out to 2.8 percent of sales to the manufacturer, and 2 percent of syrup sales to the bottler. (The bottler's actual cost is much less because his costs are based on sales of the bottled product to retailers.)

If this program is successful, the manufacturer will have obtained 8 $\times$ 2,000 or 16,000 special displays during the period of this promotion; as a result, he can expect to enjoy substantial sales increases. Whether he attains his quota at 20 percent increase will depend upon the effectiveness with which the bottler supervises the men to make sure the displays are set up and maintained properly, and to a great extent on competitive activity. Let us assume that one-half of the men made quota, and the balance equaled last year's sales at 100 percent. This would represent 110 percent or a $1,250,000 sales increase. Let us further assume that 8,000 displays were reported. The manufacturer would then pay out as follows:

```
Prize merchandise. . . . . . . . . . . . . . . . . . . . $25,000 (50% of $50,000)
Promotional costs . . . . . . . . . . . . . . . . . . . .   20,000
    Total  . . . . . . . . . . . . . . . . . . . . . . . . . . . . $45,000
```

This would represent a 3.6 percent cost factor on a sales increase of $1,250,000 which would still represent a good investment.

Hypothetical Case No. 3—Bank Services

The management of a medium-sized bank with $200 million in assets has decided to set up a six-month incentive plan which will apply to all bank services and involve all bank employees. The objectives are to obtain new business in a competitive market and to give all employees a greater familiarity with the bank's services by involving them in the selling process.

A catalog of merchandise prizes ranging in value from 3 to over one thousand dollars is the basic tool of the plan. It is distributed to all of the bank's 1,000 employees. The merchandise prizes are earned on a point system, each point being worth 1 cent.

The bank has set up a schedule of point awards for noncontact and contact employees, and officers. It gives noncontact employees twice as many points for bringing in business as contact employees, who have face-to-face dealings with customers every day, and four times as much as officers, who have even more opportunity for promoting the bank services.

Table 5.2 shows the point schedule which has been drawn up.

The bank has ten branches and 1,000 employees. The employees are divided into twelve teams, two representing the main office, and one for each of the ten branches. A senior officer is captain of each team.

TABLE 5.2

Bank services	Points		
	Noncontact	*Contact*	*Officers*
Regular checking accounts:			
$200–$1,000 initial deposit	100	50	25
Each additional $1,000 deposit	20	10	5
Special checking accounts:			
$25–$100 initial deposit	20	10	5
Over $100 additional deposit	60	30	15
Savings accounts:			
$25–$250.	20	10	5
Each additional $500	10	5	2.5
Certificates of deposit:			
Initial $1,000.	20	10	5
Each additional $1,000.	10	5	2.5
Safe deposit boxes	20	10	5
Christmas club	20	10	5
Installment loan	100	50	25
Mortgage loan	100	50	25

A sales meeting is used to kick off the incentive plan. It is attended by the team captains and leaders of the various groups of contact and noncontact employees, a total of 200 people.

Several bonus awards are set up to make the team work more efficiently. Each team, all of whose members earn some points in the first sixty days, gets a bonus of 250 points for each member. Team members who hit 100 percent point earnings in ninety days get a bonus of 125 points.

For the team which is the top producer for the entire period of the incentive plan, there is a 1,000-point bonus award for each member on that team; and each month there is a 100 point bonus for each member of the top producing team for that month.

In addition to team bonuses, there are bonuses set up for individual performance. If an employee signs up a customer for two services at one time there is a 50 percent point bonus. This bonus is good for the first sixty days of the six-month program. Naturally, management can choose to continue this arrangement if it so wishes.

The bank's management has set up an objective of $12 million in new business as a result of this promotion. Costs are calculated at 1/3 of 1 percent or $40,000 for prizes. In addition, $5,000 is budgeted for mailings, catalogs, and meetings.

If this objective is met, the program will be well worth the expense to the bank, not only because of the immediate business brought in, but also because of employees' greater awareness of the services the bank has to offer and their own ability to promote them to potential customers.

6

PRIZE TRIP PROGRAMS, RETAIL INCENTIVE PLANS, AND DEALER PREMIUMS

Retailer incentive plans employ the same basic techniques that are involved with sales incentive plans for manufacturer's salesmen and distributors. However, retailer programs cover a much greater range of activities because of the almost limitless forms and variations of distribution involved in selling various products.

Thus, in dealing with retailer incentive plans and dealer premiums, we encounter offers in which a single dealership can earn ten or fifteen trips to Europe in a year; while at the other end of the spectrum, we will cover programs in which a retailer or his salesmen win books of trading stamps worth only $3.

The major programs, those in which dealers can win glamorous trips or big ticket merchandise, involve planning and logistics akin to the sales incentive plans covered in the preceding chapter. In these promotions, the dealers are franchised by the manufacturer and are working over a period of six months or a year to win the awards. The method of determining winners is often set up on a quota based on previous performance, although the direct dollar or unit sales basis is more common.

In programs involving products with a low unit of sale which have very broad distribution through multiple types of retailers, a very different type of program is called for. In these cases, the incentives are generally low in value and are designed to produce an immediate order for merchandise.

In some situations, a separate incentive plan will be set up to reward retail sales people who are directly concerned with selling the product. This will usually supplement a program aimed at buyers or owners.

We will explore all these situations in some detail in this chapter. It is important to note at this juncture, however, that a great many sales incentive programs embrace all levels of distribution. These include the manufacturer's sales force, sales managers and salesmen; distributors, management sales force and nonselling personnel; jobbers or brokers, management and sales force; and retailers, management and retail salesmen.

A sales incentive program that includes a great many levels of distribution is really divided into a number of different programs each tailored for the particular group being motivated but held together by a single theme and similar sales objectives.

In many cases, there is also a tie-in with a consumer promotion, which may involve a consumer incentive plan or an advertising campaign. As in the case of all promotions, the greater the involvement of every level of distribution, the more effective a promotion becomes on an overall basis; providing, of course, that sufficient effort and money are available to cover each level.

SIZE AND IMPORTANCE OF RETAIL INCENTIVES

Incentive Marketing Facts, in its survey of typical manufacturers' use of premiums, covers the field of retail incentives under the heading of "dealer premiums." As is made clear in the description of their survey, they cover a wide range of applications of various forms of incentives directed at the dealer or retailer by manufacturers or distributors.

In the overall picture, dealer premiums account for $488 million in 1970, up from $346 million in 1967. These figures do not reflect cash prizes and, therefore, may be considered to be somewhat understated. However, "dealer premiums" are still considerably under the figure reported for "sales incentives" which is $924 million for 1970. Together, the two categories accounted for 34.6 percent of all premium expenditures reported for 1970.[1]

The leading users of dealer premiums are categorized by industry in the *Incentive Marketing Facts'* survey[2] shown in Table 6.1.

As can be seen from the variety of categories involved, there is a wide range of dealer organizations involved in the retail incentive business. The differences in these types of dealers determine, to a large extent, the type of program which is used to motivate them.

In the automobile, major appliance, and home furnishing categories, the average unit of sale tends to be high; and the dealers are often dealing with only a few manufacturers' lines. In this type of industry, we find major prize programs; many dealers win trips to Europe or other vacation spots.

In the food, toiletries, beer, and soft drink categories, we are more likely to find retail incentive plans which are built around a premium given in return for a purchase of a few cases.

TABLE 6.1

Category	Millions of dollars
Auto parts, accessories, tires	93
Food products	47
Petroleum	39
Toiletries	26
Heating, air conditioning	23
Fertilizer, farm supplies	17
Electronics: radio, TV	17
Building materials	17
Pharmaceuticals	16
Housewares, home furnishings	6
Electrical appliances	6
Detergents and cleansers	5
Beer, soft drinks	5
Automobiles	4

[1] *Incentive Marketing Facts*, Bill Brothers Publishing Corporation, New York, N.Y., 1970.
[2] *Incentive Marketing Facts*, Bill Brothers Publishing Corporation, New York, N.Y., 1970.

Incentive Marketing Facts' survey reveals the range and diversity of retail incentive plans in the section of their survey which reports on dealer purchase requirements to obtain premium or travel rewards:[3]

DEALER PURCHASE REQUIREMENTS*

(Dollar figures are average of all responses)

Short-term promotions	Low range	$	268
	Medium range		802
	High range		1,541
Long-term promotions	Low range		1,855
(including travel plans)	Medium range		4,888
	High range		13,343

* Low, medium, and high ranges represent cases where two or more levels of purchase were provided. Where only one level was offered, it was reported in the medium range.

MAJOR TRIP AWARD PROGRAMS FOR DEALERS

Dealer prize trip programs are a basic promotional tool of the big ticket manufacturer, who often finds that retailers have an apparently inexhaustible appetite for trips. The simplest form of program credits a dealer with one free trip with a certain volume of purchases. Additional trips can be accrued as the dealer buys more merchandise.

If a manufacturer's program is properly planned and promoted, his dealers will tend to purchase his merchandise over competitive lines. At the same time, the dealer who is excited at the prospect of the trip will buy more than he would otherwise and will, in turn, promote that particular line more aggressively. In many instances, a dealer prize trip program will be combined with an incentive program for retail salesmen, so that they are motivated to sell more forcefully, thus helping to move the merchandise in stock into the consumer's hands.

A typical example of a well-planned program was Caloric's "Come Fly with Caloric" program. Caloric is a major manufacturer of gas ranges, ovens, dishwashers, sinks, and food disposals.

Recently, Caloric offered its dealers a chance at a four-day trip to

[3] *Incentive Marketing Facts*, Bill Brothers Publishing Corporation, New York, N.Y., November 1970.

Las Vegas or Freeport, Bahamas, all expenses paid. . . . 600 Caloric dealers decided they [wanted to go].

The Come Fly program was strictly a buy and go trip. There were no quotas, targets . . . Three categories of dealer purchases were set up as "qualifying units" with a scale showing the number of units required to pay the full cost of a trip.

The scale began at the purchase of six to twelve units for which the dealer was required to pay $240 toward the trip. The dealer contribution diminished with each incremental purchase of eleven units, until with the purchase of seventy-three to eighty-four units, one trip was entirely paid for. Additional trips could be earned on the same scale.

Caloric salesmen were asked to have their dealer-customers sign a participation letter indicating they understood the program and did or did not want to participate. Participating dealers were then sent a detailed "Come Fly" kit.

The trip sections were so spaced that it was possible for the plant managers to accompany each group. Regional men, who went along on the flights, were able to make introductions as well as discount items [with their dealers] which might be peculiar to their own areas.[4]

The case of a manufacturer selling to dealers who carry competitive lines is somewhat different than that of an automotive manufacturer whose dealers generally are concentrating only on one product line. For the automobile manufacturer, there is a greater degree of control of dealer incentive plans, and a greater degree of sophistication is possible in the program.

An American Motors sales incentive plan illustrates the detailed planning and follow-through involved with this type of program.

The primary program was "Fast Start 71" running September 11 to November 10, 1970.

Dealerships were divided into three categories: Main (smaller dealers), All-American (200 cars or more annually), and Pack (500 or more cars annually). In general, dealers and their sales managers in the two higher groups competed for travel awards; in the Main group [they competed] for merchandise awards.

For the two higher categories (Pack and All-American) winning dealers and their sales managers were selected on the basis of a national competition, while the Main dealers competed in zone

[4] *Incentive Marketing Facts,* Bill Brothers Publishing Corporation, New York, N.Y., April 1970.

groups, giving an element of consideration to special [local] area conditions.

Winning points were controlled to assume at least minimum achievement by the maximum number of dealers; points were not earned until 50 percent of the assigned quota had first been achieved.

The fast-start theme was stressed by award of fifty special bonus points to any dealer achieving 50 percent of the quota by September 30.

The forty top Pack dealers and their sales managers (chosen nationally) each received a trip for two to Morocco for five nights and six days.

. . . the 150 top All-American dealers and sales managers received trips for two to Maui, Hawaii, for four nights and five days.

A special track and field contest was held for zone managers and associates with a reverse scoring system. The contest period was divided into six 10-day periods, each treated as a separate event with its own ranking of zone executives. The periods were appropriately named in sequence, 100-yard dash, 440-yard dash, low hurdles, high hurdles, high jump, and pole vault. In each period, each zone was ranked from one through twenty-three, and the rankings of the six periods were totalled at the end. Thus, the winners were the zones with the lowest scores.

The top six zone managers were given trips for two as hosts with the All-American dealer winners to Hawaii. The two top assistant zone managers [accompanied] Pack managers to Acapulco, while the next four visited All-American managers on a trip to New Orleans.[5]

While the two top-volume dealer categories had trip opportunities, the smaller-volume dealers had a kit which described the merchandise they could win: "a fantastic opportunity to win whatever you want: Christmas gifts for your wife or family (or yourself), new furniture and appliances, fine clothing, sporting goods, jewelry, carrying equipment for next summer."[6]

There are several features of the American Motors incentive plan which deserve comment. In the first place, the fact that the dealerships varied greatly in size was recognized in setting up the plan. In cases where there is a wide range between dealers, it is often desirable to set up the program so that inequities are avoided. One way to set up the program is that used by American Motors in this promotion, where they divided their dealers up by last year's

[5] *Incentive Marketing Facts*, Bill Brothers Publishing Corporation, New York, N.Y., November 1970.

[6] Ibid.

Fig. 6.1 *Promotion materials used in the American Motors
"Fast Start" promotion. Each dealer received a travel kit including luggage tags, special billfold for traveler's checks and
tickets, and a specially printed booklet with general information
and the names of the other winners who would be going on the
trip. (American Motors Corporation.)*

sales volume: one group with sales volume under 200 cars per year,
a record group between 200 and 500 cars, and a third group over
500 cars annually.

Another method is to use a quota system, similar to that commonly used in sales incentive plans, in which points are accrued starting at a certain percentage of last year's volume. On top of this can be imposed a dollar amount in order to start accruing points. For example, a plan could require 100 percent of last year's sales plus $10,000 in sales for a dealer to qualify. This would mean that all dealers would have to chalk up a $10,000 gain to win the trip or collect prize points. For a dealer who did $10,000 last year, this would mean doubling his sales; but for a dealer who did $100,000, it would mean only a 10 percent increase.

Both the dealer-grouping and the quota systems are obviously more complex to administer than the "buy-and-go" program, as exemplified by Caloric's plan.

In the second place, the American Motors incentive plan was actually a contest because one group of winners was limited to 40 dealers and their managers and another group was limited to 150 dealers and their managers. The first ones who achieved their goals won the coveted prizes. This principle is different from the "buy-and-go" concept incentive plan which is typical of most prize trip programs run in the appliance industry.

The contest approach was applicable to the American Motors situation because it was for a relatively short period of time during the new car model introduction. It therefore called for a quick burst of sales energy during this important period. Competition among dealers was a key factor here; and those who won the trips probably enjoyed the admiration of their fellow dealers as much as they enjoyed the trips. In this type of incentive plan, the status conveyed to a dealer matters a great deal.

Finally, American Motors management tied the Fast Start '71 program in with their own factory sales personnel, by applying the same principle to them. Thus, six out of twenty-three zone managers and their assistants were recognized by winning prize trips, during which they also served as hosts to the winning dealers.

A large percentage of plans involving dealer incentives combine these promotions with a sales incentive plan. Hamilton Watch Company provides a good example of a coordinated program with several interesting features.

> The Hamilton Nassau Holiday, with an opportunity for every dealer to win, was more than a travel vacation incentive, . . . prizes for award credits . . . included merchandise for varied point levels from

patio sets and golfing equipment at the 25 award credit level to luggage and a Winchester over-and-under shotgun at the 125 credit award level.

The top award was the Nassau Holiday at the 175 credit level. This included four days and three nights at the Paradise Island Hotel. The expenses, paid by Hamilton, included air fare to and from Nassau and all meals and entertainment.

These dealer awards were also available to the company's salesmen for reaching quota goals. Just as the dealer was eligible for more than one Nassau Holiday award if he met point requirements, Hamilton salesmen could (and did) win trips for [themselves and] their wives when they signed 80 percent of their dealer customers to participate in the program.

The promotion lasted from New Year's Day through May 25th.

The forty-two-page Hamilton Nassau Holiday Program Guide was sent to every Hamilton Watch salesman, spelling out rules and stressing the inducements. It was a no-limit promotion with dealers carrying off gifts and prizes based on their own ability to sell a prestige product.

Here's how dealers earned awards. Each one was assigned a dollar purchase objective, based on the previous spring billings. For reaching their base objective, dealers received an award credit. For each $1,000 of that objective they rated one award credit; and for each $20 over the objective one award credit was earned. Credits were redeemable at the 25, 50, 125, and the top Nassau Holiday level of 175 credits.[7]

The award system worked out here is quite ingenious. It gives a dealer credit awards for meeting his quota of last year's sales in $1,000 increments. As soon as he has attained that, he rapidly accrues additional credits in $20 jumps.

For example, if a dealer did $25,000 with Hamilton in spring of last year, he gets twenty-five credits as soon as his sales this year reach that amount. However, let us suppose that he hits that quota figure in mid-March. He, then, knows that each $20 will bring him an additional credit. Assume he sells an additional $10,000 between mid-March and the closing date of May 25th. He then accrues an additional 500 credits—enough to take himself and his wife to Nassau and leave 175 credits over for giving out to his retail salesmen or other store personnel in the form of prizes or an additional trip.

[7] *Incentive Marketing Facts,* Bill Brothers Publishing Corporation, New York, N.Y., January 1969.

PROMOTION OF DEALER PRIZE TRIP PROGRAMS

When major prize trip and merchandise programs are conducted on a long-term basis, much of the same promotional approach is employed as with sales incentive plans. In many instances, these programs are kicked off at major dealer meetings coincident with the introduction of a new line of products by the manufacturer.

Elaborate direct mail follow-up programs are usually set up to inform dealers of their progress and to keep enthusiasm high.

Hamilton Watch's prize trip and merchandise program, for example, was promoted with a very expertly conceived direct mail program.

> In heralding the promotion, Hamilton's sales headquarters mailed salesmen and dealers colorful teaser cards proclaiming "Nassau is Sun Country." Attached to the card was a tube of Sea & Ski Suntan Lotion, which made for profitable psychological pressure when received in the cold doldrums of winter.
>
> On the card was a sketch of a gay, laughing native steel drum player, plus copy advising, "It's not too early to start working on that fabulous tan you'll be bringing back from Nassau! Make sure that your sunning and selling efforts pay off! Make your spring sales objective."[8]

This teaser was only the beginning.

> An advance brochure stressing [the] prestige [consumer magazine advertising] programs went out to dealers. Lighthearted cartoon flyers [which] spelled out the Nassau Holiday story to dealers [were also sent out].
>
> This colorful card advised that over $30 million from sunken Spanish galleons lie beneath the waters of the Bahamas. Accompanying the copy was a battered Spanish doubloon.
>
> Even small palm trees were sent to participants by [Hamilton] along with tips on how to plant [them]. The accompanying message pointed out that "this is your palm tree—a young version of the many you'll see in Nassau."[9]

A dealer meeting kick-off and an expensive direct mail support program are affordable in cases where dealer volume is going to be substantial and where the manufacturer's product line represents a fairly important and significant part of the retailer's sales.

[8] Ibid.
[9] Ibid.

Dealer Premium Programs

The retail incentive plans, which use major trips and/or merchandise, involve, for the most part, big-ticket products such as automobiles, major appliances, furniture or carpets, and the like.

When we approach other merchandise categories, we will see other patterns emerging which fit their own particular distribution set-ups.

A case in point is the automobile after-market sometimes called TBA (standing for tires, batteries, and accessories). This industry sells, through a complicated chain of distributors and jobbers, to thousands of service stations. The category accounted for almost $94 million of the $488 million spent for dealer premiums in 1970; so they account for over 20 percent of all dealer premiums.

AC Spark Plug Division of General Motors is a good example of one of the large users of dealer premiums in this field. AC's line numbers 30 major automotive products and over 400 accessories. AC spokesmen state the situation like this:

> "As you might surmise there's a necessity to provide some incentives along the way. We have a large sales force, but it's obvious we don't have enough to get the job done all the way to the consumer level."
>
> Consequently, AC feels that it must furnish "some reason that these people at the distributor, jobber, and service station levels would give us an effort beyond that they would make without incentives."
>
> The task of the [AC] merchandising department, then, is two-fold: "to provide motivation for the people who sell our products and for those who buy our products."
>
> "What we do is [to] challenge our distributors with a purchase objective. We sell them a promotional package which is a percentage of that purchase. Upon successful achievement of their purchase objective, AC shares in the cost of the wholesaler's promotion."
>
> Recently, AC suggested that distributors then challenge jobbers by giving them [prize points] in return for meeting purchase commitments. Jobbers are encouraged to pass on the point program to all their retailers who may, if they wish, award points to their own salesmen for selling AC products.[10]

[10] *Incentive Marketing Facts,* Bill Brothers Publishing Co., New York, N.Y., 1970.

In addition they use a forty-eight-page prize catalog offering 850 items of merchandise. AC also has spot promotions, an example of which is a recent self-liquidating offer of Arrow Shirts. For a suggested price of $4 and the purchase of AC products, dealers had their choice of Perma-Iron colors with short or long sleeves. Each participant received a certificate on which he indicated size and color before mailing directly to Arrow.

> Shirt certificates could also be exchanged for prize points [in the AC prize catalog]. This shirt promotion was run from February 1 to June 30, and it was so successful it was followed up by a $5 self-liquidating Wearever Aluminum Cookware offer, which ran from September 1 to January 31. In this promotion, the participants also could use their certificates as prize points in their AC catalog if they so desired, thus extending the dealers' range of choices.
>
> As an intriguing sidelight, catalog sheets and posters advertising the shirt and the cookware offers feature AC's merchandising group and their families as models. "We don't do this because we're egotistical. We do it because it generates enthusiasm among all the people in our distribution chain."
>
> AC's marketing staff consists entirely of ex-field people. Most are familiar to many customers either from distribution annual meetings, personal sales calls, or various inducting functions. Their presence in the AC promotional material brightens the thing up and makes it a little more fun.[11]

In the AC program, we see a perfect example of a plan designed to reach a very large number of dealers, few of whom are buying a very large amount of merchandise.

In this type of program, the average dealer will be motivated to buy merchandise by premiums of relatively modest value, or even, as in the case of the AC programs, to become interested in a self-liquidator. Of course, backing up these dealers is a network of distributors and jobbers who are also motivated by their own incentive plans.

In selling a product like a line of small batteries, the manufacturer is dealing with an extremely diverse group of dealers, in a series of specialized markets.

Mallory Battery Company's incentive programs, created for two of their groups of dealers, illustrate the way in which this type of situation is approached in setting up incentive programs.

[11] Ibid.

Fig. 6.2 *AC Spark Plug premium literature. Members of AC's marketing staff posed in the Arrow Shirts offered as dealer premiums. Since many of them are familiar to the customers, their presence in the pictures gave a personal touch to this promotion (AC Spark Plug Division, General Motors Corporation.)*

"More to you from Mallory's" was a specialized program aimed at hearing aid dealers.

A list price conversion table was part of the promotional brochure package. This stated what a packing slip was worth against the quoted price of an item. The value varied according to the type of battery, and the number of batteries in the package.

The twenty-six-page, full-color prize catalog [contained] order blanks to be filled out by hearing aid dealers.[12]

For $125 in purchases, prizes like automatic percolators and golf balls were offered; at the $300 purchase level, Doter ice crushers and Teflon cookware sets were available; at the $750 purchase level, tape recorders and attaché cases were included; and an additional wide variety of incentives were also offered at

---

[12] *Incentive Marketing Facts,* Bill Brothers Publishing Corporation, New York, N.Y., April 1970.

the $1,000, $2,000, $3,000, $5,000, $8,000, $20,000, $63,000, and $100,000 plateaus.

"In the latter [category] are included a Swiss Ski Trip for two weeks, complete Westinghouse Electric Kitchen, a Crestline Norseman nineteen-foot cabin cruiser, and a Ford Econoline."

The Mallory hearing and battery program illustrates how a program covering a very wide range of dealer-purchase levels can be successfully set up.

An entirely different program was aimed at Mallory dealers who handled transistor radio and photographic flash units. It was termed the "Fun in the Sun Special."

> Featuring a distributor salesman's premium, a dealer premium, and a consumer premium, the program was backed up by trade advertising campaigns, with network [TV] spots, heavy radio [support], and ads in [leading consumer magazines].
>
> Each dealer received an illustrated brochure spelling out the advantages of the program to himself and his customers.
>
> Packed inside each assortment of Mallory Duracell batteries was a certificate that entitled the dealer to a free Early American cooler or portable grill.
>
> Both were also offered as consumer self-liquidating premiums for $4.95 each with a proof of purchase coupon from the Mallory display in the store. Distributor salesmen rated the same incentive for every twelve displays sold.[13]

The Mallory transistor radio and photographic flash battery program illustrates how a dealer premium program can be set up to include a distributor salesman's incentive, and a consumer offer built around two related premiums and a special display. It also shows how an incentive program is used to promote display of the product.

"Here too, the incentive succeeded handsomely in its goal — greater display of the product . . . And, with its special seasonal appeal to consumers, in many instances, [it] rated that prime display location adjoining the cash registers."

The type of stores involved in this Mallory promotion would be drug stores, photographic outlets, and various forms of mass merchandisers. The simplicity of the dealer offer and the consumer

---

[13] *Incentive Marketing Facts*, Bill Brothers Publishing Corporation, New York, N.Y., November 1970.

offer, plus the inclusion of a display, are important elements when planning a dealer premium program for retailers who are selling a large number of different, modestly priced products (supermarkets, drug stores, stationery stores, etc.) as opposed to dealers (auto dealers, appliance stores, furniture stores, etc.) who are selling relatively few higher-priced products.

Using dealer premiums to promote merchandise which is sold through supermarkets poses especially great challenges. The average supermarket sells more than 7,000 different items, and to get display space or merchandise orders through dealer premiums requires extremely careful planning.

One approach is to promote a self-liquidating consumer premium which is included with a display of the product. When the display has served its purpose, the store manager takes the sample premium home.

A Gillette Right Guard deodorant promotion provides a good example of a successful promotion of this type. In this case, the consumer premium was a special umbrella designed by Peter Max called a "Funbrella." The Right Guard slogan is "Helps Keep You Dry," and the umbrella tied in nicely with it.

The selection of the premium is essential to an effective promotion, but the involvement of the retailer was considered the most important element.

> "That is really the key to success," [Allen Berry, Gillette Toiletries Promotion Manager] said. "You can have a great premium, good support, complete cooperation from your marketing people and sales staff and despite all that, if you don't get display, you've lost."
> "The 'Funbrellas' that were to be used for in-store display arrived rolled up," he recalls. "It wasn't just a matter of convenience . . . it helped get the retailer involved. He had to unroll the umbrella himself, and he had to put it up himself to make the display." [14]

One reason that this form of dealer premium is favored is that the premium serves a double purpose: it is a sample of the consumer self-liquidator and a gift for the store manager. Another reason is that many supermarket chains do not allow employees to accept premium offers. In this case, however, the premium is

[14] *Incentive Marketing Facts*, Bill Brothers Publishing Corporation, New York, N.Y., November 1970.

Fig. 6.3 *The Funbrella had appeal to a particular target audience—young women sixteen to twenty-five. It tied in with the Right Guard theme, "Keeps You Dry," had tremendous appeal, and was an excellent value. The trade was given an umbrella with each pre-pack display as well as display and advertising allowances. The consumer motivation was supplied by a 12-cent price off the 5-ounce size, as well as the Funbrella. (The Gillette Company.)*

actually a functional part of the display; and therefore, if the chain accepts the promotion, it will accept the dealer premium.

A few manufacturers offer alternative promotions in the form of free goods or discounts to supermarket chains. The fact that they are a minority, 16.5 percent of respondents in the *Incentive Marketing Facts'* survey,[15] shows that most manufacturers feel that they do not wish to offer alternatives to retailers because they are afraid (with good reason) that the supermarket chains would prefer the discount because it helps their profit situation.

On the other hand, a well-planned dealer premium promotion will help the retailer sell more goods; and that accounts for the fact that while it is a constant battle for the manufacturer to get his promotions accepted by his customers, a fair percentage of them are accepted and promoted.

Dealer interviews conducted by *Incentive Marketing Facts* reveal that supermarkets accepted about 25 percent of the premium offers presented to them which shows that even though they scrutinize these offers very closely, the chance for acceptance is always there. It is important to note, however, that 45 percent of the premiums offered were backed by consumer offers; and it can be surmised that most of those accepted contained consumer promotion and advertising.

In some cases, however, the dealer premium is not related to a consumer premium but is simply an incentive to purchase merchandise and to receive something extra in return. Often a premium offer will achieve more response from retailers than will a discount, and a premium offer is often less expensive than a discount.

Applying the principles of sales incentive plans to dealer premiums, Sona Food Products Company of Los Alamitos, California, used this method of promotion successfully to help sell their Chinese food products to supermarkets.

Target of the recent campaign was the supermarket owner, buyer, and store manager in the Southern California marketing area. Each purchase of a case of merchandise of a selected list—with a minimum order of 15 cases—entitled the buyer to a specified number of

[15] Ibid.

points. They could be redeemed for merchandise at any time over a three-month . . . period.

"We know that chain buyers especially are blasé about many premiums offered [to] them" [states a Sona spokesman]. "They see so many over the course of a year. But this Album of Awards makes a difference. Here [the buyer] can actually choose the kind of premium he himself wants. After all, the catalog lists more than 1,600 different items for every taste and hobby."[16]

Types of Dealer Promotions

The *Incentive Marketing Facts'* survey reports on the types of dealer promotions used:[17]

·Type of dealer incentive	Respondents using, %*
Special deal (dollar volume).	41.9
Special deal (product assortment).	39.3
Dealer contest or sweepstakes	32.0
Display premium	20.35
Continuity coupon plan	13.9

* Exceeds 100% because of multiple answers.

As might be expected, price deals represent the largest category reported in terms of dealer promotions. In a competitive price situation, there is sometimes no way in which a marketer can avoid meeting a price reduction. However, as we have pointed out, a premium offer which is properly promoted can often result in a better, and more economical dealer incentive. In actual practice, of course, most manufacturers use a combination of approaches to the retailer depending upon his marketing program and competitive activity.

Duration of Dealer Incentive Offers

In the *Incentive Marketing Facts'* survey[18] of incentive users, the average planning time for a dealer incentive program is reported at 13.5 weeks, and the average running time is reported at 12.2 weeks.

[16] *Incentive Marketing*, Bill Brothers Publishing Corporation, New York, N.Y., October 1970.
[17] *Incentive Marketing Facts*, Bill Brothers Publishing Corporation, New York, N.Y., November 1970.
[18] *Incentive Marketing Facts*, Bill Brothers Publishing Corporation, New York, N.Y., November 1970.

The average number of dealer premium promotions reported per year is 4.8.

These statistics show that dealer premium promotions run for a much shorter period of time than sales incentive programs. This is because the manufacturer cannot keep up excitement and interest on a dealer promotion for a very long period of time. He must get into the market with his promotion, give it all the promotional backing that he can, and then when it is finished, come back again with another one. Of course, manufacturers are constantly responding to the competitive situation, so that here again a relatively short time period is usually desirable.

The number of dealer premium promotions, at 4.8 per year average, also indicates that many relatively short promotions are considered to be most effective.

Dealer Sweepstakes

As we have seen with other forms of incentive promotion, the sweepstakes is often a means of stimulating action and getting extra sales or displays, for example, on a relatively lower budget than that required for straight dealer premiums. This explains their relative popularity—that they are used by 32 percent of the respondents in the *Incentive Marketing Facts'* survey.[19]

An effective sweepstakes promotion was run by Ace Combs of the consumer products group of Amerace-Esna Corporation. Their program was called the "Jackpot of Prizes Sweepstakes." Its objectives were to

> (1) give the wholesaler salesman another talking point [in his sales calls]; (2) open new accounts despite the throughout-the-market [coverage] they already [had]; and (3) increase their sales in a soft retail market.
>
> The sweepstakes rules were as follows: all retail druggists who handled Ace Combs were eligible to participate. The program operated from May 1 through July 15.
>
> With every purchase of any Ace Comb display model, the retail dealer received an entry to the sweepstakes.[20]

---

[19] *Incentive Marketing Facts*, Bill Brothers Publishing Corporation, New York, N.Y., November 1970.

[20] *Incentive Marketing*, Bill Brothers Publishing Corporation, New York, N.Y., April 1971.

Fig. 6.4 *When dealers placed orders for Ace Combs, they were entered in the "Jackpot Sweepstakes." This form of incentive enables the sponsor to know exactly how much he must budget for his promotion ahead of time. (Amerace-Esna Corporation, Molded Products Division.)*

The prizes for the retailers were home entertainment items, with a grand prize of an RCA home entertainment center and ranging down to fifty transistor radios as fifth prizes. Wholesaler salesmen were motivated by becoming co-winners. When their customers in the first three categories won, they won a special group of prizes set up for them.

Ace Combs marketing personnel were "pleased with the success of the program. 'In a soft market we were able to increase our sales,' [they said]. This gain was made in the face of generally declining sales throughout the industry for many drugstore products."[21]

Another way of using sweepstakes in promoting to dealers is to tie a dealer and a consumer sweepstakes into one package — the dealer winners corresponding to the consumer winners just as the Ace Comb wholesale salesmen corresponded to the retailer winners in their promotion.

One successful example of this approach is shown in a promotion conducted by the John E. Cain Company, Medford, Mass.

"In the Hawaiian Carnival promotion, seven lucky couples were awarded two-week vacations in Hawaii, while 100 second prize winners received air travel flight bags. Additional travel incentives were aimed at both retailers and Cain's sales force.

"Besides the consumer prizes, the supermarket manager or store owner who supplied the winning consumers with Cain's products also won a travel incentive — a four-day trip for two to Bermuda."[22]

In addition to the consumer and retail phases of the promotion, the Cain's people added another ingenious facet to the promotion — this one related to their own salesmen.

> For its own salesmen, Cain ran a related "Stuff the Ballot Box" campaign, again offering travel as the lure. Ten winners and their wives received four-day junkets to Bermuda.
>
> While generally fitting the definition of a sweepstakes, the Ballot Box contest required both effort and the luck of the draw.
>
> For each new display a salesman gained, he rated one vote in the ballot box. For each supplementary display with an established

[21] Ibid.
[22] *Incentive Marketing Facts,* Bill Brothers Publishing Corporation, New York, N.Y., October 1970.

retail customer, he earned another ballot; and the same for each new retail customer.

Winners of the all-expenses-paid trip were drawn from the box. [23]

Dealer Contests

Another type of promotion which involves dealers is a contest, generally based on display of merchandise. Such an approach rewards retailers for the best planned or biggest display of the product. One drawback to this type of promotion is that someone has to take pictures of the displays. Generally, the company's salesmen are given this assignment, and this can be a time-consuming task as they have to arrive at the store when the display is in position. Of course, in many cases they may themselves put up the display. On the other hand, the benefit to the manufacturer of having physical proof of the display activity can make this type of promotion worthwhile.

National Sugar Refining Company, New York, instead of using their sales force to take photographs of displays, used representatives of a trade magazine, *Modern Grocer*, for this purpose.

The approach that National Sugar [took] in [this] contest . . . was [to try to] obtain prominent shelf space at the store level. Any retailer, either store operator or store manager, was eligible provided he stocked and displayed Jack Frost products.

The rules were fairly easy. Each participant was to show his merchandising skill by putting up an effective and original display of Jack Frost products, commensurate with the size of the store

The contest was promoted through *Modern Grocer* both in the news and in [advertising]. The participant [mailed] in the entry blank which was printed in the ads. . . . Upon receipt of the entry blank a representative from the magazine called on the store and took a photo of the display.

The contest judges were chosen from a list of prominent executives in the food and advertising industries. [These] two industries were chosen because they represented different points of view.

Awards were based on the following points as evidenced in the photographs:

A. Type of display
B. Preferred position
C. Accessibility of the display
D. Eye appeal

---

[23] Ibid.

TWO SWEET JACK FROST CONTESTS!

$5000 in prizes! Over 100 winners! If you don't win the Display Contest, maybe you'll win the Sweepstakes.

Jack Frost Display Skill Sweepstakes Contest Rules—Eligibility

Any retail food operator or store manager who stocks and displays Jack Frost Sugar Products is eligible to participate in this contest.

How to enter this contest.

1. Fill out the entry blank on next page and mail it to Modern Grocer immediately . (See entry form.)

2. Show your merchandising skill by putting up an effective, original display of Jack Frost products, commensurate with the size of your store. Include the 5 lb. and 2 lb. granulated sugars and at least two other Jack Frost products in other categories. For example, Confectioners 10-X, Verifine or Cubes, Light Brown, Dark Brown.

3. Upon receipt of your entry blank, a Modern Grocer Representative will call on your store and take a photograph of your display.

Jack Frost . . . the nicest sugar to make things sweet with.

4. Awards to winners in the Display Contest will be determined by judges selected from a list of prominent executives in the food and advertising industries, and the awards will be based on the following points as evidenced in the photographs of your display:

A. Type of display.
B. Preferred position.
C. Accessibility.
D. Eye Appeal.
E. Space allocations.
F. Merchandising and promotional ability.
G. Use of point-of-sale material.

5. **Skill Sweepstakes Contest — 95 Prizes.**

Awards to winners in the Skill Sweepstakes Contest will be determined by the same judges as in rule number 4 among those entrants who show the following:

A. Merchandising and promotional ability.
B. Additional space.
C. Accessibility.
D. Use of point-of-sale.

Fig. 6.5 *For Jack Frost Sugar,* Modern Grocer *conducted a double-header which combined a display contest and a sweepstakes. There were twenty-seven winners in the display contest and seventy-five in the sweepstakes. (National Sugar Company.)*

    E.   Space allocations of the products

    F.   Merchandising and promotion ability

    G.   Use of [Jack Frost] point-of-purchase material

Concurrent with the display contest, Jack Frost ran a consolation sweepstakes for those who did not receive awards in the display competition.[24]

There were a total of 27 winners of the display contest, and 75 winners in the sweepstakes, so that over 100 retailers were winners in both events.

Promotion of Dealer Premiums

Those industries which utilize the major dealer prize programs, major appliances and automobiles, represent relatively few large programs. The great majority of dealer premium programs must be promoted effectively because of differences in distribution patterns and price structures.

If a product is distributed through thousands and thousands of supermarkets and service stations or through multiple types of retailers who in turn handle many thousands of different items, the promotion of the dealer premium must become a much simpler, less expensive operation than the acts of promoting major programs.

Incentive Marketing Facts' survey[25] reports on the use of various factors in the promotion of dealer premiums as follows:

PROMOTING DEALER PREMIUMS

Own salesmen	71.9%
Direct mail	57.9%
Through wholesalers	23.7%
Trade magazines	11.7%
Literature with product	7.9%
Other	5.5%

Promoting Dealer Premium Through Salesmen

In promoting dealer premiums, personal contact with the retailer is usually of key importance. The particular role which the sales-

---

[24] *Incentive Marketing Facts*, Bill Brothers Publishing Corporation, New York, N.Y., April 1970.

[25] *Incentive Marketing Facts*, Bill Brothers Publishing Corporation, New York, N.Y., November 1970.

man will play, however, varies widely depending upon the type of distribution set up.

In cases where a manufacturer's sales force is selling directly to supermarket chains, the salesman's job is to try to convince chain buyers to take on and promote the dealer premium. The salesman's knowledge of his trade and his personal rapport with his retailers becomes a major factor in the manufacturer's ability, in a very competitive situation, to get his promotions accepted by giant retailers. A high degree of sophistication lies in the development of the program consumer advertising back-up and point-of-purchase which the salesman uses to help him sell his particular program. His competition comes not only from his own product category, but also from every product category the retailer sells. There is only so much space in the store, and this gives room for only so many promotions at any given time.

In other situations, when multiple levels of salesmen are involved, a very different situation pertains. In these cases, a major promotional effort must often be directed through the various levels of distribution, directed at the jobber's salesman or broker's salesman, to attempt to convince him to present the dealer premium offer to his customers. Here the manufacturer's job is to persuade these salesmen that the dealer premiums will enable him to sell more products by giving him a special deal to talk to his retailers about. A properly conceived dealer premium has this effect. When a jobber or broker salesman has a large number of items he is selling. a dealer premium offer may be enough to get him to place a little extra sales effort behind that particular manufacturer's product.

As we have seen, dealer premium offers are very often supplemented by special incentives for wholesale salesmen, which are tied into the particular product or products being promoted.

INCENTIVES FOR RETAIL SALES PEOPLE

The retail salesman is the final step in the distribution chain — the man or woman who deals with the all-important consumer. In terms of incentives, the retail salesman is difficult to reach effectively because he is so many steps removed from the manufacturer, and also because many retail managements do not favor attempts by manufacturers to influence what they sell in their stores.

Successful incentive programs involving retail sales people can be worked out, however, and can be an important part of an overall incentive program. The type of retail operation has much to do with the form a retail sales incentive plan will take.

In many retail operations, the sales people are not really doing any selling but are simply serving customers. Typical examples of these are supermarkets or other stores which are primarily self-service in nature; restaurants, or fast food operations (hamburger, fried chicken, donuts, etc.); and service stations.

With this form of retailer, the emphasis is usually placed on trying to motivate retail personnel to be courteous and friendly as well as neat and tidy. However, occasionally an attempt is made to involve them in suggestive selling — to ask the customer whether she would like to buy the weekly special for example.

Mystery Shopper Programs

One of the most frequently used incentive devices, which is applicable to this category of retail personnel, is the Mystery Shopper technique in which the retail people are told that during a particular period of time they can win an amount of money, usually $2 to $5, if they make certain offers or suggest certain products to an individual who poses as a customer. These individuals are, of course, hired by the manufacturer to be Mystery Shoppers.

In order to be effective, the Mystery Shopper promotion must have the cooperation of retail management. This is accomplished by persuading them that upgrading the performance of their store personnel is good for their business.

Retail management is usually furnished with a promotional program for the Mystery Shopper by the manufacturer. This program is used to instruct retail personnel on the ground rules of the promotion. Depending on the type of store, it may consist of printed material, posters and signs; or it may be in the form of instructions for a meeting to be conducted by store managers. In any event, the whole idea is for retail sales people to perform certain actions in the expectation that they may win prize money.

In order to be effective, a large enough number of retail calls must be made on each store involved so that the word gets around to the employees that they have a chance of winning if they remember to perform the proper actions to qualify.

The objectives of Mystery Shopper programs vary. Sometimes they are related to a particular product sales special but more often they have a more general aim, with a sales training purpose in which knowledge of the product and courtesy are stressed.

Using Company Sales Personnel to Rate Retail Personnel

In some cases, company personnel can be effectively used to award retail prizes to retailers, including retail sales people.

A Mystery Shopper program is quite an expensive form of promotion so that many a promoter turns to his own sales force when it comes to motivating and rating retail personnel.

A good example of a program like this was conducted by the Clark Oil and Refining Company, of Milwaukee, Wisconsin, "to stimulate dealers, managers, and attendants."

> Here are the seven winning steps of good service which must be consistently followed to attain an excellent rating in the "Lead the Leaders" program:
> 1. *Ask for the full tank.* "Good morning, Mrs. Jones, may I fill your tank?"
> 2. *Provide two-man service.* If two attendants are available, both shall service the customer's car until new customer drives in.
> 3. *Clean all windows, tail lights, and headlights.*
> 4. *Get under the hood.* Automatically open the hood and check battery, radiator, and oil.
> 5. *Get your customers to come back.* Give the customers the correct number of . . . [trading stamps]. Don't ask, "Do you save stamps?" Use the slogan "Hurry Back."
> 6. *Friendly, courteous service.* Smile, use a good word, a friendly nod, and so on.
> 7. *Keep your station and yourself neat and clean.*
> Winners in Clark's dealer incentive program were chosen on the basis of how well they completed the above seven steps as well as their sales gallonage increases on the formula shown in Table 6.2.
> Monthly excellent, good, or fair ratings . . . [were] made by nineteen Clark marketing district managers on the basis of service provided and sales gallonage increases.[26]

[26] *Premium Practice*, Bill Brothers Publishing Corporation, New York, N.Y., July 1967.

TABLE 6.2

Clark premium	Monthly service rating prize points		
Sales increases	Fair	Good	Excellent
2%	100	150	200
4%	300	350	400
6%	600	700	800
8%	1,000	1,100	1,200
10%	1,800	1,900	2,200
12%	3,100	3,300	3,500
14%	4,400	4,700	5,000
16% or more	6,200	6,600	7,000

The "Lead the Leaders" program was administered through the dealer, and the prizes were distributed among the individual employees on the basis of their contribution to the station's success. The program was run from April through September and helped to contribute to a sales increase of 10.6 percent, as compared to 4.5 percent for the industry.

The use of company sales people, as in the case of the Clark program, is pretty much confined to situations where the dealers handle one product exclusively on a dealership arrangement such as automobiles, gas, and oil; or where retail stores are wholly owned by a manufacturer.

PMs, Spiffs, and Merchandise Rewards

In many retail sales situations, the sales person does more than just ask the customer what he wants and then serve him. The products involved are big ticket items, and the sales person is often on a commission or salary plus bonus arrangement. These product categories involved would include home furnishings, major appliances, sewing machines, typewriters, firearms, sporting equipment, and so forth.

Retail sales people have much to do with the selling process, persuading a customer to buy a particular brand.

In these situations, the manufacturer has good reason to motivate a retail salesman with some kind of reward for selling his product. Sometimes, these rewards are cash called PMs (after the initials for "Push Money") or spiffs.

As in many other forms of incentive, as they relate to retail salesmen, store managements tend to refuse to allow the payment of PMs (if they know about it!). However, a prize merchandise

program to motivate retail salesmen is often considered accept-
able; and many of them are used as part of manufacturers' programs.

Columbia Bedding Company of Chicago worked out such a
prize point promotion which was effective for them.

> . . . "What is of special value," [says a Columbia officer], "as far as
> we are concerned is . . . to reach the man on the firing line—the
> retailer's salesman who meets Mr. and Mrs. Customer on an every-
> day basis and has to sell them their bedding. What we needed was a
> program which would bring us results right on the floor where that
> salesman was showing the bedding. It soon became evident that the
> merchandise prize system was the right marketing tool."
>
> The problem was expanded to a certain extent by the size of
> different retailers. The larger ones had a staff of floor salesmen,
> while many of the smaller ones are family owned and family run re-
> tail outlets. Therefore, Columbia worked out a trip-and-catalog pro-
> gram which would intrigue the entire trade, and then they went into
> the mechanics of backing it up.
>
> The common denominator used in the system was based on a
> dollar point. For example, a $49 mattress would earn 1/2 point or
> 50-cents [worth of merchandise] with other conversions as per the
> following chart:[27]

$49.00 mattress	½ point	$0.50
59.00 mattress	¾ point	0.75
69.00 mattress	1 point	1.00
79.00 mattress	2 points	2.00
89.00 mattress	3 points	3.00

As can be seen in this chart, the higher-priced mattresses
produced more points per dollar of sale than did the less expensive
ones. Thus the retail salesmen were encouraged to trade their customers up to the better merchandise.

The great majority of participants in the program were floor
salesmen who redeemed their certificates for items like McGregor
shirts at four points. However, for the small store owner, who did
most of the selling himself, there were trips running up to 1,000
points for a couple. Thus, the program recognized all types of retailers.

There was also a strong sales training aspect to Columbia's
program.

[27] *Incentive Marketing Facts,* Bill Brothers Publishing Corporation, New
York, N.Y., April 1970.

What the catalog program did was to communicate directly with the retail salesman and to give the manufacturer the opportunity to get his story across in a face-to-face meeting just at a time when the floor salesman's interest was peaking.

The mechanisms of the program were simple. The Columbia Bedding salesman would get a copy of the invoice with the certificate attached. He would then hand the certificate to the individual who sold the bedding. [When] the retail salesman accumulated the number of points he wanted, [he] sent his order blank to Columbia. With every certificate, sales literature about Springwall mattresses was attached.

[Columbia used] these tools not to build interest solely in the premium, but much more importantly, to build interest in the product itself.[28]

Sweepstakes as Incentives for Retail Salesmen

Sweepstakes can be effectively used as incentives for retail sales people—either as a means of getting across information on products or as a means of stimulating sales. From a budget viewpoint, a sweepstakes can be very desirable, creating interest and involvement at a modest cost. For those selling products in the 5 to $50 price range, this type of approach is particularly attractive.

In getting product information to retail sales people, a sweepstakes offer generally requires that entrants answer various questions with information about the product in spaces provided on the sweepstakes entry blank. This information is contained in direct mail pieces, in product literature, or in advertising.

While they are obtaining this information they are forced to read about the product and its features. Only correctly filled-out entry blanks qualify for winning prizes.

Another more direct approach to using sweepstakes to promote to retail sales people is to have each sale of an item count as an entry blank. The more sales an individual salesman makes the more chances he has to win. Here again, excitement and involvement can be generated on a relatively modest budget.

Hypothetical Case No. 1—Refrigerators, Freezers, Electric Ranges

This manufacturer of major appliances sells his product line through 4,000 dealers—appliance stores, mass merchandisers,

[28] Ibid.

and department stores. One hundred distributors handle the line, selling to an average of forty dealers each.

The manufacturer decides to put on a prize trip program to be made available to dealers through those distributors who agree to participate on a fifty-fifty basis. The timing of the program is to be February through May. The prize trip will be an eight-day trip to European capitals to be run on a charter basis. The total cost of each trip is $640.

The manufacturer figures that he can allow $4 per unit toward the trip, with another $4 per unit to be absorbed by the distributor. In addition, the manufacturer allows an extra 50 cents per unit to cover promotional costs.

The prize trip promotion is presented to the distributors individually by the manufacturer's sales force. Of 100 distributors, 90 sign up for the program. These distributors represent 3,600 dealers including a wide variety of types and sizes.

The mechanics of the program are worked out like this: one trip = $640. Unit sales needed by retailer to qualify for one trip: $640 ÷ $8 = 80 units. While the average unit sale is worth $8, the manufacturer has set up a point system on a scale of 100 points for the average unit, 8,000 points are needed to earn one trip. Point values vary from 45 points for a small, efficiency apartment stove to 250 points for a deluxe refrigerator.

In order to qualify for two trips, a dealer must sell 160 units with an average value of 100 points during a four-month period, or 40 units per month. Of the 3,600 dealers served by 90 distributors, 400 of them qualify for trips as follows:

```
    400 dealers average 3 trips each
    1,200 trips × 80 units each = 96,000 units
    Cost of trips 1,200 × $640  = $768,000
    Cost to manufacturer
      (50%)                     = $384,000
    Cost to distributors
      (50%)                     = $384,000
    Manufacturer's price of average unit, $155 × 96,000:
    Total prize trip sales during February–May period = $14,880,000
    Cost of promotion at 50¢ per unit × 96,000 =       $    48,000
    Total cost to manufacturer:
    Trips          $384,000
    Promotion        48,000
                   ─────────
                   $432,000
    Cost of promotion as % of sales = 3%
```

The promotion cost was 3 percent. Let us assume that the 400 dealers involved in the promotion accounted for 60 percent of total sales for the period. Total sales for this period are $24,800,000.

Therefore, in setting up his promotion, the manufacturer realized that this promotion would be confined to the large dealers, some of whom actually sent five or six people on the trip. Analyzing sales of his top 500 dealers for the previous year for the period February through May, he found that they sold $11,500,000 worth of product. He targeted a 20 percent increase for these dealers or a total of $13,800,000, hoping for a sales increment for this group of dealers of $2,300,000.

Actually, fewer dealers reached the target than anticipated, 400 instead of 500. But they produced an incremental sale of $3,300,000.

Hypothetical Case No. 2—Canned Tuna Fish

A canned tuna fish has a market share of 23 percent in the region where it has distribution.

The product manager is anxious to come up with a spring promotion which will help to boost share and also create goodwill in the trade.

His sales force has excellent contacts with local supermarket chain headquarters.

He decides to promote a combination of dealer premium and consumer self-liquidator—a handsome salad bowl with a serving fork and spoon at $4.95 in the mail with two proofs of purchase. While consumer appeal is primary, he believes that the item will also appeal to the supermarket managers or assistant managers as a gift to take home to their wives.

A point-of-purchase free standing display is made up which is designed to hold two cases of product. It contains a special shelf for the premium. This is to be offered to the trade with a special price (10 percent off). They must agree to put up the display for at least one week in the period April 1 to May 15.

One case of twenty-four 7-ounce cans of tuna normally sells to the store for $9.40. A 10 percent discount brings the display to the store as follows:

Regular price	*Special display price*
2 cases at $18.80	$16.92 plus display and salad bowl set free

The product manager's sales manager reports that he can place 500 displays, after checking with retail trade sources.

Two out of four chains agree to take on the display and to bulletin their store managers pointing out that they can keep the salad bowl set after the promotion is completed. These chains represent a total of 160 supers. The balance of the displays will be placed in smaller stores throughout the region.

```
500 displays                 =    1,000 cases
Sales per display            =      100 cases
100 cases × 500              = 50,000 cases
Self-liquidator redemptions = 10,000
Cost of promotion:
    Displays at $3.00 × 500 . . . . . . . . . . . . . . . . . . . . . . . . $1,500.00
    Price-off merchandise discount, 500 × 1.88. . . . . . . . . . . .    940.00
Salad set self-liquidator for store manager, 500 × $3.00 . . . .  1,500.00
                                                                   $3,940.00

Merchandise sold. . . . . . . . . . . . . . . . . . . . . . . . . . . . . . $600,000 00
```

Assuming that these same outlets would normally have sold $450,000 in merchandise during this period, the cost of the promotion was 2.8 percent on the additional $150,000 worth of sales.

7

USING CONSUMER AND SALES INCENTIVES TO IMPLEMENT MARKETING STRATEGY

The extent to which incentives are used in the marketing of a product is governed by many complex factors which will be discussed in this chapter. Great judgment must be exercised to determine what balance should be established between the two major types of incentives, consumer and trade, in any given program. Beyond that lies the equally difficult judgment as to which forms of incentives will do the most effective job to promote overall marketing objectives. Unfortunately, there are many consumer promotions which are inadequately supported by trade incentives; just as there are trade promotions which fail because consumer incentives are weak or poorly planned.

To set up successful incentive programs, it is necessary to analyze the situation thoroughly, establish clear objectives, set up balanced and practical programs with adequate budget support, and follow through to make sure that the plans are properly executed. In marketing plans where consumer and trade incentives are involved, there is often a tendency to spread resources of money and manpower too thin, rather than to be more limited in scope so that key assignments can be carried out efficiently and effectively. However, the continuing challenge and fascination in the planning of incentive programs is the diversity of situations encountered. Varied situations are not only involved with different industries, products, and competitive challenges, but also with the relationship of incentive plans with all other aspects of the marketing program. Before considering whether to use incentives in any marketing program, it is important to find out whether the consumer or trade incentives are going to be able to make a contribution in a given marketing situation. "Are incentives actually going to be able to accomplish the objectives we have set up for them?" is the key question to be asked.

In one case, a negative response would indicate that things were in such bad shape that only drastic action, a new product, a new distributor setup, or a new management team, would solve the marketing problems. In another case, a negative response might indicate that the product had an exclusive edge over competition and a dominant share of market and that incentives could make no really profitable contribution to the marketing program.

However, most products are not in such a "black and white" situation. At any given moment, most products or services must consider incentives and establish ways to evaluate them as they relate to their marketing programs.

Most businesses which sell products or services are potential users of incentives in one way or another to help their marketing efforts. They use them, however, in a vast number of different ways depending on how their products or services are produced and sold.

CONSUMER AND TRADE INCENTIVES IN THE MARKETING MIX

We have seen how the interrelationship between consumer and trade incentives can vary from one company or industry to another depending upon the needs and objectives of the marketing managers in various situations. Consumer and trade incentives will bear a relationship to each other according to a particular marketing program. They will also bear a relationship to all the other elements in a marketing program depending upon their relative importance.

Accordingly, in one case, we will find that a sales incentive plan is a very minor factor in the area of sales management, while dealer premiums and consumer incentives are of major concern. In this case, sales management may be expending major money and effort on sales training, sales personnel procurement, and sales compensation plans.

In another case, consumer incentives will not be a factor, while sales incentives at the wholesaler and dealer level occupy tremendous time and effort. In this case, the major effort directed at consumers may be concentrated on consumer advertising.

A review of the major elements concerned with a marketing program will help to place incentives in perspective with the marketing mix.

Incentives and Product Promotion

The marketing program starts with the product or service being sold. The product must be first developed. It must be priced and it must be packaged. (Even a service is "packaged," as in the case of an insurance "package" in which one policy covers several needs.)

In developing a product, the possibility of the future use of consumer and trade incentives should be kept in mind. For example, a decision on pricing, which permits the product to remain competitive, may be made to allow for a certain amount of dealing at the trade or consumer level. As another example, a decision on package design for a supermarket product might take into consideration a future need to place a special offer on the face of a carton without causing a serious effect on the visual impact of the package.

Incentives and the Distribution Process

In establishing effective distribution, the marketing managers are dealing primarily with various types of sales personnel within one or more sales organizations. Thus, we may have a sales force which is selling product direct to the customer, as in the case of a door-to-door selling organization or an industrial sales force. However, more often than not we are dealing with several levels of sales organizations. As we have seen, these levels may include the manufacturer's sales force, distributors, jobbers, and finally retailers.

Fig. 7.1 *Mrs. Paul's Fish Sticks and Fillets offered a combination of a price-off coupon and a 25-cent Mrs. Paul's Cookbook in the same advertisement. The coupon encourages purchases; the cookbook contains 150 recipes showing ways to use Mrs. Paul's products. Advertisement appeared in* Reader's Digest, *April 1972. (Mrs. Paul's Kitchens, Inc.)*

Manufacturer's Sales Force

At the manufacturer's sales force level, there are many activities which may involve the sales manager in accomplishing his job. Among these are:

Sales compensation plan
Sales meetings
Sales presentations
Sales training programs
Sales incentive plans

In most situations, the sales compensation plan is an established entity. It represents the major item of expense and fluctuates according to the level of sales performance of the sales force.

The other items included within the sales manager's budget are, in effect, competing against one another for their share of the budget dollar. It might be a matter of judgment, for example, as to whether or not a sales incentive plan at a particular time would be more effective than a series of regional sales meetings, or an audio-visual sales presentation for salesmen to use in presenting their story to the trade. How the overall program is finally formulated can have an important effect on the sales results at the end of the year.

Distributors and Jobbers

In a similar way, there are various alternatives open to the marketing manager in setting up his program with his distributors and jobbers. The various elements he deals with in formulating a marketing program are:

Basic selling terms
    Discount structure
    Credit terms
Sales meetings
Sales presentations to retailers
Trade incentives

As in the case of the sales compensation plan, the basic selling terms, while they may be changed from time to time, represent the essential determinants to establish the affordability of other elements which may be used to help make the distributor and jobber selling program work.

Here again, sales incentives must be considered in relation to their effectiveness when compared to sales meetings or sales presentations. Of course, in many programs, all these elements are used in conjunction with each other, each complementing the other.

Retail Trade

At the retail level, dealer premiums and trade incentives are generally competing with various forms of trade allowances, cooperative advertising programs, and display programs. Here again, the choice is not always between one program or another but generally involves a balance between several elements within the marketing program.

Incentives and Other Methods of Consumer Promotion

Consumer incentives represent a group of consumer motivational methods which must be considered in relation to their cost/performance ratio when compared to consumer advertising, display programs, direct mail programs, or public relations programs.

Some of these activities work more directly than others, but their main purpose is to influence a consumer to react favorably toward a product or service.

In considering the role of consumer incentives in this context, we could look upon consumer incentives as pointing at the center of a target which represents actual customers or the best prospects for a product. As each ring of the target moves away from the center, it represents diminishing consumer interest in the product.

Consumer advertising serves the purpose of covering not only the center of the target, but also moving out to cover those who are not in the immediate market but who may become customers tomorrow, next week, or within the next six months.

The marketing manager must cover both his immediate customers and tomorrow's customers; and therefore, a balance must be set up between the consumer incentive, or the immediate motivation, and consumer advertising, or the longer-range influences.

Display programs, set up in retail stores to present the product to the customer while she is shopping, lie in between consumer incentives and consumer advertising in terms of their effect on an ultimate purchase.

In setting up the consumer advertising and promotion program, decisions must be reached as to the relative performance of each activity so that a balanced and effective plan results. Generally, the consumer advertising expenditure will exceed the consumer incentive budget by many times, simply because the number of people to be reached in advertising increases so rapidly as one moves from the center of the target toward the outer rings.

PRACTICAL APPLICATIONS OF CONSUMER AND TRADE INCENTIVES IN TYPICAL MARKETING SITUATIONS

It is interesting to analyze, in some detail, how consumer and trade incentives are used in typical situations in various industries which are large users of incentives.

The following industries are covered in this section:

Supermarket products
Service station products
  gas and oil;
  tires, batteries, and accessories
Major purchase products
Medium-priced products
Banks
Insurance companies

USE OF CONSUMER AND TRADE INCENTIVES IN PRODUCTS SOLD THROUGH SUPERMARKETS

In promoting products sold through supermarkets, the marketing man must constantly be aware of the various limitations under which he must operate. At the same time, he must also be aware of the tremendous opportunities which supermarket promotion can afford him.

On the one hand, he is selling one of approximately 7,000 products which are on the shelves. He must always be conscious of the fact that his product is put to the test every day in competition, not only within his own product category, but also with every other item sold. Every inch of shelf space in a supermarket is valuable, and it is all used intensively. Within a given product category, one can observe fairly closely how various brands are selling, by the number of shelf facings they enjoy. Thus, the biggest selling brand in a category may show eight or ten facings in each of two or three sizes, while the lesser brands may have only one or two facings in only two sizes each. Naturally, product movement is watched closely by supermarket management; and when a product's sales slow to a certain point, the brand will be dropped.

Supermarkets occupy a certain finite space;[1] and as new products are constantly being introduced, something has to be given up for each new product which is taken on. The consumer, however, is the key. If the consumer does not buy a new product, it will be taken off the shelf. On the other hand, if an existing product is taken off the shelf and enough consumers complain, that product will be placed right back on the shelf again.

There are great opportunities for the marketing man, in dealing with supermarket products effectively. If he can use his skill in packaging, advertising, and promoting his products properly, he can be assured that his efforts are going to pay off; because the supermarket brings his product to the consumer at the point of purchase two or three times a week.

Consumer and trade incentives are used to give products an extra push; and if they work, they can be instrumental in moving a very large amount of extra volume. Incentives, then, take over where packaging and advertising leave off.

Incentive Marketing Facts' survey[2] gives facts on the breakdown of expenditures in consumer incentives, dealer premiums, and sales incentives by product category.

SUPERMARKET PRODUCTS

Product category	Total premiums in millions	Consumer incentives, %	Dealer premiums, %	Sales incentives, %
Food	$326	77	13	10
Detergents and cleansers	31	73	15	12
Beer and soft drinks	41	39	13	48
Paper products	24	84	8	8

Incentive Patterns in Supermarket Products

Supermarket products, as reported in this survey, account for $422 million in consumer premiums, dealer premiums, and sales incentives. The actual total would be somewhat higher as some

[1] A typical supermarket dong $60,000 per week will occupy approximately 70,000 square feet and will have available approximately 2,500 shelf feet for grocery products.

[2] *Incentive Marketing Facts*, Bill Brothers Publishing Corporation, New York, N.Y., November 1971.

TABLE 7.1

Incentive classification	Food	Soft drinks, beer	Detergents, cleansers	Paper products
	(millions of dollars)	(millions of dollars)	(millions of dollars)	(millions of dollars)
Self-liquidators	102.2	13.5	4.4	3.9
Free mail-in	49.6	0.5	1.2	7.6
Coupon plan	40.8	. . .	9.7	7.5
On-pack	2.3	. . .	0.5	
In-pack	39.5	. . .	3.5	. . .
Container	0.9	0.1	. . .	
Other direct	5.0	0.1	2.4	0.6
Sweepstakes	4.1	1.8	0.2	0.4
Dealer premiums	47.9	5.3	5.0	2.0
Sales incentives	34.0	19.7	4.3	2.0

categories (cigarettes, and health and beauty aids, for example) are not included. In addition, price-off coupons and coin refund offer redemptions would account for approximately $100 million additional. Finally, sampling of certain supermarket products, through the mails, door-to-door, and offered in consumer advertising, represents a substantial amount on top of this. Table 7.1[3] shows the breakdown by type for the classifications reported on.

We should mention that self liquidators are not, in fact, supported by manufacturers' promotional funds but instead are paid for by the consumer. This fact, of course, accounts for their popularity. It also means, however, that their effectiveness is somewhat limited as they require a purchase by the consumer.

In promoting supermarket products, a promotional mix will be established which will recognize certain very important factors within the supermarket marketing arena.

Sales volume and profitability

Each product has a particular niche in the supermarket arena. Each competes for a total volume in a category which will remain pretty even on a proportionate basis. Likewise, there are high profit items and low profit items. These factors in volume and profit will affect the degree to which a product is capable of responding to an incentive promotion and will also affect the form and shape that an incentive program will take.

[3] Ibid.

Shown in Table 7.2 are the sales volume on profit margins of selected supermarket products as reported in a study by *Progressive Grocer* magazine.[4]

In comparing one product category with another, it becomes apparent that the sales volume of categories like beer, soft drinks, and cigarettes renders them important to the supermarket. With regard to profitability, light bulbs at 45 percent and chips and snacks at 24 percent look attractive. However, it is when a combination of the two factors, volume and profitability, are involved that supermarkets are apt to back and support manufacturers' promotions.

Accordingly, a beer incentive promotion works for a product which accounts for 5.6 percent of grocery sales with a 17.9 percent profit. A promotion on light bulbs is working for a very high profit item, but it only represents .22 percent of grocery sales. Even if sales doubled, there is not going to be much effect upon overall store sales volume and profit.

Other considerations indicated in this chart reveal that baby foods with 1.2 percent of grocery sales require almost as much shelf feet (90.4) as do cigarettes (96.4) with equal profit margin

TABLE 7.2   Grocery Products

Product	% of grocery sales	Profit % margin	No. of linear shelf feet
Baby foods	1.20	5.6	90.4
Beer and ale	5.61	17.9	46.1
Cigarettes	11.58	5.7	96.4
Coffee, regular	2.67	4.0	45.8
Dry cereal	2.40	12.0	73.3
Canned tuna	1.61	9.0	18.0
Catsup	0.52	10.0	16.1
Light bulbs	0.22	45.0	10.7
Baked beans	0.51	15.0	14.6
Paper towels	1.17	10.0	15.7
Mayonnaise	0.22	12.0	5.1
Pourable salad dressings	0.51	16.0	30.2
Chips and snacks	0.96	24.0	35.2
Canned soup	2.07	8.0	53.9
Soft drinks (liquid)	6.33	17.0	70.5

[4] *Progressive Grocer*, Butterick, Div. American Can Co., New York, N.Y., April 1971.

but ten times the sales. Chips and snacks, on the other hand, with
1 percent of sales and a profitability of 24 percent, require only
35.2 linear shelf feet.

A well-conceived incentive promotion on chips and snacks or
beer is going to provide the sponsor with a good chance for acceptance from the supermarket chain. While a promotion on light
bulbs might be directed at consumer purchase, by going directly
to them through an advertised incentive, sweepstakes or premium,
for example, one would be unwise to count on very much support
from the supermarket at the point of purchase.

Another important point is that the physical space devoted to
a product is dictated by consumer demand. Baby foods need a lot
of shelf space to display their wide variety of products, even
though the amount of sales volume is not large in proportion to
shelf space occupied and profit margins are low.

In this study, nonfoods represented a total of $2,237 in weekly
sales, as compared with $24,172 for grocery sales and store-wide
sales of $59,644. However, grocery sales accounted for $3,462
gross profit with a margin of 14.3 percent. Nonfoods accounted
for $656.60 gross profit with a margin of 29.3 percent. So there is
quite a large difference in profitability between foods and nonfoods, as Table 7.3 indicates.[5]

We can immediately see the attraction of nonfoods for supermarkets. However, supermarket operators must balance their
selection of merchandise against the shelf space given to the very
profitable nonfood categories. Hence, we see that 486 linear shelf
feet of area is given to the nonfood category as opposed to 3,461

TABLE 7.3   Nonfood Products

Product	% of nonfood sales	% profit margin	Number of linear shelf feet
Deodorants	4.75	27.4	8.9
Toothpaste	5.18	17.7	13.7
Shampoos	3.10	27.4	11.1
Vitamins	1.29	36.4	2.9
Razor blades	2.56	31.7	27.0
Encyclopedias	10.00	30.0	16.0
Pet supplies	3.57	33.0	24.7

[5] Ibid.

feet for grocery products. Any higher percentage would endanger the physical ability of the super to show a full selection of grocery, frozen food, meats, or dairy products. It is apparent that the non-food category is a fertile ground for incentive promotions, as the supermarket operator can see the immediate benefits of sales increases on such profitable items.

The physical limitations of the supermarket as related to incentives

Products which are not displayed on the grocery shelves as packaged goods include self-service meats, produce, frozen meats, dairy and delicatessen products, frozen foods, service and frozen bakery, seafood, and so forth.

The ability of these products to support promotions on or in the package is somewhat more restricted than is the case with packaged goods. The frozen products are, of course, in refrigerated units; and the meat and dairy products are in chilled display units. These products are not usually able to be featured in special displays either, which tends to inhibit the degree to which they can respond to consumer incentive promotions.

Each product category must also recognize certain physical attributes which are part of its packaging.

Products packaged in cartons, powdered detergents, cereals, tea bags, potato chips, cookies, can provide space for certain types of in-packs inside the package. These products also have space on the outside of the package to advertise the in-pack offer or to feature a self-liquidator. These products are particularly suited to carry premium offers. Packages in smaller cartons, such as tooth paste or hair cream, sometimes avail themselves of on-packs using a transparent bubble pack which shows the premium attached to the carton.

Products sold in bottles, cans, or aerosol containers generally rely upon special displays or tear-off coupons in pads on the shelf near the product. These coupons are called "shelf talkers." Similarly, products in the dairy or frozen food areas generally rely upon shelf talkers to carry incentive offers to the consumer.

Soft drinks, which are generally sold in six-packs or eight-packs, can use the carton as a receptacle for premium offers, or feature offers which are printed on the carton itself.

A Gerber doll to keep your baby company

Only $2.50 with 4 Gerber labels . . . a special for Baby Week. Our little 10″ doll is a perfect image of the famous Gerber baby. It's baby-safe, too, with an all-vinyl, skin-soft body; movable head, arms and legs. Has washable cotton sleeper.

To order your Gerber doll, just send us $2.50 and 4 labels from any of these Gerber baby foods: Toddler Meals (hearty one-dish main servings), Strained or Junior High Meat Dinners (with the extra protein your baby needs), or 2 box tops from Gerber Fruit Cereals (the combination cereals babies love).

Send to:

Doll Offer

P. O. Box 1972,
Fremont, Michigan 49412

Please send me _____ Gerber baby dolls. (Sleeper packed separately.) For each doll ordered, I'm enclosing $2.50 (check or money order, no coins or stamps, please) and 4 labels from (in any combination) Gerber Toddler Meals, Strained or Junior High Meat Dinners, or 2 Gerber Fruit Cereal box tops.

Name _____
(Please print clearly)

Address _____

City _____ State _____ Zip Code _____

Please allow 5 weeks for delivery. Offer good in U.S.A., except where restricted or prohibited by law. Orders without zip code cannot be accepted.

Fig. 7.2 *During National Baby Week, in May of each year, the Gerber people run a special promotion. In this one, a replica doll of the well-known Gerber Baby is offered as a self-liqui- dator for $2.50 with four Gerber labels. This is an excellent promotion of product image developed in a special consumer premium. Advertisement appeared in* Family Circle, *May 1972. (Gerber Products Company.)*

Distribution patterns and incentives

Beer and soft drinks are sold through distributors or bottlers. They employ route salesmen who drive trucks to deliver the product to the stores. Within these categories, we find heavy use of trade incentives. Accordingly, the total beer and soft drink category places only 39 percent of their incentives in the consumer area and 48 percent in sales incentives. It should be pointed out, however, that the beer category is severely limited by law in their use of consumer incentives. Only self-liquidators are permitted in most states. It would be reasonable to expect, therefore, that the soft drink category would spend over 50 percent in consumer incentives, as the 39 percent figure includes both beer and soft drinks.

In other supermarket products, the proportion between consumer and trade incentives would be more nearly like that of the food category—77 percent consumer, 13 percent dealer premiums, and 10 percent sales incentives. Here, too, distribution methods would have an effect upon the balance. With a product which is sold direct to the supers, correspondingly more would go to consumer incentives; while with a product which was sold through brokers or rack jobbers, a greater amount proportionately would go to sales incentives.

COMBINING CONSUMER INCENTIVES, DEALER PREMIUMS, AND SALES INCENTIVES IN A SUPERMARKET PROMOTION—PRODUCT Z

To illustrate the combined use of incentives, we will review the promotion, for a period of one year, of a line of canned juices called product Z.

Product Z is sold through a manufacturer's sales force of fifteen men, who in turn sell through 500 food brokers.

A schedule of incentive promotions for the brand is set up to cover the calendar year. It represents four levels of distribution: manufacturer's salesmen, brokers, retail trade, and consumers. (See Exhibit 1.)

There are two major promotions in the year's plan. One is the introduction of a new flavor, flavor ZZ, with sell-in beginning in February; the other is a self-liquidator offer in July to help sell flavor ZZ to the consumer, as well as five other flavors in the product Z line. Both promotions will be advertised to the consumer.

EXHIBIT 1 Promotion Calendar

	Jan.	Feb.	Mar.	Apr.	May	June	July	Aug.	Sept.	Oct.	Nov.	Dec.
Manufacturers' salesmen		Flavor ZZ bonus incentive					Sales incentive plan product Z ⟶					
Brokers and broker's salesmen		Flavor ZZ Incentive sweepstakes					Self-liquidator promotion Incentive sweepstakes					
Retailers		Flavor ZZ trade deal 2 free w/10					Self-liquidator used as a dealer premium					
Consumers						Price-off coupon — Product Z ⟶						
	Product Z TV schedules			Flavor ZZ TV schedules			Self-liquidator offer		Coin refund offer product Z			
							Product Z TV schedule		Flavor ZZ TV schedule		Product Z TV schedule	

226

In addition to these two promotions, two consumer price-off promotions are planned. The first is a 7-cent price-off coupon on the product Z line, planned to reach consumers in magazines and newspapers in April and May. The second is a coin refund offer of 50 cents for four labels of product Z, to be advertised in newspapers in October only.

The Introduction of Flavor ZZ

The line of juices now contains five flavors, so the addition of flavor ZZ will increase the line to six. Flavor ZZ is a combination of two popular flavors, and it has been through extensive consumer tests. Th research indicates that it should represent 10 percent of total product Z sales at the end of the introductory year. To some degree, it is expected that flavor ZZ will "borrow" sales from other flavors in the product Z line, so its contribution to overall sales is expected to account for a 7.5 percent increase in total brand sales during the last six months of the year, after it has gained distribution.

A motivational package of trade and consumer incentive has been set up. The first element of this package is a special bonus feature which has been added to an already existing sales incentive plan for the fifteen manufacturer's salesmen. The existing program is based on point rewards for meeting and beating sales quotas on the entire line of product Z for the year. The special bonus feature on flavor ZZ is to award a salesman with a bonus of $5000 in merchandise or prize trip points if he meets his quota. As the quotas have been set at an attainable level, it is expected that the fifteen-man sales force will exceed them, gaining an average of $750 worth of extra points during the period. The budget has been set for this activity at $11, 500 (15 × $750). It is expected that this extra bonus will provide a strong incentive for the manufacturer's salesmen to promote the flavor ZZ program vigorously to their brokers, upon whom they must rely for a successful introduction.

The next element of the program is an incentive plan for brokers based on a sweepstakes. A sweepstakes approach has been agreed upon because the 500 brokers have an average of five salesmen each, for a total of 2,500. Individual incentives would have to be too small in size to be meaningful on the budget which has been established at $50,000. (This represents only $20 per man on the average.) Another consideration in selecting a sweepstakes is that it permits a fixed prize structure based on points. In this way, a predetermined budget can be set up. All brokers and their salesmen will compete for point awards on the basis of the number of cases of flavor ZZ that they sell. The more cases they sell, the more chances they have to win.

The prizes are to be drawn on the basis of each broker, not on the basis of broker salesmen. In this way, the broker has complete flexibility to determine how to set up his own point distribution within his own organization.

The ground rules have been set up so that a total of 175 prizes will be drawn, ranging in value from $100 to $2,000 worth of points. No broker can win more than once. Therefore, about one-third of the brokers will win prize points averaging $285 per winner. The same merchandise catalog which is used for the manufacturer's salesmen will be distributed to the brokers.

To illustrate the flexibility in this program, let us use a $1,000 point award as an example. One broker could distribute it evenly among his five salesmen, letting each choose gifts with points worth $200 from the catalog. Another broker with four salesmen might choose to distribute points according to each individual's sales performance on flavor ZZ. This broker might take a $200 gift for himself, and then give points to his men which would run from $100 to $300 depending on their sales performance. A third broker might split $1,000 worth between himself and his partner.

The third element in the flavor ZZ introduction is a manufacturer's trade deal, which enables the broker to offer two free cans in a case of twelve (two free with ten). The deal is offered on all sizes of flavor ZZ during the February–March introductory period.

The broker salesmen will be given an eight-page presentation to present the flavor ZZ program to the retail trade. The presentation will contain brief facts about the consumer research and the market potential for flavor ZZ. It will outline the advertising and promotion program, and it will present the two-free-with-ten trade deal.

The advertising campaign for flavor ZZ has been worked out in a special TV spot schedule which will reinforce the existing TV schedule for product Z's entire line. An introductory spot TV schedule will run for two months, April and May, and will be followed by another special effort in October and November. During the interim period, flavor ZZ will be promoted as part of the regular line in product Z advertising. The product Z spot schedules will cost $400,000, with $275,000 spent in the introductory period and $125,000 spent in the follow-up period.

On April 1st, a price-off coupon worth 7 cents is to be run in magazines and newspapers with a combined circulation of 10 million. The objective of the price-off coupon is to create extra consumer demand for flavor ZZ at the time of its introduction, stimulating product movement and exerting some pressure on the retail trade to stock the product as a result of consumer requests for the product.

Introductory Price-off coupon — Product Z

Women's magazines, circulation 5,000,000 . . . . $30,000
Newspapers, circulation 5,000,000   25,000

$55,000

Cost of coupon is 7¢, plus 3¢ handling = 10¢ total
Predicted redemption rates:*

Magazines (on-page)	4.3% × 5mm = 215,000 coupons
Newspapers	3.7% × 5mm = 185,000 coupons

Percentage of total coupons circulated, redeemed during period April through December:

Magazines   65% × 215,000 = $139,750 × 10¢ $13,975
Newspapers   84% × 185,000 =   155,540 × 10¢   15,554

Total coupon cost $29,529
Cost of space   55,000

$84,529

Total redemptions, 400,000
Product moved (allow 10% misredemption) = 360,000 units

* 1971 Study of Couponing Trends, A. C. Nielsen Co., New York, N.Y., 1971.

Self-Liquidator Promotion — Product Z

The second major promotion is a self-liquidator offer which will be run during the July–August period. The premium is a colorful 30-inch-diameter beach ball offered to the consumer for $2.25 plus three labels of product Z in the 32-ounce or 46-ounce size. One of the labels must be flavor ZZ.

A special display piece which features the beach ball itself has been developed. The primary objective of the promotion is to use the premium to get special case displays of product Z, displays which prominently feature flavor ZZ. The self-liquidator offer will be added to existing TV spots during the promotional period.

The manufacturer's salesmen and the broker incentive plans will follow the same format as that developed for the introduction of flavor ZZ.

In the manufacturer's salesmen incentive plan, bonus prize points will be given for case displays, as well as for above-quota sales of flavor ZZ made during the June period just preceding the promotion. It is expected that the average salesman will get $500 worth of extra prize points during the promotion, so the budget has been set at $7,500 (15 × $500).

The broker's sales incentive plan will work on the same basis as that of the flavor ZZ introductory promotion, except that brokers will get chances to win on the basis of the number and size of case displays set up during the promotion. Case displays will count as entries in a sweepstakes drawing with a prize purse of $25,000. Again, 175 prizes have been set up, so that about one-third of the brokers will win.

At the retail level, it has been arranged to have the retail trade get additional beach balls for certain employees. Of course, the beach ball that goes with the display is kept by the store personnel. A total of 10,000 beach balls have been put aside for the retail trade. At a cost of $1 each, a budget of $10,000 has been set up for this purpose.

The total number of case displays projected for the program has been established at 3,000.

Coin Refund Offer—Product Z

The second price-off promotion is to be advertised in newspapers with 5 million circulation the first two weeks in October. The offer is a refund of 50 cents for four 32-ounce or 46-ounce size product Z labels, one of which must be flavor ZZ.

The return is projected at 3/4 percent, and the promotion costs are as follows:

Fig. 7.3 *Muriel cigars uses an extremely interesting approach to sampling. The advertisement offers a free sample pack containing seven different cigars including ones with special flavors. Advertisement appeared in* Playboy, *October 1971. (Muriel Cigars, Consolidated Cigar Corporation.)*

10,000,000 circulation $\times$ 3/4% = 75,000
2 advertisements at 5,000,000 circulation each
Cost of redemption: 50¢ refund
                                                       25¢ postage and handling

Total . . . . 75¢
75,000 $\times$ 75¢ . . . . $ 56,250
Cost of newspaper space   45,000
                                                   $101,250
Product moved: 75,000 $\times$ 4 = 300,000 cans

The objectives of the coin refund offer are as follows:

1. Stimulate multiple purchase of product Z.
2. Stimulate trial usage of flavor ZZ.
3. Provide broker salesmen with a consumer promotion to sell to retailers along with the flavor ZZ TV schedule running during the same period.

The Combined Budget for Product Z Including Flavor ZZ Introduction

The motivational program for product Z, with the special program for flavor ZZ is shown in Exhibit 2. The cost of consumer advertising is included for comparative purposes, although it is not part of the incentive program. Of course, the motivational programs could not be effective without the advertising, and vice versa.

The relative importance of the various incentive elements in product Z's promotion for one year is indicated below:

Level of distribution	Dollars, in thousands	%
Manufacturer's salesmen	36	13
Brokers and brokers' salesmen	75	27
Retail trade	10	3
Consumer incentives (including advertising)	156	57
	277	100

Naturally, the consumer incentive area would become larger if the self-liquidator was included. If we assume that the self-liquidator will account for 50,000 beach balls, the value of consumer incentives would increase by $112,500 ($2.25 $\times$ 50,000). The cost of the premium will, of course, be paid by the consumer.

If we counted the self-liquidator with the above figures, we

EXHIBIT 2

	Product Z (general)	Flavor ZZ	Self-liquidator	Price promotions	Totals
Manufacturer's salesmen	$ 17,250	$ 11,250	$ 7,500	...	$36,000
Brokers and brokers' salesmen	...	$ 50,000	$25,000	...	$75,000
Retail trade	...	See Note 1	$10,000	...	$10,000
Consumer incentives	...	...	...	7¢ coupon: $29,529 50¢ refund: $56,250	$85,779
Consumer advertising	$650,000	$525,000	See Note 2	7¢ coupon: $25,000 50¢ refund: $45,000	$1,245,000
Totals	$667,250	$586,250	$42,500	$155,779	$1,451,779

NOTE 1: The two-free-with-ten trade allowance does not generally fall into a promotional budget category. It would, however, represent a very substantial amount.

NOTE 2: The self-liquidator offer was advertised to the consumer as part of the product Z commercial in July and August.

would have consumer incentives running at about 70 percent of the total spent for incentives.

Another way of looking at the product promotional budget would be to break it down by activities as follows:

	Incentives	%	Consumer advertising	%
Product Z (general)	$ 17,250	8.0	$ 650,000	52.0
Flavor ZZ introduction	61,250	30.0	525,000	42.0
Self-liquidator promotion	42,500	20.5		
Price-off promotions	85,779	41.5	70,000	6.0
	$206,779	100.0	$1,245,000	100.0

In the case of product Z, then, we have projected a year's budget in which 30 percent of incentives and 42 percent of advertising will be devoted to an important addition to the product line, flavor ZZ. We have established an overall budget in which consumer and trade incentives including dealer premiums will account for about 20 percent of the total advertising and promotion budget.

Note that in the promotional planning, care has been taken to set up a program which will be manageable within a year's time span. Thus, the important introduction of flavor ZZ is the prime consideration of all selling personnel, manufacturers, and brokers during the first several months of the year. During this period of time, other items in the product Z line are advertised to the consumer. After the pipelines have been filled with flavor ZZ, a heavy TV schedule promotes the new flavor to the consumer. This is followed with the price-off coupon, which, having been put out in April, will begin to take maximum effect in May and June. While it is good for any item in the product Z line, the flavor ZZ advertising and store display features will mean that consumers will tend to redeem their coupons for the new flavor during the May–June period.

In the month of June, the selling personnel will be selling the self-liquidator promotion to the trade, preparing to get display exposure to the consumer during the summer months of July and August.

The self-liquidator promotion, beginning in early July, will be backed up by the TV schedule on product Z with special ten-second

"tags" telling the consumer to look for the beach ball self-liquidator at her store.

Finally, in October, as the 7-cent price-off redemptions begin
to drop off, a couple of 50-cent coin refund offer advertisements
are run to keep consumer motivation going. At the same time, a six-
week TV schedule on flavor ZZ will be run, which will then be followed by another six-week schedule on product Z featuring flavor
ZZ as part of the product line.

USE OF CONSUMER AND TRADE INCENTIVES IN THE PROMOTION PRODUCTS SOLD THROUGH SERVICE STATIONS

Service stations are unique as a form of retail outlet. Everyone who
drives a car is dependent upon them; and since the U. S. automobile
population is over 100 million, they are located almost everywhere.
Their sheer number (over 200,000 in the U. S. alone) makes them
fiercely competitive.

While convenience is important to the motorist, it takes very
little in the form of an incentive to take him from one service station
to another located down the block. In the gasoline end of the business, it is not surprising, therefore, that consumer incentives are
extremely important. In fact the two product categories, gas and
oil, use $167 million in consumer premiums annually, two thirds of
the amount spent by the largest category, foods, with its myriad of
different products.

While gas remains the volume product of the service station,
there are many other automotive products—tires, batteries, wiper
blades, air filters, oil filters, and replacement parts and accessories that are sold through service stations. Of course, these products are also sold through many other retail outlets as well. This
huge automotive accessory business does use some consumer premiums; but due to the nature of the distribution process, dealer
premiums and trade incentive are far more important in auto parts
and accessories.

The difference in expenditure in major incentive categories
between these two product groups show how greatly they differ
in the use of incentives, due to the nature of the distribution
process and the differences in the products themselves.

SERVICE STATION PRODUCTS*

Product category	Total premiums (in millions)	Consumer incentives, %	Dealer premiums, %	Sales incentives, %
Petroleum products (gas and oil)	$220	76.0	18.0	6.0
Auto parts, accessories, tires	200	24.6	46.9	28.5
Total	$420			

*Incentive Marketing Facts, Bill Brothers Publishing Corporation, New York, N.Y., November 1971.

For each of the product categories, about $2 per U. S. automobile is spent on consumer and trade incentives. This amounts to $420 million spent on 100 million U. S. cars. For gasoline and oil, sold by brand directly to the service stations, the major emphasis (76.0 percent) is placed on consumer incentive which will help these products hold their share at an affordable price.

By contrast, auto parts and accessories are sold through a complicated chain of distributors and jobbers to service stations, at the same time gaining distribution through other retail outlets. Tires are sold through manufacturer's retail operations and through department store and mail order chains. For this reason, the proportion devoted to consumer premiums is relatively minor, with consumer premiums accounting for only 24.6 percent of the $200 million, while dealer premiums account for 46.9 percent and sales incentives 28.5 percent of the category.

Consumer Incentive Patterns in Service Station Products—Gas and Oil

In the development of consumer incentive promotions for gasoline and oil companies, there are several important factors which must be considered. They are as follows:

1. Continuity

The service station is not as interested in the promotion which attracts the motorist who stops in just once as with a promotion which will bring the customer back to his place of business again and again.

2. Universal appeal

The promoter in the oil business is looking for a premium promotion which has the broadest based appeal possible, something which almost everyone can use or enjoy. A promotion which is confined to any one group or type of consumer may be used now and then, but the most successful promotions appeal to a mass audience.

3. Cost

Just as in the case with supermarket products, the most effective way to sell more gasoline is to reduce the price. The justification for consumer incentives is in their ability to bring in repeat traffic over a period of time at a lower cost than price-cutting. This does not mean that a consumer incentive promotion can hold its own against a price reduction; but it does mean that, all other factors being equal, the various forms of consumer incentive can be of major importance in increasing sales and profits.

4. Easy handling

The promotion must be capable of being handled easily by service station attendants. A very bulky item, or one which is extremely fragile, is not practical to cope with in the service station. It is important to note that the great majority of service station consumer premium offers are physically given to the customer at the pump so that the reward is available immediately. Send-away premium offers are usually used only as back-up items in a service station promotion.

The Major Forms of Consumer Incentives in Promoting Gas and Oil

Recognizing the four major factors, continuity, universal appeal, cost, and easy handling, there are several important forms of promotion available to the gasoline marketer. These major consumer incentives are:

1. Trading stamps
2. Free giveaways
3. Self-liquidators
4. Sweepstakes and games

Trading Stamps in Service Station Promotions

Trading stamps as a continuing consumer incentive promotion fulfill the basic requirements for a service station. They are easy to handle, have universal appeal, and have a major continuity factor. However, just as in the case of supermarkets, if everyone in the same neighborhood offers trading stamps, the relative advantage cancels itself out, and the result is higher promotional costs for everyone.

In the gasoline business, the trend has been to have the decision of whether or not to use stamps made at the service station level, rather than at the district or regional level as is the case with supermarkets.

In any event, trading stamps will cost 1 to 1½ percent of sales, depending upon the extent to which all customers coming into a given station request or are given stamps. (In many situations, the customer is not given stamps unless he or she asks for them.)

Trading stamps work better, obviously, in neighborhoods where a local supermarket is giving out the same trading stamps and there are many active trading stamp savers in the area.

Free Giveaways in Service Station Promotions

A free giveaway promotion is usually planned and promoted by the gasoline marketer, regionally or nationally. It will be up to the individual station as to whether to take on the giveaway or not, however. Giveaway promotions are generally backed by consumer advertising in an area, and the individual station is paying for the advertising indirectly in the price of the product.

An effective giveaway premium should be able to boost gallonage by about 15 percent. This naturally is dependent upon the strength of the offer and the degree of competitive activity. The premium offer will run at between 6 cents and 10 cents for each $2.80 purchase, or about 3 percent on those sales which involve the premium. However, there are many sales made during the promotional period in which the premium offer is not given out, because the customer does not request it. There are also many sales made in which a premium is given out to customers who would have purchased anyway. Of course, promotionally minded gas station managers may wish to have the premium given out during the beginning weeks of a promotion to all customers, so that they are made aware of the premium offer and are motivated to return for additional premiums.

These variables will result in premiums being given out to 25 to 50 percent of all customers during a giveaway premium promotion. Cost as a percentage of total sales will run in the 1 to 2 percent range.

The most extensively used giveaway offers are glassware and flatware, because they produce the most predictable results as premium giveaways. However, there are a great many other types of giveaway premiums promoted by gas stations representing such different products as soft drinks, toys, place mats, flower seeds, and a wide variety of other premiums in the same price range.

Self-Liquidators in Service Station Promotions

Self-liquidator promotions have their usual attraction for service station promoters: they are low cost. Even when there is some price absorption, in order to make the offer more attractive, the self-liquidating premium is still the most inexpensive form of gas station consumer promotion. At the same time, of course, it produces the lowest amount of increase in gallonage, usually running at about 5 percent for a well-planned and executed program.

In service station promotions, most self-liquidators are kept at a price level under $1. The customer is essentially an impulse buyer who will stop to pick up an item for what represents a relatively modest amount.

In some cases, a self-liquidator is an essential part of a giveaway offer. A good example of this would be an assorted spices and spice rack offer. Here the spice rack, an attractive wooden rack, would be liquidated at $1.50 or $2. The spice bottles, eight or twelve of them, would then be given out using one variety of spice each week. Thus, the spice promotion would cover a period of eight to twelve weeks.

Consumer Sweepstakes and Games in Service Station Promotions

Some form of sweepstakes had always been an inexpensive form of promotion for the petroleum industry as well as for many other consumer products. However, in the late sixties, the form of sweepstakes, commonly called a "game," came to dominate promotional programming for oil companies. Games had originated in supermarkets, and the basic principle of operation was the same in both cases.

The game is based on giving out cards, coins, or other game pieces; one for each visit to the store or service station. Winning game pieces are "seeded" at random throughout the assortment, so that there are various large winners scattered throughout a region or area. Each station will be assured of having a certain number of low-denomination winners among any 1,000 game pieces.

The attraction of games in this competitive gas station business was that those who first ran the games enjoyed large increases (up to 40 percent in traffic and gallonage at very low cost, 1/2 of 1 percent or less).

However, just as with any other form of promotion, when all the competitors started running games at once—and these games were run from thirteen weeks to twenty-six weeks, the effects of the promotions were self-cancelling. Other factors which led the oil companies to move away from games were claims by the service stations associations that station owners were forced to take the games; consumers were unhappy that there were not more winners; and, finally there was a series of Congressional investigations into the practices involved in running the games related to dealer relations and the fact that consumers were not informed as to their odds of winning the prizes offered.

As a result of these adverse reactions and activities at the consumer, the dealer, and the governmental levels, the oil industry abandoned games as a form of promotion for a period during the early seventies. In some states, restrictive legislation has made games illegal for service stations as a result of this activity.

Sweepstakes and games do remain a legal form of consumer promotion for service stations in most states, however; and this form of promotion still offers a potential opportunity to increase gallonage at very low cost.

Trade Incentive Patterns in Service Station Products—Gas and Oil

As we have discussed, service station operations are not readily susceptible to large-scale trade incentives. This is partly because of the temporary status of most service station attendants and partly because of the large number of rather small retail operations involved.

The main objective of trade incentives when used at the service station level is to obtain station manager and attendant support for consumer promotions, or to use incentives to improve cleanliness in the stations and courtesy on the part of employees.

In getting the support of dealers and their personnel in consumer programs, a typical approach is to make available a certain number of sets of the premium to the manager to keep and to distribute to his personnel. This has the effect of giving him an incentive to sign up for the consumer promotion and also gives the station attendants a chance to be exposed to the premium before the promotion breaks.

In some situations, a clean-up and courtesy drive involves sales incentives at the station level. Here the control by oil company sales personnel must be the key factor because the sales force must administer any program such as the Clark Oil "Lead the Leaders" drive covered in the last chapter. This type of promotion lends itself to merchandise prize awards on the basis of all personnel at the station level.

Regional Oil Refinery W — Twelve-Week Promotional Plan

Regional Oil Refinery W has 500 service stations which pump an average of 30,000 gallons per station per month. Their marketing management has prepared a promotional plan which combines consumer and sales incentives in a twelve-week program. The objectives of this plan are as follows:

1. Increase gallonage by 15 percent over a twelve-week period.
2. Motivate service station personnel to be more courteous to customers and to increase selling efforts on automotive accessories.
3. Provide an incentive to station managers to clean up stations and to back the consumer promotion.

The program for the service station personnel consists of merchandise prize catalog sheets offering merchandise worth $5, $10, $15, or $25. Every two weeks for twelve weeks, each station is rated by increases in gallonage and by increases in sales of various accessory items such as wiper blades, air filters, gas additives, and so forth. Each station is also rated for cleanliness and courtesy by a mystery shopper, who will call on the station at least twice during the twelve-week period. These mystery shoppers will turn in their reports which will rate certain stations on cleanliness and courtesy for the twelve-week program.

Stations are graded according to a point system, worth 1 cent per point. Prize merchandise is then split up among station employees by the station owner or manager every two weeks and at the end of the promotional period.

STATION PERFORMANCE CHART — 2-WEEK PERIOD

Sales increase

Under 10%
Over 10%. . . . . 1000 points
Over 15%. . . . . 2000 points
Accessory sales: 100 points per $100

Thus if a station exceeds 15 percent increase in a two-week period, prizes worth $20 are available to the station manager. If he has four employees, he can distribute prizes worth $5 to each man.

In an average station pumping 30,000 gallons per month, the two-week increase is 15 percent of 15,000 gallons, or 2,250 gallons at 35 cents per gallon or $787.50.

Twenty dollars worth of prizes, then, will be charged against the sales increase of 15 percent. To this will be added any prize points accumulated against accessory sales.

In addition to these prizes, we will assume that stations at the end of the promotion will be given prize awards for courtesy and cleanliness on a scoring basis from one to ten. Only stations which score over six will win points. The scoring chart is shown in Table 7.4.

TABLE 7.4   Courtesy/Cleanliness Rating by Mystery Shopper

	Bonus points	Prize value
6 rating	2,500 points	$25.00
7 rating	4,000 points	$40.00
8 rating	6,000 points	$60.00
9 rating	9,000 points	$90.00
10 rating	12,500 points	$125.00

Thus, a station which gains an eight rating from the mystery shopper's calls gets $60 worth of merchandise to distribute among its employees.

We will assume that 50 percent of all stations are given a six rating or over by the mystery shoppers and will qualify for prizes with a breakdown as follows:

6 rating	25%	of	500 stations	—	125 stations
7 rating	15%	of	500 stations	—	75 stations
8 rating	8%	of	500 stations	—	40 stations
9 rating	1%	of	500 stations	—	5 stations
10 rating	1%	of	500 stations	—	5 stations
					250 stations

A glassware giveaway premium has been selected for consumer promotion, which will cost 8 cents for a glass given out for an 8-gallon minimum purchase. We shall assume that this premium is given out to 35 percent of all customers over the twelve-week period.

Now let us summarize the costs involved in this twelve-week promotion. We will assume that the overall increase for the refinery in the twelve weeks of the promotion is 16 percent. Some stations will have increases of only 5 percent, other stations will reach over 25 percent. We will also assume that accessory sales have increased by 50 percent, going from an average of $500 per week per station to $750 per week during the period of the promotion.

500 Stations — Sales Increase Awards — Twelve-Week Summary

Each 1,000 points represents a 2-week period of sales increase of over 10 percent or its equivalent; each 2,000 points represents an increase of over 15 percent in one 2-week period or its equivalent.

No. of stations	Average prize for 12-week period	Total 12 weeks (six 2-week periods)
200 stations	2,000 points	400,000 points
100 stations	5,000 points	500,000 points
100 stations	8,000 points	800,000 points
50 stations	10,000 points	500,000 points
50 stations	12,000 points	600,000 points
		2,800,000 points

Total value of prize points	$28,000

To this total, we must add the costs of accessory sales incentive awards. Accessory sales are at $750 per station average for 500 stations, which represents $375,000 in sales at one point per $100, or $3,750.

Finally, we must add the costs of the cleanliness/courtesy rating as conducted by the mystery shoppers. The budget for this segment of the program must include the mystery shopper calls and their reports, plus the point value of the awards given out.

TABLE 7.5   Cleanliness/Courtesy Program Budget
(Mystery shopper calls and reports 1,000 calls @ $10.00 each = $10,000)

Rating	%	No. of stations	Bonus points	Total points	Cost
		Cleanliness/Courtesy Point Awards			
6	25	125 stations	5,000 × 125	625,000	$6,250
7	15	75 stations	8,000 × 75	600,000	6,000
8	8	40 stations	12,000 × 40	480,000	4,800
9	1	5 stations	18,000 × 5	90,000	900
10	1	5 stations	25,000 × 5	75,000	750
Totals		250 stations			$18,700

To the sales incentive awards must be added the consumer incentive award program which is figured as follows:

Total normal monthly gallonage — 500 stations × 30,000 gallons = 15,000,000 gals per month
Normal 12-week sales 45,000,000 gallons × 35¢ per gallon = $15,750,000
Promotional increase 16% × 45,000,000 gallons = 7,200,000 gallons × 35¢ = $2,520,000
Total gain for 12 week period

	Millions of gallons	*Millions of dollars*
Normal sales	45.0	$15.75
16% increase	7.2	2.52
Total	52.2	$18.27

The consumer incentive was given out to 35 percent of total customers who purchased an average of 12 gallons each. (They averaged 50 percent more gallons than the minimum requirement of 8 gallons.) Therefore, sales involving 18,270,000 gallons (35 percent of 52.2 million) involved glassware giveaways.

18,270,000 gallons ÷ 12 = 1,522,500 glasses
1,522,500 glasses at 8¢ = $121,800

Combined promotional costs for 12 weeks regional oil refinery W

Sales increase prize awards	$ 28,000
Accessory sales prize awards	3,750
Courtesy/cleanliness prize awards	18,700
Consumer incentive premiums	121,800
	$172,250

Thus, the total promotion cost about 1 percent on total sales (2.49 on the sales increase). In addition to the sales increases derived from the program, the refinery also stimulated an improvement in courtesy among employees and in the cleanliness of individual stations. Incidentally, while the accessory sales program did not benefit the refinery directly, it helped the station manager in stimulating his employees to sell additional extras to their customers.

Incentive Patterns in Tires, Batteries, Automotive Parts, and Accessories

Dealer premiums and sales incentives become the major incentive promotional area as we move away from oil and gas and into other automotive supply products.

However, the automotive supply market does use consumer incentives, to some degree relying heavily on the lower cost incentives — self-liquidators and sweepstakes:

Premium category	*Dollars in millions*
Self-liquidators	$ 14.0
Direct premiums	5.2
Sweepstakes	25.1
All other consumer	4.8
Dealer premiums	93.8
Sales incentives	57.0
	$199.9

The products we are concerned with here have important retail distribution outside of service stations, some of them to a greater degree than others. Furthermore, they vary to a considerable degree among themselves in the following areas:

Cost of product
Extent of consumer recognition of brand
Degree of consumer influence in purchase

The various products in the TBA (tires, batteries, automotive parts) group are broken down by their characteristics in Table 7.6.

As the table indicates, there are various groupings of products within the category, which have certain characteristics in com-

TABLE 7.6

Product	Cost	Brand aware-ness	Consumer selection	Principal retail distribution channels
Tires	High	Yes	Yes	Service stations, garages, auto dealers, tire stores, mail order, and department stores
Batteries	Medium	Yes	Very little	Service stations, garages, auto dealers, tire stores, mail order and department stores, automotive chain stores
Oil and air filters	Low	Some	No	Service stations, garages, auto dealers, mail order stores, automotive chain stores
Wiper blades	Low	No	No	Service stations, garages, automotive chain stores, mail order stores
Spark plugs	Medium	Some	No	Garages, auto dealers, automotive chain stores
Mufflers	High	Some	Very little	Garages, muffler chain stores, auto dealers
Polishes and waxes	Low	Yes	Yes	Service stations, garages, automotive chain stores, mail order and department stores
Additives	Low	Yes	Yes	Service stations, garages, automotive chain stores, mail order and department stores
Fuel pumps, water pumps, PVC valves, distribu-tors, etc.	High	No	No	Garages, auto dealers

mon. These products will utilize similar forms of incentives in their promotions.

Tires

Tires are rather heavily advertised to the consumer because they are replaced several times during the life of the average car, and they are relatively high-priced. In addition, their distribution pattern does not follow the jobber route but goes from manufacturer to retailer on a fairly direct route. Thus, we find that while service stations are important outlets, some major manufacturers have retail tire chain stores of their own. Mail order chains and department stores are in the business in an important way; and, of course, automobile dealers often supply their customers with replacement tires.

Consumer incentives in the tire business are heavily sale-oriented, characterized by very competitive deal promotions. However, tire chain stores regularly offer premiums to attract store traffic, either through self-liquidators or traffic builders; and consumer sweepstakes are very actively used.

As far as the service stations are concerned, the major oil companies have their own private brands, which are sold under their brand names and are promoted aggressively to the consumer. At the same time, the major mail order chains and department stores also have their own private brands.

The tire companies often run sales incentive programs among their own sales forces.

Those major tire manufacturers who have retail store distribution run sales contests in these channels of distribution to stimulate their retail stores' sales, including tires.

Batteries, Mufflers, Filters, and Spark Plugs

Batteries, spark plugs, mufflers, air and oil filters are changed with relative frequency during the life of an automobile. This frequency of change has made it possible for the leading brands to develop sales volume and to advertise to the consumer so that he is aware of the name of the leading battery or oil filter. (Although consumer demand is certainly not a factor.) The main reason for consumer advertising is to persuade the trade that they should stock and carry the brands with which the consumer is familiar.

Then, trade incentives are used to motivate the distribution and jobber to sell these products to the retailer, and dealer premiums are used to stimulate retail purchase.

Consumer incentives, in the form of self-liquidators, can be used with this type of product; but it is very difficult to attract the attention of the consumer on products which have such a low-interest appeal to the great majority of purchasers. However, the consumer sweepstakes are also a factor here; they are popular because they can be conducted at low cost relative to the total incentive budget.

Polishes, Waxes, and Additives

Cleansers, polishes, and additives comprise a group of products which are included in the automotive classification because of their uses and form of distribution. However, they behave more like supermarket products when it comes to promotion.

Consumer advertising is an important facet of their overall promotion, and the leading products cultivate consumer demand as competitively as a detergent or a hair spray. Consumer advertising for leading brands is on a packaged goods level because these products will respond to consumer campaigns with immediate sales results.

Quite naturally, incentive programs for these products will include consumer premium offers from time to time. They also respond to trade incentive offers in which service station personnel can win prizes by selling the product to consumers through suggestive selling in the service station.

Fuel Pumps, Water Pumps, PVC Valves, Distributors, and Other Automotive Parts

Products sold in this automotive supply category number in the thousands. Their brand names (except when they are part of a known manufacturer's line of products) are not recognized by the consumer. They are anonymous and the consumer is not able to exert the slightest influence over which product is put into or onto his car. Furthermore, he really does not care which brand of fuel pump or PVC valve is put under the hood of his car.

Within this very large segment of the automotive supply market, consumer incentives are virtually nonexistent. Instead, trade incentives at every level, distributor, jobber, and retail outlet, become the important factor.

USE OF CONSUMER AND TRADE INCENTIVES IN MAJOR PURCHASE PRODUCT CATEGORIES

Major purchase products are strongly oriented toward trade incentives, with prize trip and merchandise awards motivating both the seller and the buyer. This does not mean that consumer incentives are not used within these categories of products. It simply means that trade incentives are much more important in these categories than in the packaged goods field.

In analyzing the variations within the major purchase categories, it is interesting to observe how the type of product and its form of distribution will have an important effect on the incentive list. Major purchase products can be characterized as follows:

Automobiles

Major Appliances

  TV Stereo
  Refrigerators and Freezers
  Ranges
  Washers and Dryers
  Air Conditioners

Home Furnishings

  Furniture
  Carpet
  Bedding

Business Machines

  Computers
  Typewriters
  Calculators
  Photocopiers

Farm Equipment

Incidentally, in most of these product classifications, the business or commercial customer represents an entirely different market than the consumer market, and a different method of selling must be employed than selling to the average consumer. Thus, in automobile products, there are consumer sales and there are commercial fleet sales to company purchasing agents, or to rental car companies. In major appliances and home furnishings, there are sales to individual consumers and there are sales to home builders, office builders, mobile home manufacturers, hotel builders, and the like. In business machines, there is the commercial end of the business while consumer sales of typewriters and adding machines represent the consumer segment.

For the most part, then, the manufacturers of "big ticket" products serve dual markets. As far as trade incentives are concerned, however, they sometimes employ incentive programs which cover both customer areas, consumer and commercial; except in cases where major sales are made direct to a business customer, by-passing the regular sales force and the distributor/ dealer organization.

Exhibit 3 shows where these various product categories apply their incentives to gain maximum benefit from their incentive dollar.

The fewer the levels of distribution, the more effective and efficient the incentive plan will be. Thus, in the automobile business, the distributor channel is nonexistent, so that all trade incentive activity can be focused on the dealer and dealer salesman. To take a different example, most big ticket business machines are sold to individuals who work for companies—purchasing agents, office managers, or technical people. Therefore, incentive plans are concentrated on company sales personnel except for some activity among distributors and dealers who sell typewriters to the consumer.

Automobiles

The domestic automobile manufacturers sell direct to their dealers, who concentrate on one or two makes of cars, in the great majority of cases. This combination of direct selling and one-product, one-brand dealership means that the automobile manufacturers have an opportunity to set up very effective sales incentive plans direct from the manufacturer to the dealer level.

Dealer sales incentive plans are a regular part of the marketing

EXHIBIT 3

	Manufacturer salesman	Distributor	Dealer	Dealer salesman	Consumer
Automobile	Sales incentive plans	X	Prize incentive plans	Prize merchandise, cash, sweepstakes	Sweepstakes traffic builders
Major appliances	Sales incentive plan	Prize incentive, trips, and merchandise	Prize trips, and merchandise awards	Prize merchandise	Traffic builders, free premiums (infrequent)
Home furnishings	Sales incentive plans	Prize incentives, trips, and merchandise	Prize incentive plans	X (except bedding)	Traffic builders, free premiums
Business machines	Sales incentive plans	Prize incentives, trips, and merchandise	Prize merchandise awards	Prize merchandise	Door openers
Farm equipment	Sales incentive plans	Prize incentives, trips, and merchandise	Prize merchandise awards, trips	Prize merchandise	Free premiums

mix with automobile manufacturers. They generally are run for two-month periods; and two or three plans are usually scheduled in each model year. Dealers are offered prize trips or merchandise awards for achieving quotas, and dealer salesmen are often included in the plans with opportunities to win merchandise prize awards. In many cases, factory sales personnel share in the prize trips and awards as well, winning proportionately according to their own sales performance. These sales incentive plans are financed from the manufacturer's promotional budget. According to *Sales Incentive Facts,*[6] automobile manufacturers spend over $130 million on sales incentives annually, by far the largest amount spent by any industry.

When it comes to consumer incentives, the automobile manufacturer usually turns to the dealer to pay for the programs. This is because the dealer's active participation is essential in making a consumer incentive program an effective instrument for producing sales. Unless the dealer pays for the program, he will not have an important stake in it and will not be properly motivated to make it work.

One unique aspect of automobile prospecting is that complete lists of automobile owners are available by year and make of car. Consequently, a manufacturer can put together a direct mail program which will be directed at a particular segment of the market (for example, all owners of compacts which are three to four years old). Into the program he can put a sweepstakes or free traffic-building premium to motivate these people to come into the dealer's showroom. This type of program is typical of those which are offered to dealers at cost by manufacturers. Some automobile manufacturers use advertising media to promote traffic-building promotions; but these efforts are less common than the dealer-supported direct mail efforts because they are less effective in reaching the precise target — the potential purchaser of a particular car.

An estimate of the annual amount put into consumer incentives by the automobile dealerships is in the $30 to $40 million range.

---

[6] *Sales Incentive Facts,* Bill Brothers Publishing Corporation, New York, N.Y., November 1971.

Fig. 7.4 *A big-ticket item, the New Holland garden tractor, uses a major premium offer to encourage purchases. Customers who buy between March 1 and April 30 get a free GE television or a choice of two very desirable outdoor garden and lawn appliances. This promotion offers the prospect of a really strong extra inducement to buy. Advertisement appeared in Life, April 21, 1972. (Sperry Rand Corporation.)*

Major Appliances

Major appliance manufacturers are completely oriented toward the distributor in their selling operations. This pattern of distribution originally was established because the manufacturer had to have a local organization in each market which could stock merchandise for his many dealers and provide service locally. Despite the fact that many major appliances are now serviced by factory representatives, the distributors are still an essential element in major appliance distribution.

The major appliance business uses prize trips and merchandise awards extensively in providing sales incentives for distributors and large dealers. They also offer merchandise awards to smaller dealers.

The major appliance category includes TV, stereo, washers and dryers, freezers and refrigerators, ranges, and air conditioning and heating equipment. It represents another extremely large category of sales incentive users estimated at over $100 million in volume.

Large dealers' personnel as well as distributor personnel win trips which take them all over the world. It is not uncommon for one of these promotions to involve a series of these trips which will transport as many as several thousand people to Europe, Hawaii, or the Far East.

The use of incentives in the major appliance business is, for the most part, a "loading" operation, permitting the manufacturer to get his products out of his warehouses and into the distributors' and the dealers' hands.

Major appliance dealers represent a number of different types of retail operations. They include large discount stores, department stores, mail order chains, appliance specialty stores, and public utilities such as gas and electric companies. Some of these retail outlets do not participate in incentive programs because it is against store policy; and for others, their store purchases are not large enough to make the plans attractive to them. However, to dealers who are independent businessmen with a relatively large volume, these programs obviously have tremendous appeal, as they have also for distributor personnel.

In most dealer incentive plans, the major appliance manufacturer and his distributor will split the cost of the program fifty-

fifty, so that the distributor has a responsibility for making the program work. He will therefore strive to sell his dealer merchandise and to help him, in turn, sell it to the ultimate consumer. Toward this objective, many major appliance manufacturers will also offer the distributor and dealer salesmen incentive plans based on merchandise prize awards. In these plans, the distributor will be asked to share a substantial part of the cost.

Consumer incentives are used in the major appliance business, but on a sporadic basis. They are not considered as a continuing, basic requirement in the major appliance marketing plan. The reason for this is partly that bringing consumer traffic into a store through a program run by a manufacturer or distributor may simply result in selling competitive appliances, because the major appliance retailer (except for mail order and utilities) sells a number of different brands. Another reason that consumer incentive plans are not used more often is that major appliances are very competitive in price, and it is difficult to put the cost of a consumer incentive into the retail price structure.

When consumer incentives are employed in the major appliance business, they generally take one of two forms. First is a traffic-building promotion, either a premium or a sweepstakes which requires a visit to the dealership to enter. Second is the premium which is given away with purchase of the product. Usually an item with a retail value of $10 to $20 will be given away with the purchase of an appliance with an average retail price of $250.

Home Furnishings

Big ticket products in the home furnishings business are sold partly through distributors and partly direct to the retail stores. The major segments within the category are furniture, carpet, and bedding, each segment of which has its own particular characteristics regarding the use of incentives.

Furniture

The furniture business is the largest factor in this product category and the one which is least concerned with incentive promotions. This huge industry is composed of a great number of manufacturers only a few of whom are large enough to achieve any brand name recognition among consumers. The sales force for a furniture manufacturer usually consists of a few very highly paid representatives who are not at all susceptible to the type of sales incentives program which we have seen in other industries.

At the dealer level, there would appear to be an opportunity for an aggressive manufacturer to use price incentives to expand market stores. However, the lack of dominant brand names in the industry means that there is little prospect of a meaningful response to consumer offers at the store level.

Those furniture manufacturers who advertise to the consumer, do use a form of direct incentive, brochures or catalogs which are offered in consumer magazine advertising in most cases. These full-color printed pieces are relatively expensive, and a charge is usually made of 25 cents to $1 for the literature. Another reason for charging for the color literature is to try to screen out those who are not currently in the market for furniture.

Carpet

The carpet industry, like the furniture industry, has many manufacturers. However, there are four or five brand names which have consumer recognition, and another dozen manufacturers are considered by the trade to be important factors. Some carpet manufacturers sell direct to the retailer, but more often the distributor method of selling is employed. In both cases, prize awards for distributors and dealers are prevalent and seem to be of increasing importance. These programs are similar to automotive programs on a more limited scale. They are usually based on performance over quota, although some programs are simply based on the "pay-and-go" principle in which the dealer goes on a prize trip if he buys a certain fixed amount of carpeting.

In addition to prize awards for distributors and dealers, many carpet manufacturers have sales incentive award programs for their own salesmen. At the consumer level, incentive offers tend to follow the same pattern as in the furniture industry, using offers direct to the consumer in magazine advertising. However, carpet manufacturers do use traffic-building sweepstakes or free premiums more often than does the furniture industry. The difficulty with these consumer incentive plans is that most retailers carry many different lines of carpet so that there is a strong likelihood that the retailer will end up selling a competitive carpet to the customer who was attracted by the promotion.

Bedding

The bedding industry is dominated by a few major manufacturers who sell through department stores and furniture stores. These manufacturers' most common trade incentive practice is to offer the retail salesmen incentives to sell their merchandise. They also offer incentives to store buyers and managers. However, consumer offers are rarely used in the bedding industry, which relies for the most part on price-off sales at the retail level to stimulate the consumer.

Business Machines

Most big ticket business machines are sold or leased directly to companies. For that reason, the contact is directly between company representatives and people who are responsible for the purchasing function. Some lines of business equipment are handled through distributor organizations which will sell, in turn, to various businesses; but the direct sales force comprises the most important volume category in calculators, photocopiers, business typewriters, cash registers, and computers.

Sales incentives are widely used in this industry, aimed at the direct sales force. Trips and merchandise are wrapped into very elaborate programs which generally are sustained for a period lasting from six months to a year. Typically, the direct sales force of a business equipment manufacturer is large. It may include several hundred salesmen (indeed, some include several thousand). The sales incentive plan serves as a tangible way in which sales management can reward performance, keep morale up, and give prestige to the best performers.

Consumer incentives are not big factors in the business equipment field. One reason is that it is hard to reward a man who is serving in a purchasing function. For the most part, sweepstakes or premiums are used occasionally to establish leads. A sweepstakes, for example, can be used to establish interest on the part of a prospect for a piece of equipment. ("You will have a chance to win something if you will listen to our salesman's presentation of our products.") In another application, a modest premium could be developed which would be left with a prospect *after* a sales presentation. It would serve as a reminder to call the sales representative when the prospect was ready to order — in effect saying, "Thank you for listening."

Farm Equipment

In the farm equipment industry, a wide range of incentives are used: principally trade incentives aimed at distributors and dealers, but also including consumer premiums offered to the farmer. The farmer is, of course, an extremely hard-working and busy prospect. At the same time, however, incentives directed to him provide a little extra motivation to buy. They also give him and his family some pleasure or fun in making a really large purchase, which is necessary to their livelihood.

In the farm equipment field, then, we find the use of sales incentives in the form of trips and merchandise directed at the manufacturer's sales force, distributors, and dealers. There is also some use of consumer incentives, sweepstakes or free premiums, directed at the farm equipment purchaser.

USE OF CONSUMER AND TRADE INCENTIVES IN MEDIUM-PRICED PRODUCT CATEGORIES

Between the often-purchased packaged goods products and the major purchase products, there are thousands of products priced between $5 and $100, falling into the medium-priced category. (See Exhibit 4.)

These medium-priced products use consumer and trade incentives somewhat differently than the other two categories. There is less emphasis on consumer incentives because these are, for the most part, considered purchase items as opposed to the impulse purchase nature of packaged goods, whose sales can be easily stimulated by a premium offer.

At the same time, medium-priced products use trade incentives somewhat differently than do big-ticket items. There are fewer major trip programs, and there is more of a tendency to promote shorter, less expensive trade incentives, such as sweepstakes or dealer premiums. Quite often a trade program will be built around a merchandise display, to motivate the retailer to put it on his floor or counter.

The retail channels of distribution, as we have seen, often affect the form which incentive programs will take. It will be helpful, therefore, to look at the various product categories and their retail distribution patterns.

In general, those products which are purchased fairly frequently and with which the brand name is fairly important will be able to use consumer or trade incentives most effectively. However, there is not one of these products which cannot use some form of incentive promotion. We have encountered examples of dealer loader programs with beauty aids, glassware, jewelry, cameras, sporting goods, and hardware; consumer premium incentives with clocks, housewares, flatware, games, and men's apparel; and dealer prize trips with paints, and watches.

In the medium-priced product category, however, the incentive programs are usually concentrated in one direction of effort, either trade or consumer, in an endeavor to plan and promote an affordable program which will produce results.

EXHIBIT 4   Medium-Priced Products

Product	Importance of brand name	Retail outlets*
Art items	Not important	Furniture stores
Apparel, men's	Very important	Specialty stores
Apparel, women's	Some importance	Specialty stores
Bathroom accessories	Some importance	
Beauty care cosmetics, accessories	Very important	Beauty shops
Books, records	Some importance	Book stores, record stores
Cameras, film	Very important	Camera stores, drug stores, and others
Camping equipment	Some importance	Sporting goods stores
Clocks, watches	Quite important	Jewelry stores
Cutlery flatware	Quite important	Jewelry stores
Desk items, stationery	Not important	Stationery stores
Dinnerware, glassware	Some importance	Jewelry stores
Games, toys	Some importance	Book stores, stationery stores
Garden and lawn tools	Some importance	
Housewares, general	Very important	Hardware stores
Housewares, kitchen	Very important	Hardware stores
Jewelry	Not very important	Jewelry stores
Lamps, lighting fixtures	Not very important	Furniture stores
Radios	Very important	Radio stores
Soft goods, sheets, towels, blankets	Some importance	
Sporting goods	Some importance	Sporting goods stores
Tools, hardware, paints	Some importance	Hardware stores, paint stores

All items are handled by department, mail order, and discount stores. Only *other* types of retailers are listed in this table.

Direct Selling Items

Several classifications within the medium-priced category lend themselves to direct selling to the consumer. Among such items are jewelry and art. These products often use premiums to help solicit orders from direct mail magazine or newspaper advertising.

Premiums are generally used to motivate prospects to place orders. Generally speaking, one or more additional items of the same merchandise will be offered free when the customer places an order.

USE OF CONSUMER AND TRADE INCENTIVES BY BANKS AND INSURANCE COMPANIES

Banks and insurance companies are similar in that the nature of their product is a service to the customer related to his personal or financial affairs. There is a marked difference, however, in the way in which they use incentives.

Banks are, in essence, retail establishments patronized by their customers fairly frequently, either in person or by mail. Their customers deposit paychecks, open savings accounts, set up automobile or homeowner loans, and conduct a great deal of day-to-day business with the bank. Furthermore, people in the banks are in contact with the customers daily, and their contact is an important part of helping the bank to do business.

On the other hand, insurance companies sales forces must, at the outset, have a very close and involved sales encounter with the customer, at the end of which he may or may not get the order. Once the policyholder has bought the policy, no further sales pressure is needed. The customer pays his premiums every year until the policy lapses or is dropped. The key point in insurance is, therefore, to make the initial sale.

Banks

Banks use sales incentives for employee programs which usually cover both those directly and indirectly involved with customer contact. The banks have found that getting all employees involved in the enthusiasm of a sales incentive plan is an effective tactic. Noncontact employees are generally rewarded on the basis of double points, as compared with contact employees who have a chance to meet directly with customers. However, banks have found that noncontact employees have been quite successful in stirring up extra business among friends, neighbors, and relatives.

Normally, bank sales incentive plans are run across all the bank's services: checking, savings, loans, safe deposit boxes, credit card applications, and so forth. However, in some cases, they do confine the program to just one or two services.

Banks also are extensive users of consumer premiums, which are usually offered on a particular form of bank service, savings auto loans or a special service like Christmas Club. Banks generally favor free premiums in return for a deposit of a certain size, but have on occasion used self-liquidators. In order to encourage regular savings, many banks have had excellent results using continuity premiums.

Insurance Companies

As we have indicated, insurance companies are interested in closing a sale with the prospect. To accomplish this, they are, as a group, large users of sales incentive plans offered to their agents' salesmen on a major scale. They use almost $100 million dollars worth of sales incentives per year to motivate their large sales forces, which number in the hundreds and thousands of men who must sell each customer individually. Insurance businesses have always, since their early days, been users of motivational techniques; and their good salesmen enjoy the prestige as much as they enjoy winning the tangible awards in trips and merchandise offered.

As far as consumer incentives are concerned, insurance companies generally use them as prospect-locaters through direct mail. The direct mail will contain a free offer of modest value, perhaps an appointment book or a road atlas. Those who ask for the premium indicate that they have read the mailed material and will receive a call from a salesman to set up an appointment, the first step in the chain of events which leads to the sale of an insurance policy.

INDEX

INDEX